INTRODUCTION TO BASIC PROGRAMMING

Third Edition

Steven L. Mandell
Bowling Green State University

West Publishing Company
Saint Paul ○ New York ○ Los Angeles ○ San Francisco

COVER: Victor Vasarely, *Vega-Nor*, Albright-Knox Art Gallery, Buffalo, New York
Gift of Seymour H. Knox, 1969–

COPYRIGHT © 1982   By WEST PUBLISHING COMPANY
COPYRIGHT © 1985   By WEST PUBLISHING COMPANY
COPYRIGHT © 1987   By WEST PUBLISHING COMPANY
                    50 W. Kellogg Boulevard
                    P.O. Box 64526
                    St. Paul, MN 55164-1003

Printed in the United States of America

Library of Congress Cataloging-in-Publication Data

Mandell, Steven L.
    Introduction to BASIC programming.

    Includes index.
    1. BASIC (Computer program language)   I. Title.
QA76.73.B3M36 1987   005.13'3   86-33949
ISBN 0-314-34731-3

∞

CONTENTS

BASIC SUPPLEMENT

● Section I
Introduction to BASIC

● Preface

BASIC has traditionally been accepted as the most effective programming language for instructional purposes. In recent years, business and computer manufacturers have recognized the vast potential for the BASIC language beyond education. Therefore, the availability and usage of BASIC has increased dramatically. Today most small business computer systems and home computer systems rely exclusively on BASIC programming support.

One major problem associated with such tremendous growth has been the lack of controls on the implementation of the language. Although there is a national standard (ANSI) version of BASIC, it is normally not followed by computer designers. Thus there are differences in the BASIC language found on various computers. The material in this book not only presents BASIC found on a typical large time-shared computer system (Digital Equipment Corp.), but also includes coverage of microcomputer implementations (Apple, Macintosh/Microsoft, IBM/Microsoft, TRS-80).

Color coding has been used extensively throughout the material to assist the reader. The following legend should prove valuable:

BLUE	Computer Output
BROWN SHADING	Statements Referenced in Text
RED	User Response

● Background on BASIC

BASIC, an acronym for Beginner's All-purpose Symbolic Instruction Code, was developed in the mid-1960s at Dartmouth College by Professors John Kemeny and Thomas Kurtz. It is a high-level language that uses English-like words and statements such as LET, READ, and PRINT. It is easy to learn and is considered a general-purpose programming language, because it is useful for a wide variety of tasks.

BASIC, like English and other languages used for communication, includes rules for spelling, grammar, and punctuation. In BASIC, however, these rules are very precise and allow no exceptions. They enable the programmer to tell the computer what to do in such a way that the computer is able to carry out the instructions.

BASIC was originally developed for use in a large, interactive computer environment: one or more BASIC users could communicate with the computer *during* processing and feel as though they had the computer all to themselves. As the demand for minicomputers and microcomputers increased, manufacturers of such computers felt pressure to develop simple but effective languages for them. Rather than create entirely new languages, most opted to offer BASIC because of its interactive capability—the user can communicate directly with the computer in a conversational fashion. Many altered the original BASIC, however, to suit their equipment. The result is that although the BASIC language has a universally accepted set of standard rules called **ANSI BASIC,** each manufacturer adds its enhancements, or extensions, to this standard to make use of the special features of its machines.

This supplement discusses BASIC commands common to most computer systems but will note the language variations among the different versions. The main implementation used in this text is BASIC-PLUS-2 as implemented on the DECsystem 20/60. All programming examples have been run on this system. In addition, differences between this implementation and the IBM Personal Computer, the Apple, the TRS-80, and the Macintosh have been noted. Although there are a variety of BASIC implementations available for these microcomputers, this supplement discusses only the Apple II Plus, the Apple IIe, and the Apple IIc with Applesoft, the IBM PC and Macintosh with Microsoft BASIC, and the TRS-80 Model 4 computer with Model 4 BASIC.

● Introduction to Programming

Programming is the process of writing instructions (a program) for a computer to use to solve a problem; these instructions must be written in a programming language. A program can be anything from a simple list of instructions that adds a series of numbers together, to a large, complex structure with many subsections, which calculates the payroll for a major corporation.

When computers were first developed, programming was extremely complex and programmers were happy simply to get their programs to work. There was little concern over writing programs in a style that was easy for other people to understand. Gradually, however, programmers began to realize that working with such programs was very difficult, particularly when someone other than the original programmer had to alter an existing program.

Because of this problem, programmers began developing ways to make programs easier to understand and modify. These techniques, which have been developed over the last twenty years, are referred to as **structured programming.** Structured programming has two basic characteristics: (1) the program logic is easy to follow, and (2) the programs are divided into smaller **subprograms** or **modules,** which in BASIC are referred to as subroutines. Thus, structured programming avoids large, complex programs in favor of more manageable subprograms, each designed to perform a specific task. Because the logic of structured programs is easier to follow than that of unstructured programs, they are more likely to be free of errors and are easier to modify at a later date.

This supplement will emphasize the concepts of structured programming. Because many versions of BASIC were developed before the concept of modularization was thoroughly understood, these older versions do not lend themselves to structured programming. We will try to present techniques for working around these difficulties whenever possible.

● The Programming Process

Software is a program or a series of programs that tells the computer hardware what to do. Since the computer must be able to read and interpret each instruction, the program must be precisely written. To know what instructions are required to solve a problem, the programmer follows five steps, commonly called the **programming process:**

1. Define and document the problem.
2. Design and document a solution.
3. Write and document the program.
4. Submit the program to the computer.
5. Test and debug the program and revise the documentation if necessary.

DEFINING AND DOCUMENTING THE PROBLEM

Misunderstandings concerning the desired results of a program can lead to programs that do not meet the user's needs. Therefore, before the programmer begins work, the problem must be clearly defined and documented in writing. **Documentation** consists of any comments, diagrams, or other information that explains the program to people. This documentation should include a description of program input and output:

1. What data is necessary to obtain the desired output? From where will this data be obtained? How will this data be entered? The programmer should make it as easy as possible for the user to enter the data that a program needs.
2. All output and the manner in which it is to be formatted must be described. Formatting here refers to the way in which the output is to be displayed or printed to make it easy for the user to read and use. For example, placing output in table form with appropriate headings is one way of formatting it.

Let's practice defining and documenting a simple problem. Suppose you need a program to convert a given number of feet to miles. The output is the number of miles in the stated number of feet. The input is the number of feet to be converted. You will also need to know the conversion formula (that is, how many feet there are in one mile). You now have all the information needed to solve the problem. This information could be documented as follows:

Problem Definition

Write a program to convert a given number of feet to miles.

Needed Input

The number of feet to be converted.

Needed Output

The number of miles in a given number of feet. The output will be formatted like this:

There are xxx.xx miles in xxxx.xx feet.

The programmer must understand the problem thoroughly, and must also write the statement of the problem in a clear, concise style. Documenting the problem makes it apparent whether or not the problem is clearly understood.

DESIGNING AND DOCUMENTING A SOLUTION

Once the programming problem is thoroughly understood and the necessary input and output have been determined, it is time to write the steps needed to obtain the correct output from the input. The sequence of steps needed to solve a problem is called an **algorithm.** In an algorithm, every step needed to solve a problem must be listed in the order in which it is to be performed. Developing an algorithm is an important step in all programming.

Computers, *cannot* make assumptions as humans can. Therefore, when developing an algorithm for a computer to follow, take care that no steps are left out.

Let's develop an algorithm for the problem of converting feet to miles. The steps could be stated like this:

1. Read the number of feet to be converted to miles.
2. Find the number of miles by dividing the number of feet by 5,280 (the number of feet in one mile).
3. Print the number of miles.

Top-Down Design

Using a computer to solve a problem is considerably different than most people think. The programmer needs to know only a little about the computer and how it works, but he or she must know a programming language. The most difficult aspect of programming is learning to organize solutions in a clear, concise way. This is where **top-down design** becomes helpful. The term "top-down design" means that the programmer proceeds from the general to the specific, attempting to solve the major problems first and worrying about the specific details later.

The process used in top-down design is called **stepwise refinement,** which is the gradual breaking down of a problem into smaller and smaller subproblems. Sometimes this is referred to as the "divide-and-conquer" method, because it is easier to deal with a large job by completing it a small step at a time. This approach prevents the programmer from becoming overwhelmed by the size of the job at hand.

Top-down design can be applied to solving all types of everyday jobs. For example, cleaning a room, which is a single job, is actually comprised of many smaller tasks, such as these:

- Pick up and organize small items.
- Clean floor surfaces.
- Clean walls and/or windows.
- Clean furniture.

Each of these tasks can be further divided; for example, the second one might be broken into smaller tasks like this:

- Clear floors of all items.
- Vacuum all carpet.
- Shake rugs (outside).
- Sweep wood surfaces.
- Mop tile surfaces.

Of course, it would be possible to divide each of these tasks into even smaller subtasks.

The diagram in Figure I–1 is called a **structure chart.** This chart graphically represents the stepwise refinement process by connecting general tasks with their associated subtasks. Level 0 contains the general statement of the problem and Level 1 contains the first level of refinement. Note that the second step (clean floor surfaces) is the only task that has been further refined in this example, as shown in Level 2. A complete structure chart to clean a room would be much larger and have many more levels of refinement.

Flowcharting

Once a solution has been reached, it must be documented. One way is by using a structure chart as we did in the room-cleaning example. The structure chart graphically depicts the levels of refinement of the problem and demonstrates how the separate tasks (also referred to as modules) are related to one another. Two other commonly used ways to document solutions are flowcharts and pseudocode.

One way of graphically representing the steps necessary to solve a programming problem is by using a **flowchart.** A flowchart shows the actual flow of the logic of a program, whereas a structure chart simply contains statements of the levels of refinement used to reach a solution. The meanings of different flowchart symbols are stated in Figure I–2. At this point, do not worry if you do not understand them all.

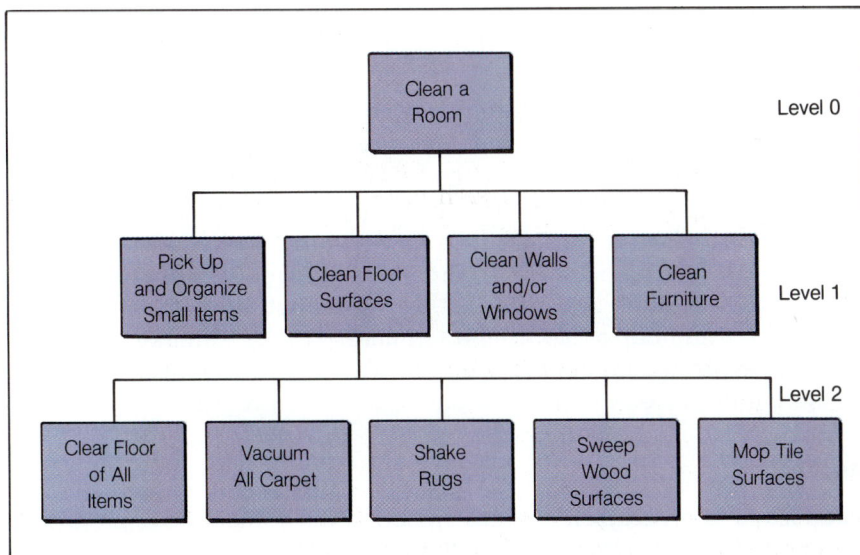

● FIGURE I–1
Structure Chart for Cleaning a Room

Processing Step

Process symbol Used to represent calculations or other processing operations.

Input or Output Step

Input/output symbol Represents either inputting data or outputting results.

Start or Stop Step

Terminal symbol Used to indicate the start or end of a program.

Decision Step

Decision symbol Represents a comparison. The action taken next depends on the result of the comparison.

Connector

Connection symbol Indicates exit from or entry to another part of the flowchart.

Preparation

Preparation symbol Indicates the dimensions of arrays or represents initialization procedures.

Subprogram

Subroutine Indicates the execution of a subroutine.

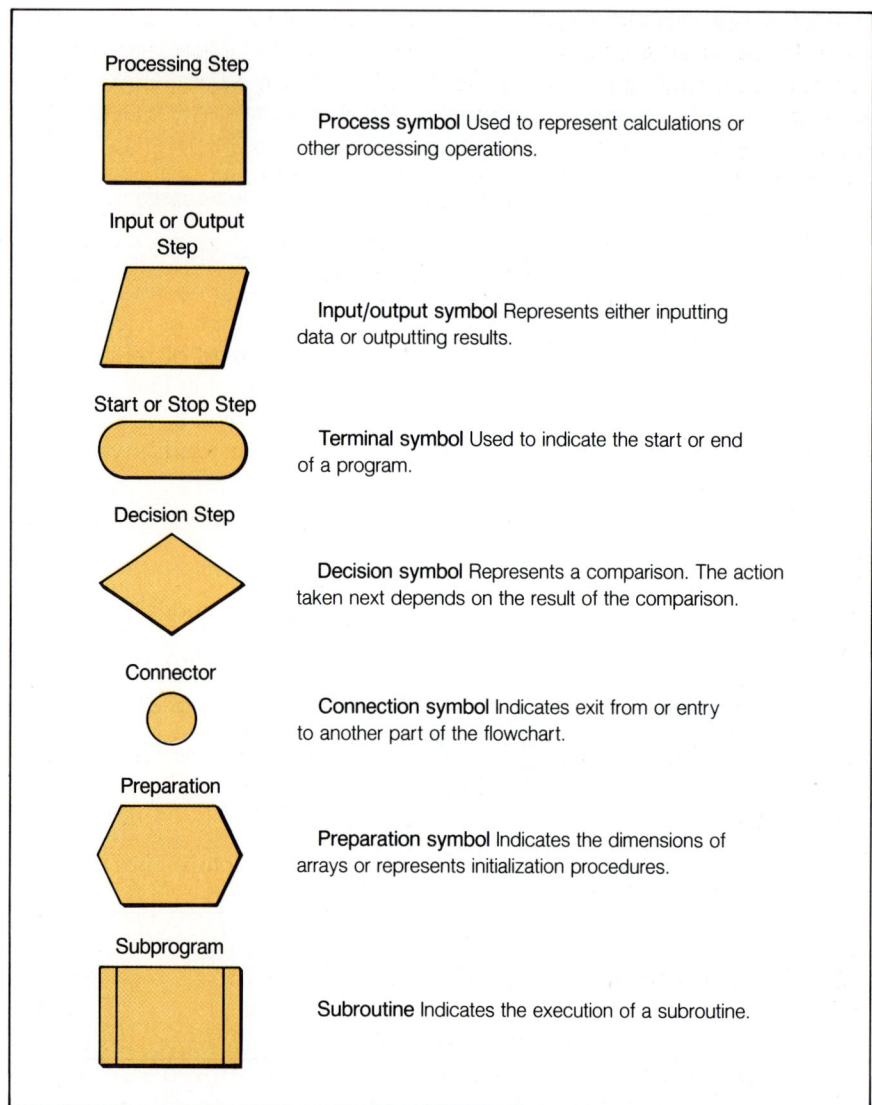

Figure I–3 shows a flowchart depicting the steps of the programming example. Notice how the symbols are shown in logical order, top down, connected by arrows. The first symbol shows the start of the program. It may correspond to one or more remarks at the beginning of the program. The second symbol shows an input step—we enter the feet. The third shows the processing done by the program—conversion of feet to miles. After that, we want to see the result, so we output the number of miles in the stated number of feet to the terminal. Finally, another start/stop symbol signifies the end of the program. The flowchart makes it easy to see the input, processing, and output steps of the program.

Pseudocode

Pseudocode is an English-like description of the solution to a programming problem. It is a type of algorithm in that all of the steps needed to solve the problem must be listed. However, algorithms can be written to solve all types of problems whereas pseudocode is developed specifically to solve programming problems. Unlike a flowchart, which is a graphic representation of the solution, pseudocode is similar to the actual program. It lets the programmer concentrate on a program's logic rather than the **syntax** or grammatical rules, of a programming language. All of the logical structures present in programs can be written in pseudocode. There are no rigid rules concerning the writing of pseudocode, but once you have developed a style, it is a good idea to follow it consistently.

The problem solution shown in the flowchart in Figure I–3 could be written in pseudocode like this:

Begin
Input the number of feet
Convert the feet to miles
Print the number of miles in the stated number of feet
End

WRITING AND DOCUMENTING THE PROGRAM

If the solution has been designed carefully, the third step—writing and documenting the program—should be relatively easy. All that is required is to translate the flowchart into BASIC statements. Figure I–4 shows this program written in BASIC. As you can see, many BASIC words, such as INPUT and PRINT, are easy to interpret. The symbol / means "divide." The REM statements in lines 10–80 are used to document the program. Compare the coded BASIC statements in Figure I–4 to the flowchart in Figure I–3; the correspondence between the two is obvious.

In the program in Figure I–4, each statement starts with a **line number.** Line numbers tell the computer the order in which to execute statements.

Lines 10–80 are comments describing the program. (We know this because they all start with the word REM.) During execution, the computer ignores all such statements; they are for documentation purposes. Line 90 tells the computer to print a statement (shown in quotes)—your cue to enter the number of feet—and then to accept the input after you type it in. Line 100 is an example of an assignment statement, which assigns a

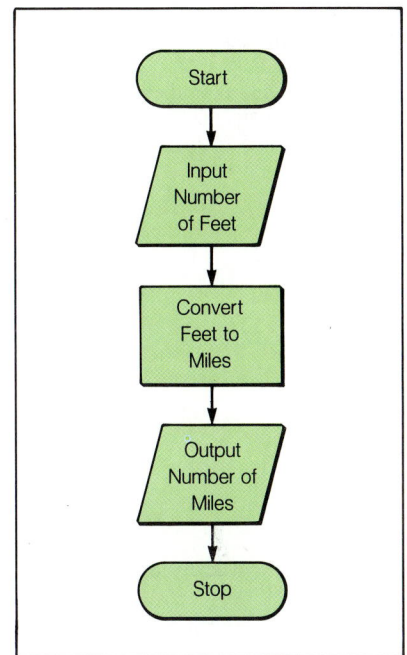

● **FIGURE I–3**
Flowchart for Conversion Program

● **FIGURE I–4**
Conversion Program

```
00010 REM ***                              CONVERSION                    ***
00020 REM ***
00030 REM ***   THIS PROGRAM CONVERTS FEET TO MILES GIVEN THAT THERE     ***
00040 REM ***   ARE 5280 FEET IN A MILE.                                 ***
00050 REM ***   MAJOR VARIABLES:                                         ***
00060 REM ***      FEET            NUMBER OF FEET                        ***
00070 REM ***      MILES           FEET CONVERTED TO MILES               ***
00080 REM
00090 INPUT "ENTER THE NUMBER OF FEET";FEET
00100 LET MILES = FEET / 5280
00110 PRINT "THERE ARE";MILES;"MILES IN";FEET;"FEET."
00999 END
```

value on the right side of the equal sign to special variables on the left (this is discussed in Section 3). Line 110 instructs the computer to print the headings shown in quotes, along with the number of feet and miles. Finally line 999 tells the computer to stop processing.

SUBMITTING THE PROGRAM TO THE COMPUTER

When students first start programming, they tend to rush through solution development and coding. They want to enter their programs into the computer and see them run. This feedback is one of the most exciting aspects of programming; it is a good feeling to have mastery over such a complex, sophisticated machine. Nonetheless, the beginning student should not hurry the early steps of the programming process. A little time spent carefully developing a solution can help to avoid a lot of frustrating time in the computer lab attempting to correct program errors.

The method used to submit programs to the computer is highly dependent on the system being used. For more detailed instructions, consult your instructor, the documentation for your BASIC system, or some other appropriate source.

DEBUGGING AND TESTING THE PROGRAM

Structured programming techniques encourage the development of programs with easy-to-follow logic and fewer errors than unstructured programs. Nonetheless, programs of any significant length virtually always contain some errors, and correcting them can account for a large portion of time spent in program development.

Debugging is the process of locating and correcting program errors. The most common errors made by a beginning programmer are simple typing mistakes, referred to as **syntax errors.** Carefully proofreading program statements as they are typed can prevent the majority of these errors.

Once the computer is able to run your program, you will need to test it with a variety of data to determine if the results are always correct. A program may obtain correct results when it is run with one set of data, but incorrect results when run with different data. This type of error is referred to as a **logic error.** It is caused by a flaw in the program's algorithm.

How the programmer is able to determine that a program contains an error depends upon the type of error that has been made. If a typing error is made, the computer usually will not be able to execute the program and an error message will be printed. If the programmer makes a logic error, the program may stop executing prematurely or it may execute properly but obtain incorrect results. Once errors are corrected in a program, the programmer must remember to also revise any corresponding documentation.

Figure I–5 shows the output of the conversion program. The conversion example is relatively simple, but it shows each of the steps required to develop a program. Although other problems may be more complex, the steps involved are the same. Successful programming can only come about through application of the five steps in the programming process.

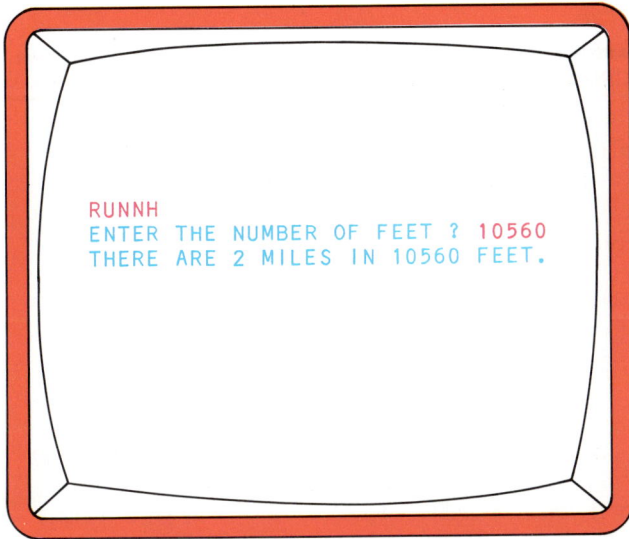

```
RUNNH
ENTER THE NUMBER OF FEET ? 10560
THERE ARE 2 MILES IN 10560 FEET.
```

● Interacting with the Computer

An important step in BASIC programming is learning to control the computer. Although this supplement cannot present the full operational details for each computer, we will discuss the principles of how to turn the computer on, make contact with BASIC, retrieve a program from external storage, display the program, alter the program, and save it for future use.

BASIC programming requires the use of different types of instructions; these instructions can be divided into two categories: BASIC statements and BASIC commands. Some of the instructions—for example, LET, READ, and INPUT—are BASIC statements. These statements are assembled into programs to solve specific business, scientific, engineering, and mathematical problems. This BASIC supplement describes their characteristics and how they are used.

BASIC commands (see Table I–1) are used by the programmer to communicate with the operating system of the computer in order to perform functions like saving programs for future reference and making changes in programs. Some commands—for example, LIST, RUN, and DELETE—are almost universally used but are not covered by ANSI standards. The rest of this section will describe such commands as they relate to the DECsystem 20, IBM Personal Computer (PC), Macintosh, Apple II, II Plus, and IIe, and Radio Shack's TRS-80 Model A microcomputer.

DECsystem 20/60

The computer used to run the program in this text is the DECsystem 20, Model 60, (DECsystem 20/60). The DECsystem 20/60 is a large minicomputer that can contain up to several million bytes of addressable internal storage for programs. The implementation of BASIC used in this textbook is BASIC-PLUS-2.

● Table I–1
Common System and Editing Commands

	DECsystem	APPLE	MACINTOSH	TRS-80	IBM
POWER SWITCH LOCATION	Left rear of terminal	Left rear of computer	Left rear of computer	Right front under keyboard	Right rear of computer
SIGN-ON PROCEDURES					
User	Control-C	No response	No response		No response
Computer response	TOPS-20 MONITOR	APPLE II*	Icon of disk with blinking question mark	TANDY CORPORATION LOGO DATE MM/DD/YY? (flashing cursor)	Enter today's date (m-d-y): time The IBM Personal Computer DOS Version 1.10 (C) Copyright IBM Corp. 1981, 1982 A >
User	LOG ACCT. # PASSWORD	No response	No response; insert appropriate disk	Enter date	Respond to date query
STARTING BASIC					
User	BASIC	Comes up in BASIC	Insert MS-BASIC disk	Type BASIC	Type BASIC or BASICA (For Advanced BASIC) after computer types A >
Computer response	READY	Flashing cursor**	Display directory of MS-BASIC disk	READY	OK
User	NEW	Begin typing program	Double-click MS-BASIC icon	Begin typing program	Begin typing program
Computer response	NEW FILENAME—		Command box appears		
User	Enter name of program; begin typing program		Begin typing program		
SYSTEM COMMANDS					
List	LIST	LIST	LIST	LIST	LIST
Execute a program	RUN	RUN	RUN	RUN	RUN
Store program on secondary storage	SAVE	SAVE name	SAVE "name"	SAVE "name"	SAVE "name"
Retrieve program from disk	OLD OLD FILENAME—	LOAD name or RUN name	Load "name" or LOAD "name", R	LOAD "name"	LOAD "name"
SIGN-OFF PROCEDURES					
User	GOODBYE or BYE	No response	Select QUIT from File Menu (see Appendix E)	No response	No response
Computer response	KILLED JOB	No response	Displays directory window	No response	No response
User	Power off	Power off	Select CLOSE, then EJECT from File Menu; Power off	Power off	Power off

* For APPLE IIe and APPLE IIc the computer response is (LOADING INTEGER BASIC)
** For APPLE IIc the computer response is **BE SURE CAPS LOCK IS DOWN**, then a flashing cursor

● COMPUTERS AND INFORMATION PROCESSING

A description of hardware for this system depends heavily on which CRT terminal is used with this computer. A user's guide provided by the manufacturer of the specific model can provide further hardware information. The CRT discussed here is the standard VT-100 terminal.

Starting the Computer

The power switch (toggle variety) is on the lower left at the back of the terminal. Press the <CTRL> (control) and C keys at the same time to provide the link between the terminal and the computer. A header will appear, followed by the symbol @:

```
TOPS-20 Monitor 5.1(5622)

@
```

This is the prompt for the TOPS-20 monitor. (A *monitor* is the housekeeping program that controls the computer.) You must now type LOGIN, followed by an account identifier and a password. The password should be known only to those who need access to the programs in that particular account. For example, the programs for this book were kept in an account called IACCT.MANDELL. The screen looks like this after you have logged in:

```
@LOGIN IACCT.MANDELL
```

Notice that the password does not appear on the screen. The monitor knows that any characters following the blank after an identifier are not to be made public.

After you have logged in properly and pressed the <RETURN> key, the computer responds with a header giving the date and time. Then the monitor prompt @ is displayed. If you hear beeps as you attempt to log in, it is an indication that you forgot to press <CTRL> C or that the computer is down. Try pressing <CTRL> C once again.

To use the BASIC language, just type BASIC after the monitor prompt. When the computer is prepared to accept BASIC commands, it responds with the prompt READY. To display a summary of all the available BASIC commands, you can type HELP.

To create a program, type NEW. The computer then asks for a name for the program:

```
READY
NEW
New program name -- IRENE.1

READY
```

If you press <RETURN> without supplying a name, the computer will call the program NONAME. You can now proceed to type in your program.

Saving and Loading Programs

We assume this computer uses magnetic disks for secondary storage. To save a program named IRENE.1, type SAVE IRENE.1:

```
READY

SAVE IRENE.1
```

To load the program again, type OLD followed by the filename. If you do not specify a filename, the computer will ask for the old program's name. Type IRENE.1:

```
READY
OLD
Old file name -- IRENE.1

READY
```

After the computer again responds READY, you may run or list the program or perform editing operations on it.

IBM PERSONAL COMPUTER

The IBM Personal Computer runs an enhanced version of Microsoft BASIC. Although it is possible to use cassette storage with the IBM, we will be discussing the hardware configuration for disk storage only.

Starting the Computer

Place the disk operating system (DOS) diskette into Drive A, the left drive. Then turn on the computer. The power switch is located at the right rear of the machine. Remember to turn on the monitor and to turn up the brightness dial, too. As soon as the computer is turned on, it will attempt to load the DOS. (If there is no diskette in the disk drive, the computer will "come up" in Cassette BASIC.)

Once the DOS has been booted, or loaded, the computer asks for the date and time. If you do not wish to enter the date and/or time, merely press the <←> (return) key after the prompts, which appear as follows:

```
Current date is Tues 1-01-1986
Enter new date (mm-dd-yy):
Current time is  0:00:52.83
Enter new time:
```

After you have responded to the time prompt and pressed <←>, the computer responds with a display similar to the following:

```
The IBM Personal Computer DOS
Version 3.10 (C)Copyright International Business Machines Corp 1981, 1985
           (C)Copyright Microsoft Corp 1981, 1985
A>
```

The A> is the system prompt. Simply type BASIC and press the <←> to load the disk BASIC translator. Then you will see the BASIC prompt:

```
Ok
```

Now you are ready to type your program.

Saving and Loading Programs

The IBM DOS has a convenient file-by-name catalog system. To save a program (for example, one named TESTS), type the following:

```
SAVE "TESTS"
```

The length of the program file name should be less than or equal to eight characters. Do not embed any spaces within the program name. To load the program from a disk, type:

● COMPUTERS AND INFORMATION PROCESSING

```
LOAD "TESTS"
```
The ending quotation marks are optional.

MACINTOSH

The implementation of BASIC used on the Macintosh for this supplement is Microsoft 2.0.

Starting the Computer

Turn on the Macintosh power switch, which is located on the lower left side of the back of the terminal. Now place the Microsoft BASIC disk in the disk drive. When the screen comes on, you will be in the "Finder" or monitor mode. On the lower half of the screen you will see several icons, or symbols, representing the various forms of BASIC that are available for use; choose the one that best fills your needs. The "mouse," or control box, is a feature of the Macintosh that requires some explanation. It works like a remote control: you move the box in the direction you wish the screen's cursor arrow to go. Once you have maneuvered the cursor arrow over the appropriate icon, "double-click" the button on the mouse: press the button twice, rapidly. The computer will now load the chosen version of Microsoft BASIC. The Command window, appearing at the bottom of the screen, indicates that you are now in BASIC. Type the word NEW in the Command window as shown, then press <Return>:

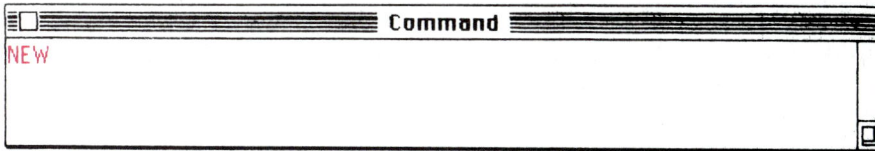

```
┌─────────────────────── Command ───────────────────────┐
│ NEW                                                    │
│                                                        │
│                                                        │
│                                                    ▣  │
└────────────────────────────────────────────────────────┘
```

You can then begin typing your BASIC program, which will appear in the list window in the right portion of the screen.

In addition to the Command window and the list window, the Microsoft BASIC screen displays two other regions: a menu bar at the top of the screen and an output window. Program manipulating commands can be performed either by using the Command window or by using the other features. Only the Command window method will be dealt with in this supplement; consult your system manual for details on the alternative methods for the operations described here.

Saving and Loading Programs

To save a program named "TESTS", for example, type SAVE "TESTS" (note that the filename must be in double quotation marks) in the Command window and press <Return>:

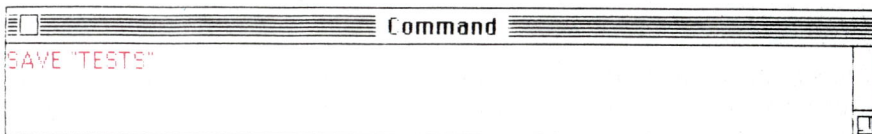

```
┌─────────────────────── Command ───────────────────────┐
│ SAVE "TESTS"                                           │
│                                                        │
│                                                        │
│                                                    ▣  │
└────────────────────────────────────────────────────────┘
```

BASIC SUPPLEMENT ● B-13

To load the program from a disk, type LOAD "TESTS" in the Command window, then press <RETURN>:

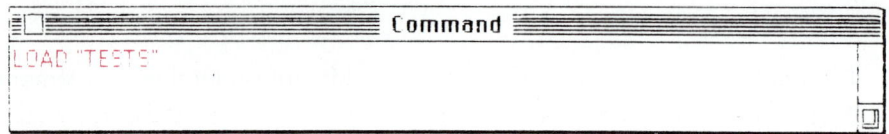

```
▤□▤▤▤▤▤▤▤▤▤▤▤▤▤  Command  ▤▤▤▤▤▤▤▤▤▤▤▤▤▤
LOAD "TESTS"
                                                                    ▫
```

APPLE II, II PLUS, AND IIe

The Apple II initially contains INTEGER BASIC, which lacks many important features of ANSI BASIC. Therefore, our discussion is limited to the use of this computer after Applesoft floating-point BASIC has been loaded. The Apple II Plus and the Apple IIe computers automatically "come up" in Applesoft BASIC.

Starting the Computer

The power switch is located on the left rear portion of the computer. An external monitor or cathode-ray tube (CRT) is required, so you must remember to turn on power to this device also. If a disk drive is attached, it will whir and try to boot the disk operating system (DOS), so be sure that a diskette is placed in the disk drive before the computer is turned on. (When the disk drive boots the DOS, it loads from a diskette the instructions that tell the computer how to manage the disk. This must be done before the computer can perform any disk-related tasks.) The computer automatically "comes up" in Applesoft BASIC, as indicated by the prompt] character.

Saving and Loading Programs

Programs commonly are accessed from disk on this system. The Apple has a convenient file-by-name catalog system for the DOS. To save an Applesoft program—for example, one named TESTS—on disk, type the following:

SAVE TESTS

and press <Return>. To load the same program from disk, type this:

LOAD TESTS

and press <Return>. You can now run the program. Alternatively, you can type RUN TESTS without first loading the program; this causes the DOS both to load and to run the program.

TRS-80 MODEL 4

The following description of the TRS-80 computer refers to the Model 4, with Model 4 Disk BASIC.

Starting the Computer

Place the system diskette with Model 4 Disk BASIC into Drive 0 (zero), the bottom drive. Turn on the power switch, which is located under the right side of the keyboard. As soon as the computer is turned on, it will load

● COMPUTERS AND INFORMATION PROCESSING

the disk operating system (TRSDOS). You will see the TRSDOS start-up logo and a prompt to enter the date. Enter the date in MM/DD/YY format and press <ENTER>. For example, to enter the date December 16, 1987, type:

```
12/01/87
```

The computer converts these numbers to Mon., Dec. 16, 1987 and displays this information. Then the following system prompt message appears:

```
TRSDOS Ready
```

This message indicates that you are at the operating system level. To load BASIC into the system, type:

```
BASIC
```

A paragraph with copyright information appears on your screen, followed by:

```
Ready
```

You may now begin using BASIC.

Saving and Loading Programs

To save a program, you need to assign it a "filespace" or filename. For example, if you write a program concerning authors, you could assign it the filespec AUTHOR and type the following command:

```
SAVE "AUTHOR"
```

It takes a few seconds for the computer to write your program to the disk, but when this process is completed, the Ready prompt appears.

The filespec of the program can have a maximum of eight alphanumeric characters. It can also have an optional extension of up to three characters. A slash (/) must be included between the filespec and the extension. The first character of both the filespec and the extension must be a letter. If a file with this filespec already exists, its contents will be lost, because the file will be re-created. For example:

```
SAVE "AUTHOR/BOK"
```

You may also add a drive number to the filespec by typing a colon (:) and the drive number:

```
SAVE "AUTHOR:1"
```

The drive number tells the computer to save the program on the disk in Drive 1. If no drive number is specified, the computer defaults to Drive 0. If you specify a disk drive, make sure you have a disk in that drive.

If you want to use this program again, you must load it back into memory. To do this, type:

```
LOAD "filespec",R
```

The trailing R is optional; if it is included, the filespec will be loaded and run. If the R is not included, the filespec will simply be loaded.

As with SAVE, you can specify a disk drive by typing a colon and the drive number. For example:

```
LOAD "AUTHOR:1"
```

The drive number tells the computer to load the program from the disk in Drive 1. If no drive is specified, the computer defaults to Drive 0. If you specify a drive number, make sure that you have a disk in that drive and that the program you specified is on that disk; otherwise, an error will occur. BASIC will return to the command mode after the load and/or run has been completed.

● BASIC Commands

BASIC commands are **immediate-mode** (or **direct**) instructions; that is, they are executed as soon as the carriage control key (<Return> or <Enter>) is pressed. They differ from BASIC language statements, which are not executed until the program is run. The most commonly used commands are discussed here. Table I–1 summarizes these commands for the five computers.

NEW.   The NEW command tells the computer to erase any program currently in active memory. After typing this command, you can start entering a new program.

LIST.   After typing in a long program, you may want to admire the finished product. Type LIST to see the program statements displayed at the terminal. If you have a very short program, LIST can display the whole program on the screen. However, if the program has more lines than the screen does, only the last part of the program will remain on the screen.
   Some screens permit only twenty-four lines to be displayed. You can display portions of programs by specifying the lines to be listed—LIST 250–400, for example. Most computers also allow you to suppress scrolling, that is, to freeze the listing temporarily (see "Controlling the Scroll" later in this section).

SAVE.   After you have typed many program lines, you will want to avoid losing them when the computer is turned off. To do this, you have to move a program from main memory to an auxiliary storage medium such as a magnetic tape or disk. This move is accomplished by the SAVE command. There are generally several options to this command; for example, you may supply a name that distinguishes this particular program from all others.

LOAD.   This command moves the designated program from auxiliary storage to main computer memory. Before moving the program, LOAD closes all open files and deletes all variables and program lines currently residing in memory. On the DECsystem, the OLD command is used instead of LOAD.

CONTROLLING THE SCROLL.   If your program's output consists of forty lines of information but your screen only has a twenty-four-line capacity, how will you see all your output? The forty lines will be displayed so quickly that you will not be able to read them until the listing is finished.

By then, however, the first sixteen lines will be gone—scrolled off the top of the screen.

Most computers have a means of controlling the scroll of the screen. The programmer can simply push one or two keys to freeze the display and then press the same keys to resume listing when desired. This method also can be used to freeze the output listing of a program during execution. Table I–2 summarizes the method of scroll freezing used on each of the five computers.

● Editing a Program

Everyone makes typing mistakes. You should quickly learn how to correct yours. You may find a mistake before you press the RETURN key, or you may find it later. These two conditions call for different methods of correction.

BEFORE RETURN HAS BEEN PRESSED.   Suppose you type LOST when you wish to LIST a program. If you notice the error before pressing RETURN, you can move the computer's cursor back to the O in LOST by pressing the DELETE key (on the DEC), the ← key (on the Apple, IBM, and TRS-80), or the Backspace Key (on the Macintosh). Then you can retype LIST correctly.

AFTER RETURN HAS BEEN PRESSED*.   If you notice an error after RETURN has been pressed, the simplest correction, in principle, is to retype the whole line. This may get tiresome for long lines, however—especially if you need to change only one character. Each computer has a means of correcting mistakes within a given line. There is not enough space

*The Macintosh has a variety of ways to edit, therefore we suggest you refer to your manual.

● **Table I–2**
Scroll Control

	SCROLL STOP	SCROLL START
DECsystem	No Scroll Key	No Scroll Key
IBM PC	Ctrl-NUMLOCK	Press any key
Macintosh	*	*
Apple II, II Plus, IIe	Ctrl-S	Press any key
TRS-80 Model III	Shift-@	Press any key

1. Ctrl-S means to hold down the control (<Ctrl>) key and the S key at the same time.
2. Shift-@ means to hold down the Shift key and the @ key at the same time.

* When a program is listed, scrolling is controlled by clicking the vertical and horizontal scroll arrows and boxes on the right side and bottom of the List window.

To stop scrolling output, click the Run menu at the top of the screen, and then click Suspend, which is found in the Run menu. To continue processing, click the Run menu again. Then click Continue, found in the Run menu.

here for a full explanation of these methods, but there are two general kinds—the screen editor and the line editor.

To use the screen editor, list the portion of the program containing the error. Then move the cursor to the position of the error—typically by pressing four keys with arrows that move the cursor up, down, left, or right. The incorrect characters then can be typed over or deleted, or new characters can be inserted between existing characters.

The line editor works on individual lines. The user specifies the line containing the error and uses commands such as REPLACE, INSERT, and DELETE instead of moving the cursor to the error.

● Summary Points

● BASIC (Beginners All-purpose Symbolic Instruction Code) was developed in the mid-1960s by Professors John G. Kemeny and Thomas E. Kurtz.

● Structured programming languages were developed to encourage the writing of easy-to-understand, more error-free programs. They have two basic characteristics: the logic of the program is easy to follow, and the program is divided into subprograms, each performing a specific task.

● The following are the five steps in the programming process: (1) define and document the problem; (2) design and document a solution; (3) write and document a program; (4) enter it into the computer; and (5) test and debug the program, and revise the documentation if necessary.

● Programs are best designed by using a top-down approach, in which a large task is divided into smaller and smaller subtasks, moving from the general to the specific.

● Program design can be documented by structure charts to show top-down design and by flowcharts to display the order and type of program steps to be performed.

● BASIC has rules of grammar (syntax) to which programmers must adhere.

● BASIC commands are used by the programmer to communicate with the operating system of the computer. Some commonly used ones are NEW, LIST, RUN, and SAVE.

● Editing commands help the programmer correct mistakes.

● Review Questions

1. What is BASIC?
2. What is software?
3. What are characteristics of structured programs?
4. What is an algorithm and how is it used in the programming process?
5. Name the five steps of the programming process.
6. What is documentation, and why is it important?
7. What is a syntax error?
8. Explain the function of the system command NEW.
9. Explain the function of the system command LIST.
10. Explain the function of the system command SAVE.

● Section II
BASIC Fundamentals

● Introduction

One of the best ways to learn any programming language is to examine sample programs. This and the remaining sections in this text will intersperse discussions of the language's general characteristics with program examples and practice problems to promote the learning process.

This section discusses some BASIC fundamentals: line numbers, BASIC statements, constants, character strings, and variables. All are demonstrated so that you can use them properly when you write programs.

● Fundamentals of the BASIC Language

A program is a sequence of instructions which tells the computer how to solve a problem. Figure II–1 is an example of a BASIC program that calculates the gross pay of an employee who worked 40 hours at $4.50 per hour.

Each line in a BASIC program is called a BASIC statement. All BASIC statements are composed of special programming commands (key words recognized by the BASIC system) and elements of the language: constants, variables, and operators. BASIC statements are divided into two general categories: executable statements and nonexecutable statements. Whether or not a line is executable is determined by the command used in the statement. In the example in Figure II–1, the first two lines of the program are nonexecutable. The computer simply ignores these statements, skipping over them and moving on to the next statement. All of the remaining lines of the program in Figure II–1 are executable. This means that the computer does something when these lines are encountered.

On the DECsystem there are two commands, RUN and RUNNH, that can be used to execute (run) a program. If RUN is used, as in Figure II–1, the computer will print a header giving the name of your program (that is, the name under which it is stored in your directory, CH2FIG1.CBP in this example), the date, and the time as well as the output of the program. The RUNNH (Run No Header) command will eliminate the header and print only the output of the program. Throughout the remainder of this book we will use the RUNNH format.

```
00010    REM *** THIS PROGRAM COMPUTES AN ***
00020    REM *** EMPLOYEE'S GROSS PAY.     ***
00030    LET HOURS = 40
00040    LET RTE = 4.5
00050    LET GROSS = HOURS * RTE
00060    LET MESSAGE$ = "GROSS PAY IS"
00070    PRINT MESSAGE$;GROSS
00099    END
```

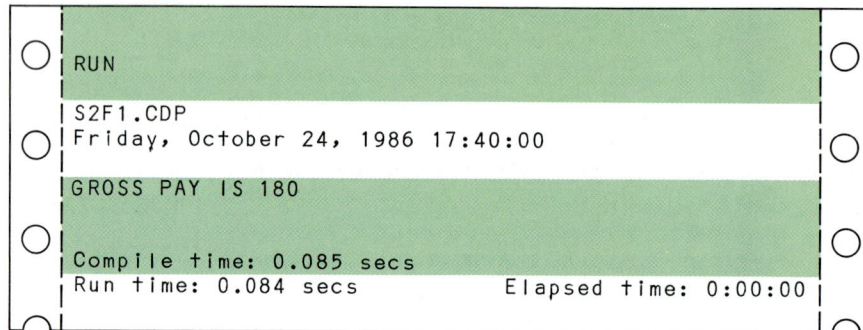

```
RUN

S2F1.CDP
Friday, October 24, 1986 17:40:00

GROSS PAY IS 180


Compile time: 0.085 secs
Run time: 0.084 secs              Elapsed time: 0:00:00
```

● FIGURE II-1
Gross Pay Program

● Line Numbers

As we mentioned earlier, BASIC commands are executed in immediate or direct mode. BASIC statements, or instructions, may be executed in either direct mode or **indirect mode.** In indirect mode, the statements are not executed until the RUN (or RUNNH) command is given. **Line numbers** tell the computer that the statements following them are to be executed in indirect mode. Therefore, the computer does not execute these statements until it is instructed to do so.

Line numbers also determine the sequence of execution of BASIC statements. (Later on, we will learn ways to alter the order in which statements are executed.) Execution starts at the lowest line number and continues in ascending numerical order to the highest number. Line numbers must be integers between 1 and 99999, although the upper limit may be lower, depending upon the system being used (Table II-1). No commas or embedded spaces can be included in a line number. Table II-2 contains examples of valid and invalid line numbers. Line numbers in BASIC are often considered labels, because they refer to specific statements in the program. In Figure II-1, the number 70 is the label for the statement PRINT MESSAGE$; GROSS.

Line numbers do not have to be in increments of 1. In fact, it is best to use increments of 10 or 20, in order to allow for insertion of lines at a later time if necessary. Instructions need not be entered in ascending numerical order: the computer will rearrange them in this order for execution. This feature of BASIC makes it easy to insert new lines between existing lines. For example, if you type:

```
00010 LET NAM$ = "SAM"
00020 PRINT MESS$,NAM$
00099 END
```

● COMPUTERS AND INFORMATION PROCESSING

COMPUTER	LOWEST NUMBER	HIGHEST NUMBER
DECsystem	1	99999
Apple	0	63999
IBM/Microsoft	0	65529
Macintosh/Microsoft*	0	65529
TRS-80	0	65529

*Line numbers are not required

and then realize you forgot a statement that should go between lines 10 and 20, you can simply add the needed statement like this:

```
00015 LET MESS$ = "MY NAME IS "
```

Now when the program is listed, it will appear like this:

```
00010 LET NAM$ = "SAM"
00015 LET MESS$ = "MY NAME IS "
00020 PRINT MESS$,NAM$
00099 END
```

Because we incremented the line numbers by 10 in this example, it was a simple matter to insert a line. If the statements had been numbered in increments of 1 instead, we would have had to retype the entire program in order to insert a line. For this reason, programmers generally use increments of at least 10.

If you find that you have made an error on a line, simply retype the line number and the correct BASIC statement. This procedure corrects the error because, if two lines are entered with the same line number, the computer saves and executes the most recently typed one. To demonstrate this fact, assume that line 160 should print SUM, but the following was typed instead:

```
00160 PRINT SUN
```

To correct this, simply retype line 160:

```
000160 PRINT SUM
```

The computer will discard the current line 160 and replace it with the newest version of line 160.

● Table II–2
Valid and Invalid Line Number Examples

VALID	INVALID
00010 PRINT "MY NAME IS SAM"	00010.5 PRINT "MY NAME IS SAM"
00020 LET NME$ = "SAM"	02,000 LET NME$ = "SAM"
00099 END	000 99 END

● BASIC Statement Components

In the remaining portion of this chapter, we will take a closer look at numeric and character string constants and numeric and string variables.

CONSTANTS

Constants are values that do not change during the execution of a program. There are two kinds of constants: numeric and character string.

Numeric Constants

A **numeric constant** is a number that is included in a BASIC statement (other than the line number). Numbers can be represented in two ways in the BASIC language: as real numbers, which include a decimal point (also called floating-point numbers), or as integers (numbers with no decimal portion). When using numbers in BASIC, remember these rules:

1. No commas can be included in numbers. The computer interprets the digits before and after a comma as two separate numbers. For example, the computer would interpret 3,751 as the number 3 and the number 751. The valid form of the number is 3751.

2. If a number has no sign, the computer assumes it is positive. For example, 386 is the same as +386.

3. If a number is negative, the negative sign must precede the digits, as in the example −21.

4. Fractions must be written in decimal form. For example, 2.75 is the correct representation for 2¾.

A **real constant** is a number with a decimal part. The following are all valid real constants.

```
  6.0        6.782
   .95       0.58
 -7.234     -0.09
```

Very small or very large numbers can be represented in scientific notation (also called exponential notation). The following format is used ±x.xxxxE±n. The E represents base 10, and the signed number following the E is the power to which 10 is raised. The number preceding the E is called the mantissa and in most systems lies between 1.000 and 9.999. A plus sign (+) by the power indicates that the decimal point is to be shifted to the right that number of places, whereas a minus sign (−) indicates that the decimal point should be shifted left that number of places.

The following are examples of exponential notation:

DECIMAL FORM	POWER EQUIVALENT	EXPONENTIAL NOTATION
5278	5.278×10^3	5.278E+03
0.0000021	2.1×10^{-6}	2.1E−06
−923180	-9.2318×10^5	−9.2318E+05
−0.00069	-6.9×10^{-4}	−6.9E−04

● COMPUTERS AND INFORMATION PROCESSING

On many BASIC systems, real numbers can be stored as either single-precision or double-precision numbers.

Single-precision numbers take less storage space than double-precision numbers, and the computer can perform single-precision number calculations more rapidly. Single-precision numbers have fewer digits and therefore are usually less accurate than double-precision numbers. This difference can be important in programs that perform a number of calculations and require a high degree of accuracy. However, caution must be used, because in some cases the BASIC internal functions might not be any more accurate with double-precision than with single-precision. You should consult the manual for your system.

An integer is a number with no decimal portion. The following numbers are examples of integer constants:

29   123434
3432   −8
205   −101

Character String Constants

A **character string** constant is simply a collection of symbols called **alphanumeric data.** These can include any combination of letters, numbers, and special characters including dashes, commas, blanks, and others. The character string is enclosed in double or single quotation marks, depending on the system. All of the systems covered in this textbook require double quotation marks to delimit character strings.

You can include single quotation marks within a string constant delimited by double quotation marks. The following are examples of valid character string constants delimited by double quotation marks:

"He said, 'Good morning.' "
"This is a string constant."
"Gary's Tennis Racket"

The following character string constant is invalid:

"The letter "A" is a vowel."

In the last example, the system would recognize the double quotation mark before the letter A as indicating the end of the string. Actually, the quotation mark at the end of the line is supposed to indicate the end of the string. This character string constant could be correctly written as:

"The letter 'A' is a vowel."

The length of a string constant is determined by counting all of its characters. For example, the two character strings below will not be stored in the computer in the same way:

"SATURDAY   "
"SATURDAY"

The first string will be stored as SATURDAY plus three blanks (the computer can store a blank, just as it can store any other character). The second string will be stored simply as SATURDAY. Therefore, the computer will store eleven characters for the first string and only eight for the second one.

The maximum number of characters allowed in a character string depends upon the system being used. On all the BASIC systems used in this textbook, the maximum character string length is 255 characters.

The program in Figure II–1 contains a character string in line 60:

```
00060 LET MESSAGE$ = "GROSS PAY IS"
```

VARIABLES

Before we explain BASIC programming any further, it is important that you understand how data is stored in the primary storage unit of a computer.

To visualize a computer's primary storage unit, imagine a block of post office boxes. Each box has an assigned number that acts as an address for that particular box (see Figure II–2). The addresses of these boxes always remain the same, but their contents will almost certainly change over a period of time. Similarly, the primary storage unit in a computer is divided into many separate storage locations, each with a specific address. A storage location containing a value that can change during program execution is referred to as a **variable.** A variable can contain only one value at a time; when a new value is assigned to a variable, the old value is lost.

In BASIC the programmer is allowed to assign names to storage locations and then refer to each location by its name. In the example in Figure II–2, HOURS and RTE are **variable names** used to identify specific storage locations. The value (or contents) of the locations named HOURS and RTE are 40 and 4.50 respectively.

The number of characters allowed in a variable name differs from computer to computer, but most computers permit variable names of various lengths. Therefore, the programmer can use descriptive variable names, that is, names that describe the value they identify. Good programming habits include the use of descriptive variable names, because

● **FIGURE II–2**
Post Office Boxes Are Similar to Variables

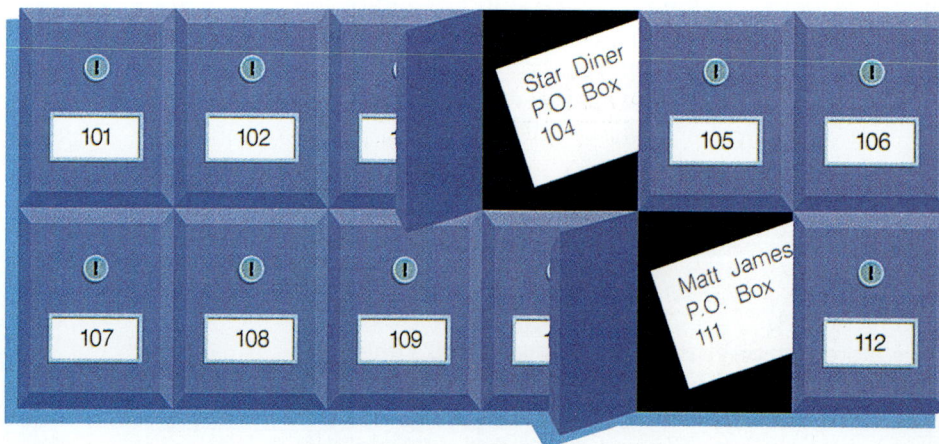

● **COMPUTERS AND INFORMATION PROCESSING**

such names make programs easy to read. For example, the name STU-DENT is more descriptive than ST.

There are some BASIC systems, however, that recognize only the first two characters of a variable name (see Table II–3). These systems would recognize the variables QUANTITY and QUEUE as being identical, for example. When using these computers, the programmer must make sure that the first two characters of each variable name are unique.

Variables are classified as *numeric* or *string*. Each of these types will be discussed here.

Numeric Variables

A **numeric variable** is used to store a number that is either supplied to the computer by the programmer or internally calculated during program execution. A numeric variable name must begin with a letter, followed by letters and/or digits with no embedded blanks.

As with numeric constants, there are both integer and real numeric variables. Integer variable names must have a percent sign (%) as the last character. Table II–4 shows some valid and invalid variable names for real and integer numbers.

It is possible to assign an integer to a real variable because the computer can convert the integer to a real number without changing its value.

● Table II–3
Maximum Number of Characters Recognized in Variable Names

COMPUTER	MAXIMUM ALLOWED	MAXIMUM RECOGNIZED
DECsystem	30	30
Apple	238	First 2
IBM/Microsoft	Any length	First 40
Macintosh/Microsoft	40	First 40
TRS-80	40	First 40

● Table II–4
Valid and Invalid Numeric Variable Names

VALID	INVALID AND REASON	
SUM (real)	225	(Variable name must start with a letter)
M1% (integer)	M2&	(No special characters allowed except those used to designate type of variable)
D6E7 (real)	RT%DAY	(The percent sign must be the last symbol)
BIG47(real)	B2$	($ symbol used to designate a string variable)
AMT% (integer)	D M6	(Variable name cannot include a blank)

For example, the integer 17 can be changed to the real number 17.0. The reverse is not true, however; if a real number is assigned to an integer variable, part of the number is lost. For example, it would be impossible to store 17.65 accurately as an integer. On the DECsystem, if a real value is assigned to an integer variable, the value is cut off at the decimal point. Therefore, if the value 17.65 were assigned to the variable X%, it would be stored as 17.

String Variables

A **string variable** is used to store a character string, such as a name, an address, or a social security number. As with numeric variables, string variables can store only one value at a time.

A string variable name begins with a letter followed by letters or digits and must be terminated with a dollar sign ($). All computers require the first character to be alphabetic and the last character to be a dollar sign, which is what enables the computer to distinguish it as a string variable name. Table II–5 gives examples of string variable names.

In the sample program in Figure II–1, lines 60 and 70 contain the string variable name MESSAGE$:

```
00060 LET MESSAGE$ = "GROSS PAY IS"
00070 PRINT MESSAGE$;GROSS
```

In line 60, the character string GROSS PAY is stored in the location named MESSAGE$; in line 70, the value stored in location MESSAGE$ is printed.

RESERVED WORDS

Certain words have specific meanings to the BASIC compiler or interpreter. These are **reserved words,** which cannot be used as variable names. Table II–6 lists a few of the most common reserved words.

Some systems, such as the Apple, scan all BASIC statements for reserved words. Any reserved words embedded in a variable name are seen by the computer as reserved words and cannot be used in a variable name. For example, RATE cannot be used as a variable name on such a system because it contains the reserved word AT.

● **Table II–5**
Valid and Invalid String Variable Names

VALID	INVALID AND REASON	
C$	$	(First character must be a letter)
HEADING$	4$	(First character must be a letter)
DAY$	E2%	(A string variable name must have a $ as the last character)
EMP$	EM$P	(The $ symbol must be the last character)
M1$	M 1$	(No blanks allowed)
SSNO$	SS-NO$	(Hyphen not allowed)

● **COMPUTERS AND INFORMATION PROCESSING**

● Table II–6
Reserved Words

ABS	END	GOSUB	LOG	REM	STEP
BASE	EXP	GOTO	NEXT	RESTORE	STOP
CALL	FN	IF	ON	RETURN	TAB
COS	FOR	INPUT	OPEN	RND	TAN
DATA	ELSE	INT	PRINT	SIN	THEN
DEF	GET	LET	PUT	SGN	TO
DIM	GO	LIST	READ	SQR	UNTIL
VAL	WHILE				

● Summary Points

● A BASIC program is a series of instructions. Each one is composed of a line number and a BASIC statement.

● The line numbers serve (1) as labels by which statements can be referenced and (2) as instructions to specify the order of execution of the statements in a program.

● Using line numbers in increments of 5 or 10 permits easy insertion of new statements.

● BASIC statements contain special reserved words (programming commands), numeric or character string constants, numeric or string variables, and formulas.

● Constants are values that do not change. A valid numeric constant is any real number expressed as an integer, a decimal fraction, or in exponential notation. Character strings are alphanumeric data enclosed in quotation marks.

● Variable names are programmer-supplied names that identify locations in storage where data values may be stored. Numeric variable names represent numbers. String variables contain alphanumeric values and their names are distinguished from numeric names by the symbol $.

● Review Questions

1. What is a BASIC program?
2. Indicate whether each of the following line numbers is valid or invalid.
   a. 000 99
   b. 136
   c. 2,893
   d. 9999

3. Convert these numbers from exponential notation to regular decimal form.
  a. 7.24396E + 03
  b. 1.99E − 02
  c. 4.972E + 05
  d. 8.05E − 04

4. Give the exponential power equivalent to these numbers using standard notation:
  a. 90206
  b. 23.785
  c. − 275210
  d. .00321

5. What is a constant? Name two types.

6. Which of these are invalid numeric constants?
  a. 0.73
  b. 1072 −
  c. 2.9171E − 02
  d. 5.346 + 05
  e. 7,942
  f. + 6029

7. Which of these are invalid character string constants in an expression?
  a. BOWLING GREEN, OHIO
  b. "APPLE"
  c. "7747"
  d. "PICKLE, DILL"

8. What is a variable? Name two types, and explain how they differ.

9. How many values can a memory location hold at one time?

10. Which of the following are illegal variable names, and why?
  a. 7$
  b. D
  c. 5B
  d. H$
  e. M$
  f. R
  g. Z9
  h. W*
  i. 25
  j. $F

● Section III
Getting Started with BASIC Programming

● Introduction

This section describes four elementary BASIC statements—REM, the assignment statement, PRINT, and END. The assignment statement is used to assign data to variables and to perform arithmetic calculations. The PRINT statement allows the programmer to see the results of processing. Processing is stopped with the END statement. The REM statement is presented here to underscore the importance of program documentation. The section also will discuss how to place multiple statements on the same physical line.

● Documenting a Program

The REM, or remark, statement provides information for the programmer or anyone else reading the program. It is ignored by the computer; in other words, it is a nonexecutable statement. This information is referred to as documentation and its function is to explain to humans the purpose of the program, what the variable names represent, or any special instructions to the user. Because REM statements do not affect program execution, they can be placed anywhere in the program. The only restriction is that the program line must begin with the reserved word REM.

The general format of the REM statement is

line# REM comment

The comment can be any statement that the programmer regards as appropriate documentation. The word REM must be included exactly as shown; "line#" indicates that a valid line number must be inserted here.

Figure III–1 is a sample program that uses the REM statement. Lines 10 and 20 describe the purpose of the program. Lines 30 through 70 explain the major variables that are used throughout the program. These seven lines are helpful to someone who may be reading the program but who is not the original programmer. Notice that line 80 contains no comment after the REM statement. This line improves readability by separating the opening remarks from the executable statements listed later in the program.

```
00010   REM *** THE PURPOSE OF THIS PROGRAM IS    ***
00020   REM *** TO COMPUTE AN AVERAGE TEST SCORE.  ***
00030   REM *** MAJOR VARIABLES:                    ***
00040   REM ***      FTEST - FIRST TEST            ***
00050   REM ***      STEST - SECOND TEST           ***
00060   REM ***      TTEST - THIRD TEST            ***
00070   REM ***      AV    - AVERAGE               ***
00080   REM
00090   LET FTEST = 89
00100   LET STEST = 85
00110   LET TTEST = 78
00120   LET AV = (FTEST + STEST + TTEST) / 3
00130   PRINT "AVERAGE",AV
00999   END
```

MICROCOMPUTERS	DIFFERENCE
Apple	None
IBM/Microsoft	None
Macintosh/Microsoft	None
TRS-80	None

Notice also the asterisks that surround the descriptive comment. Although this device is simply a matter of personal taste, many programmers use asterisks to separate comments from the rest of the program. This technique allows the REM statement to be easily identified when the programmer is looking through long program listings.

Remarks may also be placed in the body of the program in order to explain a BASIC instruction or a series of instructions. For example, if an arithmetic calculation is performed, it is sometimes helpful to explain the purpose of that particular calculation immediately before the lines that perform it. We could add the following remark to the sample program in Figure III-1.

```
00115 REM *** COMPUTE AVERAGE OF THREE TEST SCORES ***
```

A more descriptive remark can be used for more complicated calculations.

Many systems allow comments to be placed on the same line as an executable statement. In these cases, a special symbol must be used to mark the beginning of the comment. On the DEC system this symbol is an exclamation point (!) used as follows:

```
00120 LET AV = (FTEST + STEST + TTEST) / 3      ! CALCULATE THE AVERAGE
```

The BASIC system will recognize CALCULATE THE AVERAGE as a comment because it is preceded by an exclamation point. This same type of comment can be indicated on the IBM and the Macintosh by the use of a single quotation mark (') like this:

```
120 LET AV = (FTEST + STEST + TTEST) / 3      'CALCULATE THE AVERAGE
```

Adding a comment at the end of a BASIC statement can be a very useful way to document a program.

● The Assignment Statement

The LET statement is an **assignment statement;** that is, a statement that stores a value in main memory in the location allotted to the stated variable. In a flowchart, an assignment statement is illustrated by a processing symbol ([___]). The general format of the LET statement is:

line# LET variable = expression

The variable can be a numeric or string variable. If it is a numeric variable, the expression can be a numeric constant, an arithmetic formula, or another numeric variable. If the variable is a string variable, the expression can be either a string constant or another string variable.

The LET statement can be used to assign values to numeric or string variables directly or to assign the result of a calculation to a numeric variable. In either case, the expression on the right side of the equal sign is assigned to the variable on the left side. This operation causes the value of the expression to be placed in the memory location identified by the variable name on the left side of the LET statement.

Here are some of the assignment statements from the sample program in Figure III–1:

```
00090 LET FTEST = 89
00100 LET STEST = 85
00110 LET TTEST = 78
00120 LET AV = (FTEST + STEST + TTEST) / 3
```

Lines 90 through 110 assign three numeric constants (in this case, test scores) to three numeric variables. Line 120 assigns the result of an arithmetic calculation to the numeric variable AV, which represents the average of the three scores.

The following table lists examples of assignment statements along with short descriptions of how they would be executed.

ASSIGNMENT STATEMENT	COMPUTER EXECUTION
00100 LET HOURS = 30.5	The numeric value 30.5 is assigned to the storage location called HOURS.
00110 LET SUM = A + B	The values in locations A and B are added together and the result is stored in location SUM. A and B remain unchanged.
00120 LET NUMBER = 1	The value in location 1 is also stored in location NUMBER. 1 remains unchanged.
00130 LET EMPL$ = "JON"	The character string enclosed in quotes (but not the quotation marks themselves) is placed in the location called EMPL$.
00140 LET CNT = CNT + 1	The value 1 is added to the current value in CNT. This new value replaces the previous value of CNT.

Only a variable name is permitted on the left side of the LET statement. For example,

```
00130 LET A + 1 = B
```

is *not* a valid statement.

The LET Statement is often used to assign a beginning value to a variable; this is called initialization. For example:

```
LET X = 0
LET Y = 1
LET NME$ = " "
```

BASIC, however, automatically initializes variables to a default value if the programmer does not initialize the variables to a specific value. Numeric variables default to the value zero and string variables to the null string (a blank space). Although this feature is available, it is not considered good programming practice, therefore we do not recommend the use of automatic initializations.

On most BASIC systems, including all those covered in this textbook, the use of the reserved word LET is optional. These systems see the following two statements as identical:

```
00010 LET TEST1 = 36
00020 TEST1 = 36
```

For simplicity's sake, we will discontinue using LET in programs after this section.

ARITHMETIC EXPRESSIONS

In BASIC, arithmetic expressions are composed of numeric constants, numeric variables, and arithmetic operators. The arithmetic operators that can be used are defined in the following table.

OPERATOR	OPERATION	ARITHMETIC EXPRESSION	EXPRESSION IN BASIC
+	Addition	$A + B$	A + B
−	Subtraction	$A - B$	A − B
*	Multiplication	$A \times B$	A * B
/	Division	$A \div B$	A / B
^	Exponentiation	A^B	A ^ B

Some examples of valid expressions in assignment statements follow:

```
00010 LET M = 5 + 4
00020 LET T = N1 + N2 + N3 + N4
00030 LET J = A - B
00040 LET X = 3 * C
00050 LET Y = (P * D) * C
00060 LET Q = N ^ 5
00070 LET C = 6.4 + P / X
```

Again, some compilers and interpreters do not require the LET statement. If such is the case, all these statements could be written without using LET.

In an addition operation such as

```
00010 LET X = A + B
```

the value in the memory location identified by the variable A is added to the value in the memory location identified by the variable B. The result then is placed in the memory location identified by the variable X. For example, if A equals 5 and B equals 3, the computer would add 5 + 3 and place the result, 8, into the storage location identified by X.

For the example $X = A - B$, the same steps occur except that the value stored in B is subtracted from the value stored in A.

The multiplication operator (*) is used in multiplying two values. For example,

$$X = A * B$$

multiplies the value in the memory location identified by A by the value in the memory location identified by B and places the product in the memory location identified by X.

The division operator (/) is used in dividing two values. For example,

$$X = A / B$$

divides the value in the storage location A by the value in the storage location B and places the result in the storage location identified by X.

The result or product of an arithmetic operation can be used in subsequent calculations; for example,

```
00050 LET X = M + N
00060 LET Y = X * 6
00070 PRINT X,Y
```

The last arithmetic operation we will talk about here is **exponentiation,** or raising a number to a power. For example, A^3 is the same as A * A * A. The ^ operator is used in exponentiation. In the statement

```
00050 LET Y = X ^ 3
```

X would be cubed (X * X * X), and the result would be stored in the storage location identified by Y.

In the example using arithmetic operators, note that we have left a space on each side of the operators. This spacing is not necessary, but it greatly improves the readability of the program.

HIERARCHY OF OPERATIONS

When more than one operation is to be performed in a single arithmetic expression, the computer follows a **hierarchy of operations** that states the order in which arithmetic expressions are to be evaluated. When parentheses are used in an expression, the operations inside the parentheses are performed before the operations outside the parentheses. If parentheses are nested, the operations inside the innermost set are done first. Thus, in the expression

(6 + (5 * 2) / 3.12) + 10

the first operation to be performed is to multiply 5 by 2.

Parentheses aside, operations are performed according to the following rules:

Priority	Operation	Symbol
First	Exponentiation	^
Second	Multiplication/division	*, /
Third	Addition/subtraction	+, −

Operations of high priority are performed before operations of lower priority. If several operations are on the same level, they are performed from left to right. Table III–1 gives some examples of how BASIC evaluates expressions.

● The PRINT Statement

The PRINT statement is used to display or print the result of computer processing. It is flowcharted using an input/output symbol (⬜). The general form of the PRINT statement is as follows:

line# PRINT { variable
literal
arithmetic expression
any combination of the above

● **Table III–1**
Examples of Evaluating Arithmetic Expressions

EXPRESSION	EVALUATION PROCESS
1. Y = 2 * 5 + 1	
First: 2 * 5 = 10	Process highest priority
Second: 10 + 1 = 11	Process next priority
Result: Y = 11	
2. Y = 2 * (5 + 1)	
First: 5 + 1 = 6	Perform process within parentheses
Second: 2 * 6 = 12	Perform next priority
Result: Y = 12	
3. Y = (3 + (6 + 2) / 4) + 10 ^ 2	
First: 6 + 2 = 8	Process innermost parentheses
Second: 8 / 4 = 2	Perform next priority
Third: 3 + 2 = 5	Process rest of outer parentheses
Fourth: 10 ^ 2 = 100	Perform next priority
Fifth: 5 + 100 = 105	Perform lowest priority

If more than one item is included in the PRINT statement, the items are separated by commas. These commas are also used to format or arrange the output; this topic will be discussed in detail in Section 4. For now, it is sufficient to know that the commas automatically space the items across the output line.

PRINTING THE VALUES OF VARIABLES

We can tell the computer to print values assigned to storage locations simply by using the reserved word PRINT with the variable name after it. If there is more than one variable to be printed, the names must be separated by commas:

```
00160 PRINT HRS,PERHR,TPAY
```

Printing has no effect on the contents of the storage location being printed. The PRINT statement only gets the value of a variable and prints it to the terminal screen.

PRINTING LITERALS

A **literal** is a group of characters containing any combination of alphabetic, numeric, and/or special characters. It is essentially the same as a constant. The term *literal*, however, is applied to constants used in PRINT statements. There are two types, character string literals and numeric literals.

Character Strings

A character string literal is a group of letters, numbers, and/or special characters enclosed in quotation marks. Whatever is inside the quotation marks is printed exactly as it is. For example,

```
00190 PRINT "SAMPLE @%OUTPUT 12"
```

would appear on the screen as

```
SAMPLE @%OUTPUT 12
```

Note that the quotation marks are not printed.

Literals can be used to print headings in output. To print column headings, for example, put each heading in quotation marks and separate them with commas. Here is an example:

```
00040 PRINT "NAME","RANK","SERIAL NO."
```

When this statement is executed, the following output will appear on the screen:

```
NAME          RANK          SERIAL NO.
```

Headings can be set off from the rest of the output in two ways: by underlining or by using a blank line. One way to underline headings is by including a separate PRINT statement that contains the necessary underscore lines, as shown below:

```
00040 PRINT "NAME","RANK","SERIAL NO."
00050 PRINT "____","____","_____"
```

The output would be:

```
NAME            RANK            SERIAL NO.
____            ____            _____
```

Note that the underline is slightly separated from the heading. This is caused by the separate PRINT statement.

A blank line in output makes the output more readable, and can be achieved by using a PRINT statement alone:

```
00140 PRINT
```

To skip more than one line, simply include more than one such statement:

```
00140 PRINT
00150 PRINT
```

Numeric Literals

Numeric literals are numbers placed within the PRINT statement which are to be printed in the output. They do not have to be enclosed in quotation marks. For example, the statement

```
00100 PRINT 103
```

will print

```
103
```

PRINTING THE VALUES OF EXPRESSIONS

The computer can print not only literals and the values of variables, but also the values of arithmetic expressions. Look at the following program:

```
00010 LET A = 15.00
00020 LET B = 26.00
00030 PRINT (A + B) / 2, A / B
00099 END
```

The computer will evaluate each expression in line 30, according to the hierarchy of operations, and then print the results:

```
20.5            .5769231
```

The computer can print only a certain number of digits for each value. Look at the second value printed. In this case, the computer cannot print more than nine digits. If the computer did not have this limit, an infinite number of digits would have been printed, because the full answer is:

```
.576923076923076923076 . . .
```

The last six digits repeat infinitely. An extremely large or small value may be printed in exponential notation instead.

● The END Statement

The END statement instructs the computer to stop program execution. In a flowchart, it is indicated by the termination symbol (⊂⊃). The general format of the END statement is

line# END

The END statement is always the last line of a program that is executed. On the DECsystem, it must also be the last physical line of the program. To make the END statement readily identifiable, many programmers give it a line number of all 9s. All programs in this book will follow this practice.

● Multiple Statements on a Single Physical Line

Most BASIC systems allow multiple statements to be placed on a single physical line. On the DECsystem, this can be accomplished by separating the statements with backslashes (\). For example, if we wanted to skip two lines, instead of using two physical lines as illustrated previously, we could accomplish the same result more efficiently with the following line:

```
00110 PRINT \ PRINT
```

Many microcomputer systems use the colon (:) instead of the backslash (\) to place multiple logical lines on the same physical lines. For example,

```
00110 PRINT : PRINT
```

The sample program in Figure III–2 demonstrates the use of the REM and assignment statements and implements all four options of the PRINT statement.

● A Programming Problem

PROBLEM DEFINITION

A local stereo shop was advertising the following discounts:

● 5 percent off the purchase of a receiver and a pair of speakers
● 20 percent off the purchase of a receiver, a pair of speakers, and a turntable
● 40 percent off the purchase of a receiver, a pair of speakers, a turntable, and a cassette deck

Being a small shop, it only carries one model of each item. The price for each is as follows:

Item	Price
Receiver	$423.00
Pair of speakers	$300.00
Turntable	$185.00
Cassette	$210.00

Before going to the stereo shop, you decide to write a program to tell you the discounted price of each of the advertised options.

```
00010  REM ***                        PURCHASE COST                      ***
00020  REM ***                                                           ***
00030  REM *** THIS PROGRAM PRINTS THE ITEMS AND THEIR PRICES IN A CHART. ***
00040  REM *** IT THEN DETERMINES THE TOTAL PURCHASE COST AND PRINTS THE ***
00050  REM *** RESULTS.                                                   ***
00060  REM *** MAJOR VARIABLES:                                           ***
00070  REM ***      P#  - PURCHASED ITEMS                                 ***
00080  REM ***      C#  - COST OF EACH ITEM                               ***
00090  REM
00100  REM *** ASSIGN ITEMS AND PRICES ***
00110  LET P1$ = "RECORD"
00120  LET P2$ = "SNEAKERS"
00130  LET P3$ = "BOOK"
00140  LET C1 = 8.98
00150  LET C2 = 24.82
00160  LET C3 = 6.50
00170  REM
00180  REM *** PRINT HEADINGS, CHART AND RESULTS ***
00190  PRINT "ITEM #","PURCHASE","PRICE"
00200  PRINT
00210  PRINT 1,P1$,C1
00220  PRINT 2,P2$,C2
00230  PRINT 3,P3$,C3
00240  PRINT
00250  PRINT "TOTAL PURCHASE COST",C1 + C2 + C3
00999  END
```

```
RUNNH
ITEM #            PURCHASE        PRICE

  1               RECORD          8.98
  2               SNEAKERS        24.82
  3               BOOK            6.5

TOTAL PURCHASE COST               40.3
```

MICROCOMPUTERS	DIFFERENCE
Apple	None
IBM/Microsoft	None
Macintosh/Microsoft	None
TRS-80	None

● FIGURE III-2
Purchase Cost Program

SOLUTION DESIGN

The general problem of finding the discount price can be divided into three steps: assigning the price of each component, determining the discount price by option, and printing the prices.

The first step in the program is to enter the price of each component. Next, determine the discount price for each option by adding the total

● **FIGURE III-3**
**Structure Chart for Stereo Discount
Price Program**

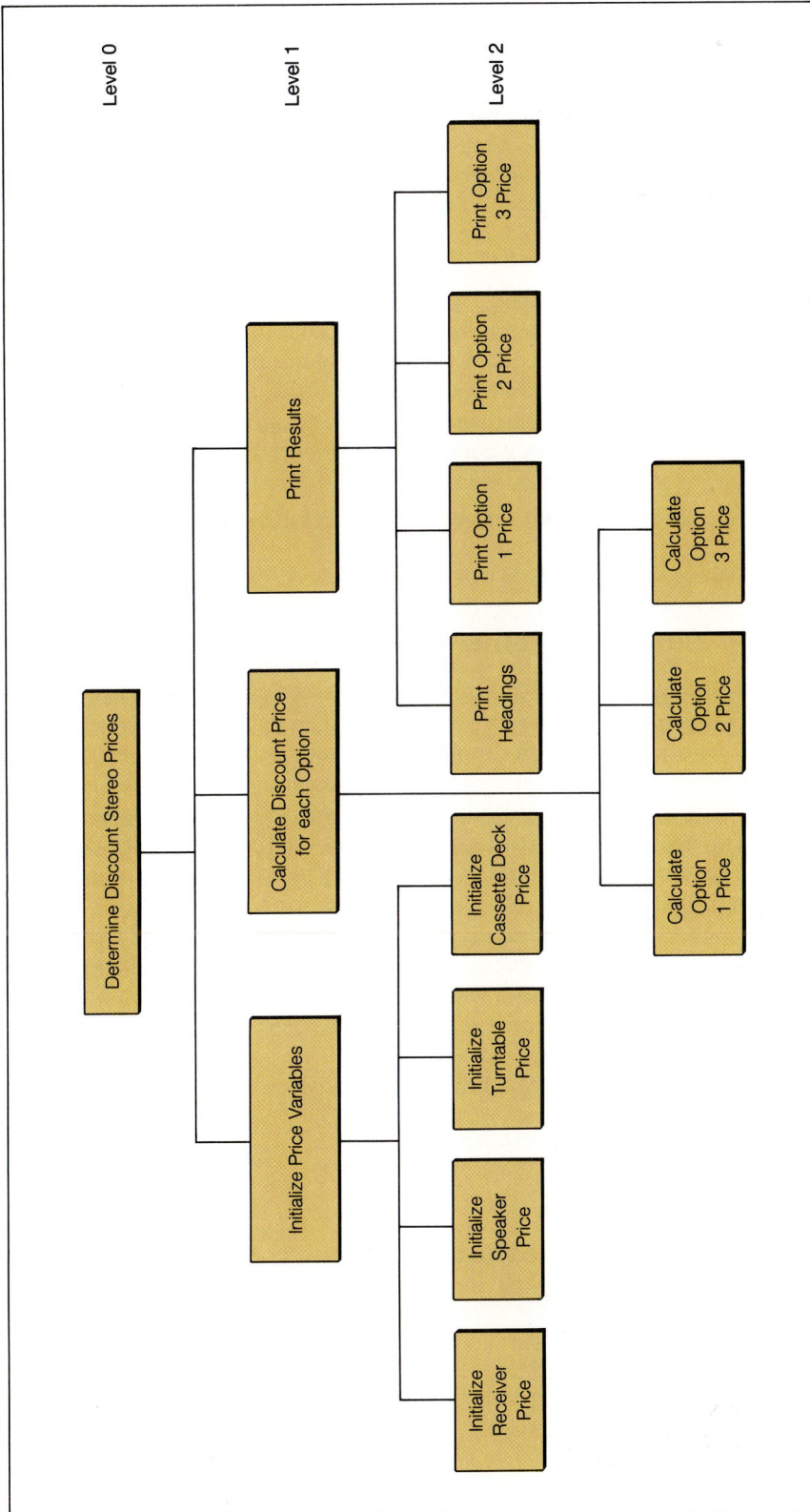

price of the items in an option and multiplying by the appropriate discount factor. You will notice we multiplied by 0.95, 0.8, and 0.6 for the respective options instead of 0.05, 0.2, and 0.4. This is because we are interested in what we have to pay rather than the discount amount itself. Finally, we want to print the results. A structure chart in Figure III–3 diagrams the outline of the problem.

THE PROGRAM

Figure III–4 shows the flowchart, the program listing and output of the program. The REM statements in lines 10 through 130 document the purpose of the program and the meaning of the variables. The REM statement in line 130 is used to set off the remarks from the executable statements. Lines 140 through 170 use assignment statements to enter the price of each stereo component. Lines 180 through 200 calculate the discounted price for each option. The headings are printed out in lines 210 through 230 and the results are printed out in lines 240 through 260.

● Summary Points

● REM statements are used to document a program; they are not executed by the computer.
● The purpose of the assignment statement is to assign values to variables; LET is an optional keyword in some BASIC implementations.
● The assignment statement is not evaluated as an algebraic equation. The computer first evaluates the expression on the right side of the equal sign and then assigns that result to the variable on the left side of the equal sign.
● Arithmetic expressions are evaluated according to the following hierarchy of operations: (1) operations in parentheses, (2) exponentiation, (3) multiplication or division, and (4) addition or subtraction. Multiple operations at the same level are evaluated left to right.
● The PRINT statement is used to print or display the results of processing.
● The END statement indicates the physical end of a program and stops execution.

● Review Questions

1. What is the purpose of the REM statement?
2. What is the purpose of the assignment statement?
3. In a LET statement, why can only a variable name be on the left side of the equal sign?
4. Evaluate the expression 10 LET A = 2.5 + (X * (Y ∧ 2) / C) * (8 + X) where X = 2, Y = 4, and C = 8.
5. What hierarchy, or priority, of arithmetic operations does BASIC follow?
6. What is the purpose of the PRINT statement?

● COMPUTERS AND INFORMATION PROCESSING

Start

Initialize Variables

Calculate Discounted Price for Combination 1

Calculate Discounted Price for Combination 2

Calculate Discounted Price for Combination 3

Print each Price Option

Stop

Pseudocode

Begin
Initialize prices of components
Package 1 = price of receiver and speakers *.95
Package 2 = price of receiver, speakers and turntable *.8
Package 3 = price of receiver, speakers, turntable, and cassette *.6
Print headings
Print price of each option
End

```
00010 REM ***                    DISCOUNT PRICES                    ***
00020 REM ***                                                       ***
00030 REM ***   THIS PROGRAM CALCULATES THE DISCOUNT PRICE FOR      ***
00040 REM ***   THREE STEREO SYSTEMS.                               ***
00050 REM ***   MAJOR VARIABLES:                                    ***
00060 REM ***      R  - PRICE OF RECEIVER                           ***
00070 REM ***      S  - PRICE OF A PAIR OF SPEAKERS                 ***
00080 REM ***      T  - PRICE OF TURNTABLE                          ***
00090 REM ***      C  - PRICE OF CASSETTE DECK                      ***
00100 REM ***      T1 - DISCOUNT FOR R $ S PACKAGE                  ***
00110 REM ***      T2 - DISCOUNT FOR R,S, & T PACKAGE               ***
00120 REM ***      T3 - DISCOUNT FOR R,S,T, & C PACKAGE             ***
00130 REM
00140 LET R = 423
00150 LET S = 300
00160 LET T = 185
00170 LET C = 210
00180 LET T1 = (R + S) * 0.95
00190 LET T2 = (R + S + T) * 0.80
00200 LET T3 = (R + S + T + C) * 0.60
00210 PRINT ,"STEREO PRICES"
00220 PRINT
00230 PRINT "PACKAGE OPTIONS"," PRICE"
00240 PRINT "1. R & S",,T1
00250 PRINT "2. R, S & T",,T2
00260 PRINT "3. R, S, T & C",T3
00999 END
```

```
RUNNH
                    STEREO PRICES

PACKAGE OPTIONS                    PRICE
1. R & S                           686.85
2. R, S & T                        726.4
3. R, S, T & C                     670.8
```

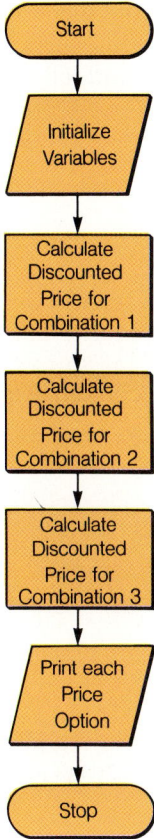

MICROCOMPUTERS	DIFFERENCE
Apple	None
IBM/Microsoft	None
Macintosh/Microsoft	None
TRS-80	None

7. What is the output of the following program segment?

```
10 LET X = 952
20 LET Y = 56
30 PRINT 5.3 + X / (Y * 10)
```

8. Define a character string, and give three examples.

9. What is the purpose of the END statement?

10. Identify which of the following statements are invalid, and tell why:

a. 10 LET P = 5 * (A + B)

b. 10 PRINT TOTAL PRICE =

c. 10 LET N = "NAN"

d. 10 LET N = N + M

e. 10 LET X = 5 + P$

● Debugging Exercises

Identify the following programs or program segments that contain errors, and debug them.

1.
```
00010 REM *** THIS PROGRAM CALCULATES   ***
00020 REM *** AN AVERAGE OF TWO NUMBERS. ***
00030 LET 10 = A
00040 LET 20 = B
00050 LET X = A + B / 2
00060 PRINT X
00099 END
```

2.
```
00100 REM *** THIS PROGRAM FINDS    ***
00110 REM *** THE CUBE OF A NUMBER. ***
00120 REM
00130 LET X = 5
00140 LET C$ = X ^ 3
00150 PRINT C$
00999 END
```

● Programming Problems

1. You want to know how much it would cost you to fly your plane to Hollywood for the Oscars. Hollywood is 2,040 nautical miles from your home. Your plane gets 14 miles per gallon, and you can get gas for $10.50 per gallon. Your output should have the following format:

DISTANCE	TOTAL COST
XXX	$XXX.XX

2. A cassette tape with a list price of $8.98 is on sale for 15 percent off. Write a program that will calculate and output the sale price of the tape.

3. You own an apartment building with eight identical apartments, each having two rooms that need carpeting. One room has a length of twelve feet and a width of nine feet, and the other has a length of ten feet and a width of eight feet. The carpeting costs $9.50 a square yard. Write a program that will calculate the amount of carpeting needed to carpet the entire building, as well as the total cost of the carpeting. The output should include both figures. The area of a room is equal to the length multiplied by the width. Be sure to document your program.

4. Write a program that will print the date, time, and telephone number of the following telephone log entries:

8/9/90	8:09 am	(419)353-7789
9/1/90	3:51 pm	(614)366-6443
1/7/91	6:42 am	(313)577-5864

The output should have the following format:

DATE	TIME	TELEPHONE #
X/X/X	X:XXxx	(XXX)XXX-XXXX
.	.	.
.	.	.

5. Write a program that converts 72 degrees Fahrenheit to its centigrade equivalent and prints the result, appropriately labeled. Use the formula $C = 5/9(F - 32)$, where C equals the degrees centigrade and F equals the degrees Fahrenheit.

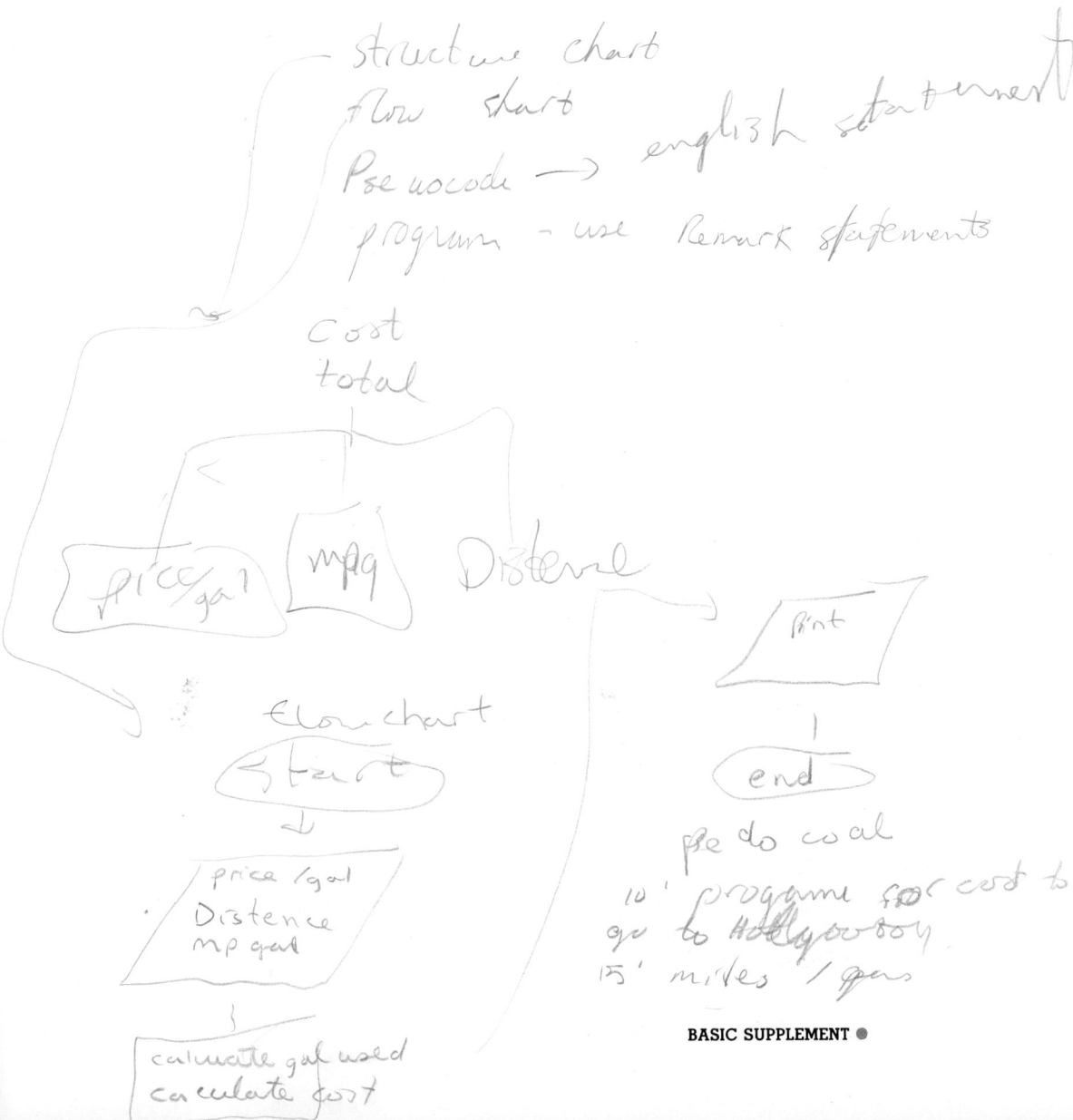

(handwritten notes)

- structure chart
- flow chart
- Pseudocode → english statement
- program - use Remark statements

Cost
total

price/gal   mpg   Distance

Print

Flow chart
Start
price/gal
Distance
mp gal

end

calculate gal used
calculate cost

pseudo coal
10' program for cost to
go to Hollywood
15' miles/gas

●Section IV
Input and Output

● Introduction

The first part of this section explains ways of entering data to a program. The two methods introduced here are the INPUT statement and the READ and DATA statements. The INPUT statement allows the user to enter data while the program is running. When the READ and DATA statements are used, the data is entered as part of the program itself.

The remainder of the section discusses ways of printing program results. It explains how output can be printed so that it is attractive and easy to read. Printing output in table form is also explained.

● The INPUT Statement

In many programs, the data changes each time the program is executed. For example, think of a program that calculates the gas mileage for your car. Each time you run this program, you will want to be able to enter new values for the number of miles traveled and the amount of gas used. If such a program used assignment statements to assign these values to variables, these statements would have to be rewritten every time you wanted to calculate your gas mileage. A more practical approach to this programming problem is to use the INPUT statement.

The INPUT statement allows the user to enter data from the keyboard while the program is executing. The format of the INPUT statement is:

line# INPUT variable list

For example,

```
00140 INPUT L
00150 INPUT W
00160 INPUT H
```

These also could be combined into one line as follows:

```
00140 INPUT L,W,H
```

Note that one or more variables may be listed in a single INPUT statement. If there is more than one, the variables must be separated by commas.

The variables listed in the INPUT statements may be string or numeric. Just be sure to enter the correct value to be assigned to each variable. In other words, the type of data must be the same as that designated by the variable.

INPUT statements are placed where data values are needed in a program. This is determined by the logic of the program.

When a program is running and an INPUT statement is encountered, the program temporarily stops executing and a question mark appears on the terminal screen. The user must then enter the required data and press the RETURN key. After each value entered is stored in its corresponding variable, program execution continues to the next statement. More than one variable can be listed in the INPUT statement; the user must know how many values to enter.

On some systems when there is not enough data entered, another question mark is displayed, or a message to ?REDO FROM THE START is printed and the user must enter all data requested by the INPUT statement. On the DECsystem an error message is printed, telling the user that there is insufficient data. For example, when line 140 is executed with only one value entered, the result would look like this:

```
00140 INPUT L,W,H
RUNNH
 ? 28.5
? 59 Insufficient data at line 00140 of MAIN PROGRAM
 ?
```

The computer will continue telling the user that more data is needed until enough data has been entered. Then the program will continue executing.

If the user attempts to enter a character string to a numeric variable, another error message will appear:

```
? 52    Invalid floating point number at line 00010 of MAIN PROGRAM
```

The user can, however, assign a numeric value to a character string variable. The computer treats the numeric value as a string of characters and stores it in the corresponding string variable, but it cannot perform calculations with this value.

If the user knew what entries to make and how many, the output would look like this:

```
RUNNH
 ? 28.5,25,10
```

The variable L would have the value 28.5, W would be assigned the value 25, and H would contain 10. As you can see, the INPUT statement offers a great deal of flexibility. Each time the program is executed, new values can be entered without changing any program statements.

● Prompts

In the previous example, when the INPUT statement was executed, only a question mark (?) appeared on the terminal screen when it was time for the user to enter data. The user was not told what type of data or how many data items to enter. Therefore, the programmer should also include a **prompt** to tell the user what is to be entered. A prompt can consist of a PRINT statement, placed before the INPUT statement in the program, which tells the user the type and quantity of data to be entered.

Figure IV–1 shows a short program that calculates the volume of a box. The length, width, and height of the box are entered and the volume is output. Note the spelling of the variable names LNGTH and WDTH. It might seem more appropriate to name these variables LENGTH and

● **FIGURE IV–1**
Program Demonstrating the INPUT
Statement

```
00010 REM *** PROGRAM USING THE INPUT STATEMENT TO READ THE ***
00020 REM *** DIMENSIONS OF A BOX AND CALCULATE ITS VOLUME. ***
00030 REM
00040 PRINT "ENTER THE LENGTH, WIDTH, AND HEIGHT OF THE BOX"
00050 INPUT LNGTH,WDTH,HEIGHT
00060 VOLUME = LNGTH * WDTH * HEIGHT
00070 PRINT "VOLUME OF THE BOX IS ";VOLUME
00099 END
```

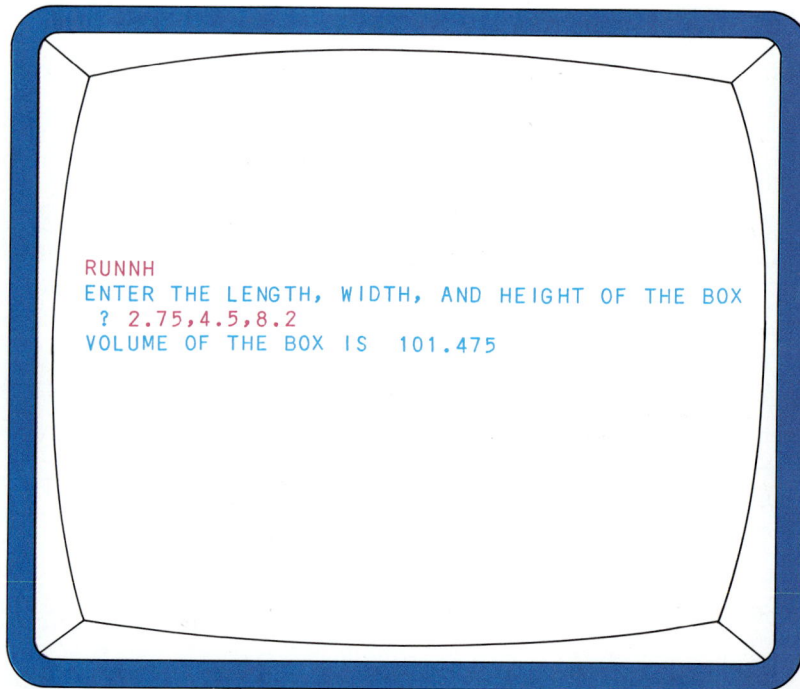

```
RUNNH
ENTER THE LENGTH, WIDTH, AND HEIGHT OF THE BOX
? 2.75,4.5,8.2
VOLUME OF THE BOX IS  101.475
```

MICROCOMPUTERS	DIFFERENCE
Apple	None
IBM/Microsoft	None
Macintosh/Microsoft	None
TRS-80	None

● **COMPUTERS AND INFORMATION PROCESSING**

WIDTH, but all or part of these words are reserved words in at least one of the BASIC implementations covered in this textbook. Therefore, it was necessary to alter these variable names to make them different from the reserved words.

Line 40 of the program in Figure IV–1 contains the prompt:

```
00040 PRINT "ENTER THE LENGTH, WIDTH, AND HEIGHT OF THE BOX"
```

Line 50 is the INPUT statement:

```
00050 INPUT LNGTH,WDTH,HEIGHT
```

After line 50 is executed, the computer will stop and wait for the user to enter the desired length, width, and height. Then execution will continue, and the volume of the box will be calculated and printed on the screen.

Most computers allow the prompt to be contained within the INPUT statement itself. If this were done for the program in Figure IV–1, lines 40 and 50 could be replaced with a single statement:

```
00040 INPUT "ENTER THE LENGTH, WIDTH, AND HEIGHT OF THE BOX";LNGTH,WDTH,HEIGHT
```

When this program is run, the question mark and the prompt appear on the same line:

```
RUNNH
ENTER THE LENGTH, WIDTH, AND HEIGHT OF THE BOX ? 2.75,4.5,8.2
VOLUME OF THE BOX IS  101.475
```

Using this format simplifies the writing of the program and makes the logic easy to follow.

This method of data entry, in which the user enters a response to a prompt printed on the screen is called **inquiry-and-response,** or **conversational mode.**

data is entered as part of the program

● The READ and DATA Statements

The READ and DATA statements provide another way to enter data into a BASIC program. These two statements always work together. Values contained in the DATA statements are assigned to variables listed in the READ statements.

The general format of the READ and DATA statements is this:

line# READ variable list
line# DATA value list

The READ and DATA statements differ from the INPUT statement in that data values are not entered by the user during program execution, but instead are assigned by the programmer within the program itself.

The following is a list of rules explaining the use of the READ and DATA statements.

● A program may contain any number of READ and DATA statements.
● The placement of READ statements is determined by the logic of a given program. The programmer places them in the program at the point at which data needs to be read.

● DATA statements are nonexecutable and can therefore be placed anywhere in the program before the END statement. This book follows the common practice of placing all data statements immediately before the END statement, so that they are easy to locate.

● The computer collects the values from all the DATA statements in a program and places them in a single list, referred to as the **data list.** This list is formed by taking the values from the DATA statements in order, from the lowest to the highest line number and from left to right within a single statement.

● When more than one data value is placed in a single DATA statement, the values are separted by commas. Character string values may or may not be placed in quotes. However, if the character string contains leading or trailing blanks, commas, or semicolons, it must be enclosed in quotation marks.

● When the program encounters a READ statement, it goes to the data list and assigns the next value from that list to the corresponding variable in the READ statement. If the variable is numeric, the data value must also be numeric. If it is a character string variable, however, the computer will allow a numeric value to be assigned to it, as previously explained for the INPUT statement. Again, computations cannot be performed with numbers that have been assigned to character string variables.

● If there is inadequate data for a READ statement (that is, if there are no more data values in the data list), an OUT OF DATA error message occurs and the program stops executing at that point.

● If there are more data values than variables, these extra data values simply remain unread.

Figure IV–2 shows a program segment containing READ and DATA statements. When the computer executes this program, it first encounters the READ statement in line 100. The statement instructs it to read four data values from the data list and assign these values to the corresponding variables. Therefore, the values JACOBS, 48, 60, and 53 are assigned to the variables NME$, S1, S2, and S3 respectively. After this task is completed, program execution continues to line 110, where the next value in the data list, GUINARD, is assigned to the variable NME$. This new value of NME$ replaces JACOBS, which was the previous value.

Note that the computer "remembers" where it is in the data list. Whenever it encounters another READ statement, it assigns the next value in

● **FIGURE IV–2**
Examples of READ and DATA Statements

		AT LINE#:	NME$	S1	S2	S3
			CURRENT VALUES OF VARIABLES			
00100	READ NME$,S1,S2,S3	100	JACOBS	48	60	53
00110	READ NME$	110	GUINARD	48	60	53
00120	READ S1,S2	120	GUINARD	62	58	54
00130	READ S3	130	GUINARD	62	58	54
00140	DATA JACOBS,48					
00150	DATA 60,53,GUINARD					
00160	DATA 62,58					
00170	DATA 54					

● **COMPUTERS AND INFORMATION PROCESSING**

the list to that variable. Study Figure IV–2 to make certain you understand how the READ and DATA statements are used in reading data values. Notice that the columns on the right side of the figure state the current values of each of the variables for lines 100 through 130.

The program in Figure IV–3 shows how READ and DATA statements can be used to read the dimensions of a box and to calculate and print the volume. Note that line 40 contains a single READ statement that reads all three dimensions of the box. The DATA statement in line 70 contains the three values to be assigned to the three variables in the READ statement.

● Comparison of the INPUT and the READ/DATA Statements

There are certain situations where the INPUT statement is particularly useful, and other situations in which READ/DATA statements are more suitable. As you become adept at programming in BASIC, you will easily be able to choose the most appropriate data entry method for a given situation. Here are some guidelines to help you decide which method to use:

● The INPUT statement is ideal when data values change frequently, because it allows the data to be entered at the keyboard during program execution.

● **FIGURE IV–3**
Program Demonstrating the READ and DATA Statements

```
00010 REM *** PROGRAM USING THE READ/DATA STATEMENTS TO READ     ***
00020 REM *** THE DIMENSIONS OF A BOX AND CALCULATE ITS VOLUME. ***
00030 REM
00040 READ LNGTH,WDTH,HEIGHT
00050 VOLUME = LNGTH * WDTH * HEIGHT
00060 PRINT "VOLUME OF THE BOX IS ";VOLUME
00070 DATA 2.75,4.5,8.2
00099 END
```

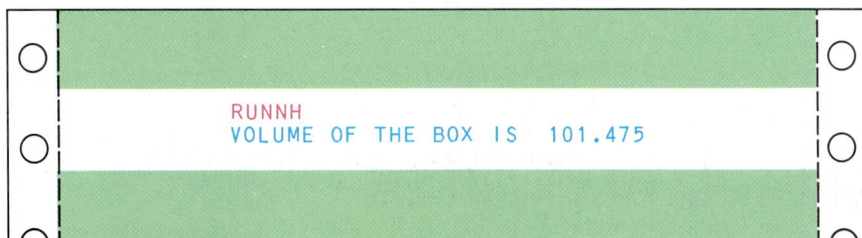

```
RUNNH
VOLUME OF THE BOX IS   101.475
```

MICROCOMPUTERS	DIFFERENCE
Apple	None
IBM/Microsoft	None
Macintosh/Microsoft	None
TRS-80	None

• The READ and DATA statements are well suited for programs using large quantities of data, because the user does not have to enter a long list of data values during program execution, as would be necessary with the INPUT statement.

• The READ and DATA statements are most useful when data values will not be different for each program execution. The main disadvantage of using the READ and DATA statements is that the program itself must be altered when the data values change.

● Using Print Zones

Section 3 explained that the PRINT statement let us have the results of processing printed. When more than one item is to be printed on a line, commas can be used to control the spacing output.

The number of characters that can be printed on a line varies with the system used. On some terminals each output line consists of eighty print positions. Each line is divided into sections called print zones. The zone size and the number of zones per line depend on the system. The print zones on the DECsystem are 14 characters wide, with five zones per line. The beginning columns of the five print zones are shown below:

ZONE 1	ZONE 2	ZONE 3	ZONE 4	ZONE 5
COL	COL	COL	COL	COL
1	15	29	43	57

Commas can be used within a PRINT statement to control the format of printed output. A comma indicates that the next item to be printed will start at the beginning of the next print zone. The following example shows how this works:

```
00010 READ W1$,W2$,W3$
00020 PRINT W1$,W2$,W3$
00030 DATA "BE","SEEING","YOU"
```

The first item in the PRINT statement is printed at the beginning of the line, which is the start of the first print zone. The comma between W1$ and W2$ causes the computer to space over to the next print zone; then the value in W2$ is printed. The second comma directs the computer to space over to the next zone (Zone 3) and print the value in W3$. The output is as follows:

ZONE 1   **ZONE 3**

RUNNH
BE   SEEING   YOU

If there are more items listed in a PRINT statement than there are print zones in a line, the print zones of the next line are also used, starting with the first zone. Notice the output of the following example.

```
00010 READ SEX$,AGE,CLASS$,MAJ$,HRS,GPA
00020 PRINT SEX$,AGE,CLASS$,MAJ$,HRS,GPA
00030 DATA "M",19,"JR","CS",18,2.5
```

RUNNH
M   19   JR   CS   18
  2.5

If the value to be printed exceeds the width of the print zone, the entire value is printed, regardless of how many zones it occupies. A following comma causes printing to continue in the next print zone, as shown in the following example:

```
00010 SPOT$ = "BAGHDAD"
00020 PRINT "YOUR NEXT DESTINATION WILL BE",SPOT$
```

```
RUNNH
YOUR NEXT DESTINATION WILL BE              BAGHDAD
```

Table IV–1 presents the formatting differences among the five computer systems discussed in this book. Columns 2 and 3 give the number of columns and rows available on each system and columns 4 and 5 give the number of print zones per line and zone widths. Note that some systems enable the user to determine the screen and zone dimensions. Columns 6 and 7 indicate whether leading and trailing spaces are provided for numeric values. Column 8 gives the maximum number of digits that will be printed for a single-precision number.

A print zone can be skipped by the use of a technique that involves enclosing a space (the character blank) in quotation marks. This causes the entire zone to appear empty:

```
00010 PRINT "ARTIST"," ","ALBUM"
```

Most computers (including all those covered in this text) also enable the user to skip a zone by typing consecutive commas:

```
00010 PRINT "ARTIST",,"ALBUM"
```

Both of these techniques cause the literal ARTIST to be printed in Zone 1, the second zone to be blank, and the literal ALBUM to be printed in Zone 3:

```
RUNNH
ARTIST                          ALBUM
```

● Table IV–1
Computer Display Characteristics

COMPUTER	SCREEN WIDTH (CHARACTERS)	SCREEN HEIGHT (LINES)	NUMBER OF PRINT ZONES	ZONE WIDTH	SPACE FOR SIGN?	SPACE AFTER NUMBER?	NUMBER OF DIGITS PRINTED, SINGLE PRECISION
DECsystem	80/132*	24/16*	5/9*	14	Yes	Yes	7
Apple	40**	24	3	16	No	No	9
IBM/Microsoft	80	24	5	14	Yes	Yes	7
Mac/Microsoft	***	***	***	***	Yes	Yes	7
TRS-80	64/32*	15	4/2*	16	Yes	Yes	6

*The slash indicates that both options are available to the user.
**Screen width may be 80 columns if the computer is equipped with an 80-column card.
***These can be determined by the user. See your manual.

If a comma appears after the last item in a PRINT statement, the output of the next PRINT statement encountered will begin at the next available print zone. Thus, the statements

```
00010  READ  NME$,AGE,SEX$,VOICE$
00020  PRINT  NME$,AGE,
00030  PRINT  SEX$,VOICE$
00040  DATA  "SHICOFF",32,"M","TENOR"
00099  END
```

produce the following output:

```
RUNNH
SHICOFF          32              M              TENOR
```

● Using the Semicolon

Using a semicolon instead of a comma causes output to be packed more closely on a line. This alternative gives the programmer greater flexibility in formatting output. In the following examples, notice the difference in spacing when semicolons are used instead of commas:

```
00060  PRINT  "JASON","JACKSON"
```

```
RUNNH
JASON            JACKSON
```

```
00060  PRINT  "JASON";"JACKSON"
```

```
RUNNH
JASONJACKSON
```

The semicolon between the items tells the computer to skip to the next **column** to print the next item—not to the next print zone, as with the comma.

The above example shows what happens when semicolons are used with character strings. Since letters do not have signs, they are run together. The best way to avoid this problem is to enclose a space within the quotes:

```
00060  PRINT  "JASON";" JACKSON"
```

```
RUNNH
JASON JACKSON
```

When numbers are printed, most computers (the Apple is an exception) print the number with a preceding space if the number has no sign, such as 104 or 48. If the number has a sign, such as -176 or $+32$, no preceding space is printed, because the sign is printed in that position. In either case, a space is left after the number for greater readability. Therefore, on most computers, when numeric values are separated by a semicolon, the printed digits are not adjacent as in the case of the character strings. The following example demonstrates this point:

```
00010  PRINT  100;-200;300
```

```
RUNNH
 100 -200  300
```

Notice that the output shows only one space before −200. This is because the computer left a space after printing the number 100. But there are two spaces before 300: Not only was a space left after −200 was printed, but a space was left for the sign (an assumed positive) of the number 300.

If the semicolon is the last character of the PRINT statement, carriage control is not advanced when the printing of the statement is completed; therefore, the output generated by the next PRINT statement continues on the same line. For example,

```
00060 PRINT 495207;
00070 PRINT "JASON";" JACKSON"
```

RUNNH
 495207 JASON JACKSON

Line 60 causes 495207 to be printed out. The semicolon after this number keeps the printer on the same line; then, when line 70 is encountered, JASON JACKSON is printed on the same line.

● The TAB Function

The comma causes the results of processing to be printed according to predefined print zones. The semicolon causes them to start printing in the next position on the output line. Both are easy to use, and many reports can be formatted in this fashion. However, there are times when a report should be structured differently.

The TAB function allows output to be printed in any column in an output line, providing the programmer greater flexibility to format printed output.

The general format of the TAB function is this:

TAB(expression)

The expression in parentheses may be a numeric constant, variable, or arithmetic expression; it tells the computer the column in which printing is to occur.

When a TAB function is encountered in a PRINT statement, the computer spaces over to the column number indicated in the expression. The next variable value or literal found in the PRINT statement is printed starting in that column. The TAB function is separated from the items to be printed by semicolons. For example, the statement

```
00050 PRINT TAB(10);"HI THERE!";TAB(25);"BYE!"
```

causes the literal HI THERE! to be printed starting in column 10. Then, starting in column 25, the literal BYE! is printed.

On some computers, however, such as the DECsystem and the TRS-80, the string HI THERE! would begin in column 11 and BYE! in column 26. In other words, the computer tabs to the tenth column and the semicolon instructs it to begin printing in the *next* column (column 11). Check your manual to determine how this works for your system.

It is best to have the expression in the TAB function evaluate as an integer, because this makes it clear in which column the output will start printing. However, it is possible to use a real value for an expression, as in the following statement:

```
00050 PRINT TAB(15.7);"HI THERE!"
```

On the DECsystem, the number 15.7 will be rounded to 16, the computer will tab to the sixteenth column, and the character string will be printed starting in column 17.

The program in Figure IV–4 illustrates the use of the TAB function. This program prints a simple table by using the TAB function to place the printed values in columns.

Note that we have used the semicolon as the punctuation mark with the TAB function. The semicolon separates the expression from the values to be printed. If commas were used instead, the printer would default and use the predefined print zones, ignoring the columns specified in parentheses. For example, if line 50 of the program in Figure IV–4 had been

```
00050 PRINT TAB(5),"ITEM",TAB(25),"QUANTITY"
```

the output would have been

```
RUNNH
            INVENTORY REPORT

            ITEM                        QUANTITY

      PENCILS        1000
      ERASERS        200
      PAPER          500
```

The computer spaced over the five columns indicated by the first TAB function, but when it saw the comma following the parentheses, it skipped over to the next predefined print zone to print ITEM. The same thing happens again with QUANTITY.

When using the TAB function, it is important to be aware of spacing. On the DECsystem, there can be a space between the word TAB and the left parenthesis, because the DEC recognizes the reserved word TAB. On some systems, however—for example, the IBM—there cannot be a space between TAB and the left parenthesis. This is because the reserved word that these systems recognize is TAB(. Without the opening parenthesis following it, TAB is taken as a variable name TAB and the value in parentheses is taken as an array subscript. (Arrays will be discussed in Section 9). The following statement would be invalid on systems that recognize TAB(as a reserved word:

```
00010 PRINT TAB (5);"ITEM";TAB (25);"QUANTITY"
```

The statement would be correctly written like this:

```
00010 PRINT TAB(5);"ITEM";TAB(25);"QUANTITY"
```

As another caution, remember that when the TAB function is used, the printer cannot be backspaced. Once a column has been passed, the printer cannot go back to it. This means that if more than one TAB function is used in a PRINT statement, the column numbers in parentheses must increase from left to right. For example,

Valid:

```
00020 PRINT TAB(5);3;TAB(15);4;TAB(25);5
RUNNH
      3          4            5
```

The following statement does not use the TAB function properly:

```
00020 PRINT TAB(25);5;TAB(15);4;TAB(5);3
RUNNH
                        5  4  3
```

The invalid statement above demonstrates the action taken by most systems when the column numbers do not increase from left to right. The statement instructs the computer to print the number 5 in column 25, which it does. However, because there can be no backspacing to columns 15 and 5 as the next two TAB functions instruct, the TAB function is ignored and the numbers 4 and 3 are printed where indicated by the semicolons.

● FIGURE IV–4
Program Demonstrating the TAB Function

```
00010 REM *** INVENTORY REPORT ***
00020 REM
00030 PRINT TAB(10);"INVENTORY REPORT"
00040 PRINT
00050 PRINT TAB(5);"ITEM";TAB(25);"QUANTITY"
00060 PRINT
00070 READ I$,Q
00080 PRINT TAB(5);I$;TAB(25);Q
00090 READ I$,Q
00100 PRINT TAB(5);I$;TAB(25);Q
00110 READ I$,Q
00120 PRINT TAB(5);I$;TAB(25);Q
00130 DATA "PENCILS",1000,"ERASERS",200,"PAPER",500
00999 END
```

```
RUNNH
            INVENTORY REPORT

    ITEM              QUANTITY

    PENCILS            1000
    ERASERS             200
    PAPER               500
```

MICROCOMPUTERS	DIFFERENCE
Apple	None
IBM/Microsoft	None
Macintosh/Microsoft	None
TRS-80	None

The IBM and Macintosh systems respond to this situation in a different way. When a TAB function specifies a column to the left of the current print position, the computer spaces to that column on the next line. The following BASIC statement was run on the IBM:

```
20 PRINT TAB(25);5;TAB(15);4;TAB(5);3
RUN
                                            5
                        4
            3
```

● The PRINT USING Statement

Yet another convenient feature for controlling output is the PRINT USING statement. This feature is especially useful when printing table headings or aligning columns of numbers. All of the computers covered in this text, except the Apple, have a PRINT USING capability. The syntax for the PRINT USING statement varies considerably among different computers. This section briefly describes its use on the DECsystem; the principles are similar for other computers with this feature.

The general format of the PRINT USING statement on the DECsystem is as follows:

line# PRINT USING image statement line#, expression-list

The expression list in the format description consists of a sequence of variables or expressions separated by commas, similar to the expression list in any PRINT statement. The PRINT USING statement instructs the computer to print the items in this expression list using the format described by the *image statement*, the line number of which is given.

An image statement is identified in the program by a colon following the line number. Its format is as shown here:

line#: format control characters

The image statement, like the DATA statement, is nonexecutable and can appear anywhere in the program. The PRINT USING statement, however, is placed where the program logic demands. A single image statement can be referred to by several PRINT USING statements.

Special format control characters are used in the image statement to describe the output image and to control spacing. The most commonly used DECsystem format control characters are listed in Table IV–2.

The PRINT USING statement can easily be used to center character strings within a field. For example, the statements:

```
00100 PRINT USING 140,"HALSTON & LING, INC."
00110 PRINT USING 140,"ATTORNEYS AT LAW"
00120 PRINT USING 140,"749 S. MAIN"
00130 PRINT USING 140,"ALTOONA,MI"
00140 :'CCCCCCCCCCCCCCCCCCCCCCCCCCCCCCCC
```

will cause the following output:

```
RUNNH
        HALSTON & LING, INC.
         ATTORNEYS AT LAW
           749 S. MAIN
           ALTOONA,MI
```

Table IV–2
Format Control Characters for the DECsystem

CHARACTER	CONTROL IMAGE FOR	EXAMPLE
#	Numeric data; used in a mask*; one symbol for each digit to be printed; zeros are added to the left of the number to fill the field.	###.###
$	Dollar sign; printed exactly as is.	$### ##
$$	Causes dollar sign to be printed immediately before first digit.	$$##.##
**	Leading asterisks; printed in place of blanks.	***##.##
.	Decimal point; printed exactly as is.	####.##
E	Alphanumeric data; preceded by apostrophe ('); permits overflow to be printed to the right; if necessary, blanks are added to the left of the data to fill the field.	'E
L	Alphanumeric data; preceded by apostrophe ('); used as a mask; aligns output at the left side of the field.	'LLLLLL
R	Alphanumeric data; preceded by apostrophe ('); used as a mask; aligns output at the right side of the field.	'RRRRRR
C	Alphanumeric data; preceded by apostrophe ('); used as a mask; centers output in the field.	'CCCC

*A mask specifies the maximum number of characters to be printed in a field.

The same image statement (at line 140) has been used for all four PRINT USING statements. When these headings were printed, all four were centered in a field of length 30, because the image statement in line 140 contains 30 C's. (As explained in Table IV–2, the character C causes the output to be centered within the field specified.)

Suppose the same program segment is run again, but with the image statement altered:

```
00100 PRINT USING 140,"HALSTON & LING, INC."
00110 PRINT USING 140,"ATTORNEYS AT LAW"
00120 PRINT USING 140,"749 S. MAIN"
00130 PRINT USING 140,"ALTOONA,MI"
00140 :'LLLLLLLLLLLLLLLLLLLLLLLLLLLLL
```

The output now looks like this:

```
RUNNH
HALSTON & LING, INC.
ATTORNEYS AT LAW
749 S. MAIN
ALTOONA,MI
```

The use of the letter L in the image statement causes the output to be lined up at the left margin of the field.

PRINT USING statements are very useful in aligning columns of numbers. Consider the following program segment.

```
00010 READ V1,V2,V3,V4
00020 PRINT USING 90,V1,V2,V3,V4
00030 READ V1,V2,V3,V4
00040 PRINT USING 90,V1,V2,V3,V4
00050 READ V1,V2,V3,V4
00060 PRINT USING 90,V1,V2,V3,V4
00070 READ V1,V2,V3,V4
00080 PRINT USING 90,V1,V2,V3,V4
00090 : ######.##
00100 DATA 14.56,78.905,10234.1,0.03,6.73,12322.4,943.05,17.65
00110 DATA 65.56,945.7,125447.80,0.17,175.35,78.92,319.00,4.56
```

The output of this program segment is as follows:

```
RUNNH
     14.56      78.90   10234.10      0.03
      6.73   12322.40     943.05     17.65
     65.56     945.70  125447.80      0.17
    175.35      78.92     319.00      4.56
```

Note that all of the numbers have been aligned at the decimal point.

The program in Figure IV–5 illustrates how PRINT USING statements can be used to print a table. Notice the use of the two dollar signs in the image statement in line 290:

```
00290 : 'LLLLLLLLLLLLLLL          $$##.##              $$##.##
```

This causes the dollar sign to "float," so that it is always printed immediately before the first digit of the number following it.

The PRINT USING statements of the IBM, Macintosh, and TRS-80 are somewhat different. The general format for all of these systems looks like this:

line# PRINT USING format expression; expression-list

The format expression can be a string constant or a string variable consisting of formatting characters.

The following example illustrates this format:

```
100 A$ = "**$###,###.## DOLLARS"
110 PRINT USING A$;P
```

Figure IV–6 demonstrates how the program shown in Figure IV–5 would be implemented on these computer systems. Table IV–3 contains a list of the format control characters for the various BASIC implementations.

● A Programming Problem

PROBLEM DEFINITION

Baymont High School would like a program to generate absentee percentages per class. Design the program so that they can run it every day

```
00010 REM *** PRINT PROGRAM TO ILLUSTRATE PRINT USING ***
00020 REM
00030 PRINT
00040 PRINT USING 280,"ITEM","TOTAL","SALES"
00050 PRINT USING 280,"PURCHASED","PRICE","TAX"
00060 PRINT
00070 READ A$,X
00080 Y = X * .06
00090 PRINT USING 290,A$,X,Y
00100 READ A$,X
00110 Y = X * .06
00120 PRINT USING 290,A$,X,Y
00130 READ A$,X
00140 Y = X * .06
00150 PRINT USING 290,A$,X,Y
00160 READ A$,X
00170 Y = X * .06
00180 PRINT USING 290,A$,X,Y
00190 READ A$,X
00200 Y = X * .06
00210 PRINT USING 290,A$,X,Y
00220 REM
00230 REM *** DATA STATEMENTS ***
00240 DATA TOASTER,27.50,BLENDER,18.45
00250 DATA BLANKET,9.90,KNIVES,34.99,FAN,29.99
00260 REM
00270 REM *** IMAGE STATEMENTS ***
00280 : 'LLLLLLLLLLL        'CCCCCCCCC          'CCCCCCCCC
00290 : 'LLLLLLLLLLLLLLLL    $$##.##             $$##.##
00999 END
```

```
RUNNH

ITEM               TOTAL                SALES
PURCHASED          PRICE                  TAX

TOASTER            $27.50               $1.65
BLENDER            $18.45               $1.11
BLANKET             $9.90               $0.59
KNIVES             $34.99               $2.10
FAN                $29.99               $1.80
```

MICROCOMPUTERS	DIFFERENCE
Apple	No PRINT USING
IBM/Microsoft	See Figure IV-7
Macintosh/Microsoft	See Figure IV-7
TRS-80	See Figure IV-7

Program Demonstrating the PRINT US-
ING Statement on the IBM, Macintosh,
and TRS-80

```
10   REM *** PROGRAM TO ILLUSTRATE PRINT USING ***
20   REM
30   PRINT
40   PRINT USING "\         \         \         \           \        \";"ITEM","TOTAL","SALES"
50   PRINT USING "\         \         \         \           \ \";"PURCHASED";"PRICE";"TAX"
60   PRINT
70   READ A$,X
80   Y = X * .06
90   PRINT USING "\       \       $$##.##         $$##.##";A$,X,Y
100  READ A$,X
110  Y = X * .06
120  PRINT USING "\       \       $$##.##         $$##.##";A$,X,Y
130  READ A$,X
140  Y = X * .06
150  PRINT USING "\       \       $$##.##         $$##.##";A$,X,Y
160  READ A$,X
170  Y = X * .06
180  PRINT USING "\       \       $$##.##         $$##.##";A$,X,Y
190  READ A$,X
200  Y = X * .06
210  PRINT USING "\       \       $$##.##         $$##.##";A$,X,Y
220  REM
230  REM *** DATA STATEMENTS ***
240  DATA TOASTER,27.50,BLENDER,18.45
250  DATA BLANKET,9.90,KNIVES,34.99,FAN,29.99
999  END
```

```
RUN

ITEM            TOTAL           SALES
PURCHASE        PRICE           TAX

TOASTER         $27.50          $1.65
BLENDER         $18.45          $1.11
BLANKET          $9.90          $0.59
KNIVES          $34.99          $2.10
FAN             $29.99          $1.80
```

MICROCOMPUTERS	DIFFERENCE
Apple	No PRINT USING
IBM/Microsoft	None
Macintosh/Microsoft	None
TRS-80	None

IBM and MACINTOSH

CHARACTER	EXPLANATION
#	Same as DECsystem.
.	Same as DECsystem.
$$	Two dollar signs cause the dollar sign to be floating, meaning that it will be in the first position before the number.
**$	Vacant positions will be filled with asterisks, and the dollar sign will be in the first position to the left of the number.
+	When a + sign is placed at the beginning or end of a number, it causes a + sign to be printed if the number is positive and a − sign if the number is negative.
−	When a − sign is placed at the end of a number, negative numbers will be followed by a negative sign and a space will appear after the number for positive numbers.
^^^^	This causes the number to be printed in exponential format.
\spaces\	This specifies a string field to be 2 plus the number of spaces between the slashes.
!	This causes only the first string character to be printed.
&	This specifies a variable-length field. The string is output exactly as it is entered.
___	The underscore causes the next character in the format string to be printed. The character itself may be underscored by preceding it with two underscores (_____).
%	If the number to be printed is larger than the specified field, a percent sign will appear before the number. If rounding causes the number to exceed the field, the percent sign will be printed in front of the rounded number.

TRS-80

CHARACTER	EXPLANATION
#	Same as DECsystem.
.	Same as DECsystem.
$	Same as DECsystem.
$$	Two dollar signs cause the dollar sign to be floating, meaning that it will be in the first position before the number.
**$	Vacant positions will be filled with asterisks, and the dollar sign will be in the first position to the left of the number.
+	When a + sign is placed at the beginning or end of a number, it causes a + sign to be printed if the number is positive and a − sign if the number is negative.
−	When a − sign is placed at the end of a number, negative numbers will have a negative sign, and a space will appear after the number for positive numbers.
^^^^	This causes the number to be printed in exponential format.
%spaces%	This specifies a string field to be 2 plus the number of spaces between the percent signs.
!	This causes only the first string character to be printed.

in order to compare the daily figures and determine if there is any pattern. Format the output as follows:

DAILY ABSENCE REPORT FOR (current date)

CLASS	TOTAL NUMBER OF STUDENTS	NUMBER ABSENT	PERCENTAGE ABSENT
XX	XXX	XX	XX
XX	XXX	XX	XX
XX	XXX	XX	XX
XX	XXX	XX	XX

Use INPUT statements to allow the user to enter the current date and the following data:

Class	#Students	#Absent
9	345	4
10	321	28
11	367	10
12	298	32

SOLUTION DESIGN

The general problem of generating an absentee percentage per class report can be divided into two subproblems—the task of processing each class, and the task of printing the information in table format.

1. Process each class
2. Report the information in a table format

Step 1 can be further broken down into several smaller tasks that must be performed for each class:

1a. Enter the total enrollment per class
1b. Enter the number absent per class
1c. Calculate the percentages per class

Step 2 can also be divided into smaller problems:

2a. Print the headings
2b. Print the per class information
2c. Print the footer

The structure chart in Figure IV–7 diagrams this outline of the problem.

THE PROGRAM

Figure IV–8 shows the flowchart, the program listing and the output of the program. Lines 10 through 100 explain the purpose of major variables used in the program. Input statements with prompts are used in lines 120 through 200 to allow the user to enter the total enrollment and number absent per class. Lines 230 through 260 calculate the absentee percentage by dividing the number absent by the total enrolled and multiplying by

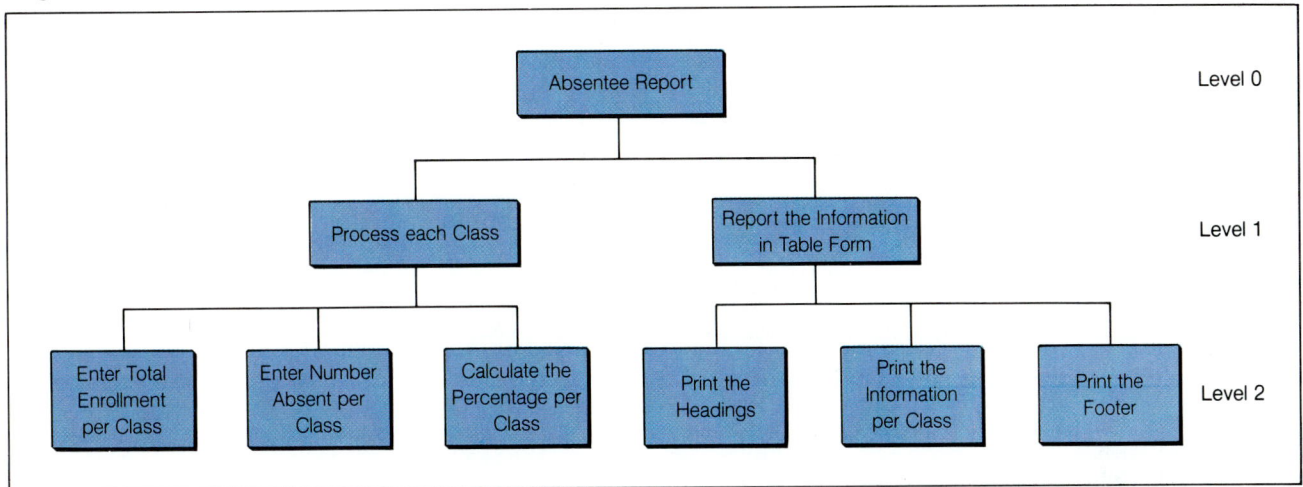

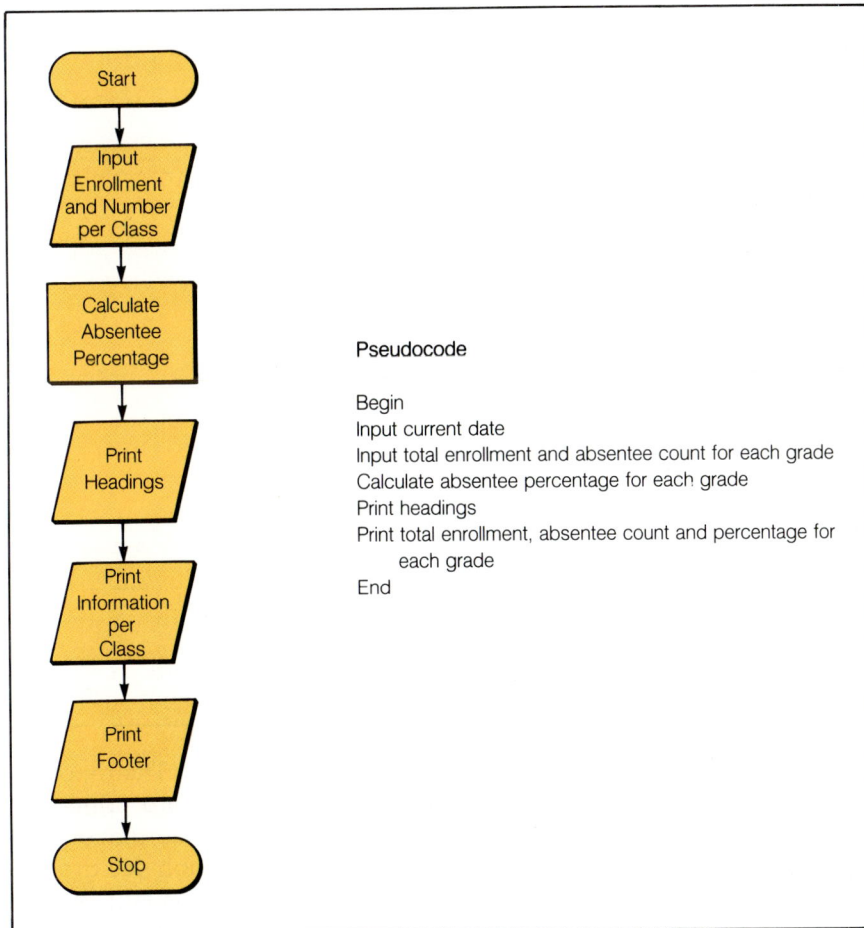

Pseudocode

Begin
Input current date
Input total enrollment and absentee count for each grade
Calculate absentee percentage for each grade
Print headings
Print total enrollment, absentee count and percentage for
    each grade
End

(Continued Next Two Pages)

```
00010 REM ***                       ABSENCE PERCENTAGES                    ***
00020 REM
00030 REM *** THIS PROGRAM GENERATES ABSENTEE PERCENTAGES PER CLASS  ***
00040 REM *** FOR ANY GiVEN DAY                                      ***
00050 REM *** MAJOR VARIABLES:                                       ***
00060 REM ***   DT$              DATE FOR PERCENTAGE DETERMINATION   ***
00070 REM ***   TTAL             NUMBER OF STUDENTS / CLASS          ***
00080 REM ***   ASENT            NUMBER OF STUDENTS ABSENT / CLASS   ***
00090 REM ***   PER              PERCENTAGE OF ABSENT / CLASS        ***
00100 REM
00110 REM *** INPUT DATE, TOTALS, AND ABSENTS ***
00120 INPUT "ENTER TODAY'S DATE IN THIS FORM MM/DD/YY ";DT$
00130 INPUT "ENTER 9TH GRADE TOTAL ENROLLMENT";NTTAL
00140 INPUT "             NUMBER OF ABSENT";NASENT
00150 INPUT "ENTER 10TH GRADE TOTAL ENROLLMENT";TTTAL
00160 INPUT "             NUMBER OF ABSENT";TASENT
00170 INPUT "ENTER 11TH GRADE TOTAL ENROLLMENT";ETTAL
00180 INPUT "             NUMBER OF ABSENT";EASENT
00190 INPUT "ENTER 12TH GRADE TOTAL ENROLLMENT";WTTAL
00200 INPUT "             NUMBER OF ABSENT";WASENT
00210 REM
00220 REM *** CALCULATE PERCENTAGES ***
00230 NPER = NASENT / NTTAL * 100
00240 TPER = NASENT / TTTAL * 100
00250 EPER = EASENT / ETTAL * 100
00260 WPER = WASENT / WTTAL * 100
00270 REM
00280 REM *** PRINT HEADINGS AND RESULTS **
00290 PRINT
00300 PRINT USING 440,DT$
00310 PRINT USING 450,
00320 PRINT
00330 PRINT USING 460,
00340 PRINT USING 470,
00350 PRINT USING 450,
00360 PRINT
00370 PRINT USING 480,9,NTTAL,NASENT,NPER
00380 PRINT USING 480,10,TTTAL,TASENT,TPER
00390 PRINT USING 480,11,ETTAL,EASENT,EPER
00400 PRINT USING 480,12,WTTAL,WASENT,WPER
00410 PRINT USING 450,
00420 REM
00430 REM *** IMAGE STATEMENTS ***
00440 :             DAILY ABSENCE REPORT FOR 'LLLLLLLLL
00450 :_____
00460 :            TOTAL NUMBER          NUMBER          PERCENTAGE
00470 :  GRADE     OF STUDENTS           ABSENT            ABSENT
00480 :    ##          ###                ###              ##.##
00999 END
```

100 in order to get a percentage as opposed to a decimal. The report in table format is obtained via print usings. The headings are printed in lines 290 through 360. Lines 370 through 400 print the information per class and line 410 prints the table footer. Lines 440 through 480 are the image statements to accompany the PRINT USING statements. They are nonexecutable; therefore the program goes to line 999, which stops execution.

```
RUNNH
ENTER TODAY'S DATE IN THIS FORM MM/DD/YY  ? 01/06/92
ENTER 9TH GRADE TOTAL ENROLLMENT ? 345
              NUMBER OF ABSENT ? 4
ENTER 10TH GRADE TOTAL ENROLLMENT ? 321
              NUMBER OF ABSENT ? 28
ENTER 11TH GRADE TOTAL ENROLLMENT ? 367
              NUMBER OF ABSENT ? 10
ENTER 12TH GRADE TOTAL ENROLLMENT ? 298
              NUMBER OF ABSENT ? 32


        DAILY ABSENCE REPORT FOR 01/06/92
```

GRADE	TOTAL NUMBER OF STUDENTS	NUMBER ABSENT	PERCENTAGE ABSENT
9	345	4	1.16
10	321	28	1.25
11	367	10	2.72
12	298	32	10.74

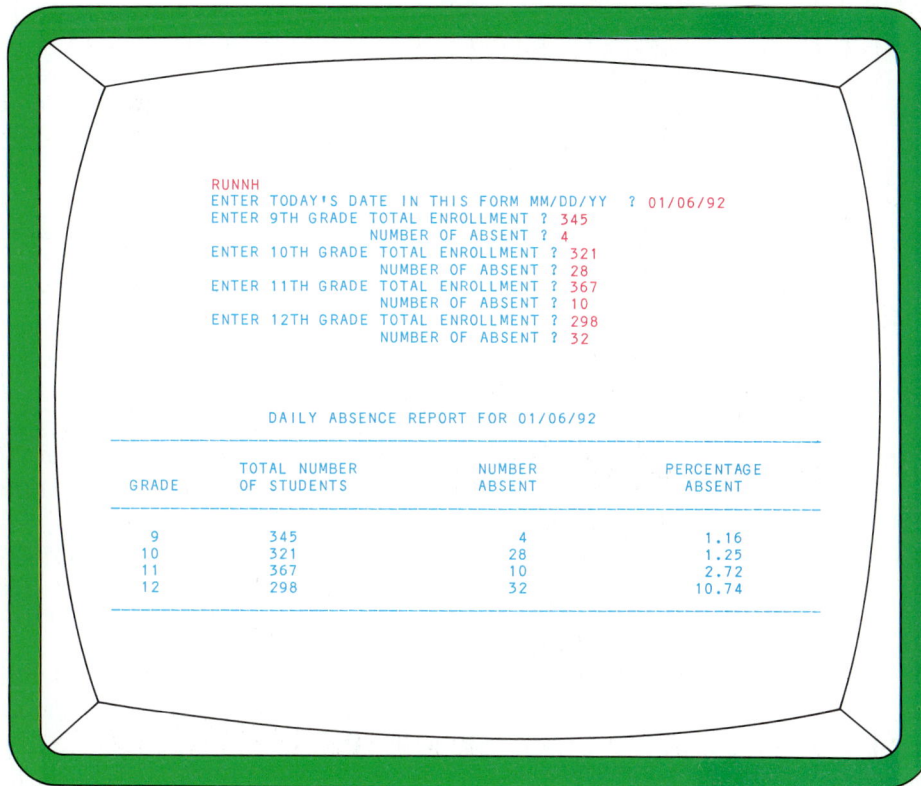

MICROCOMPUTERS	DIFFERENCE
Apple	No PRINT USING
IBM/Microsoft	No separate image line for PRINT USING
Macintosh/Microsoft	No separate image lines.
TRS-80	No separate image lines.

● Summary Points

● The INPUT statement allows the user to enter data while the program is running. Therefore, the values used can change each time the program is run.

● When an INPUT statement is encountered during program execution, the program stops running until the user enters the needed data and presses the RETURN key. Each data value entered is then assigned to the corresponding variable in the INPUT statement.

• When data must be entered by the user, the program should display a prompt telling exactly what data are to be entered.

• Another way of entering data into a program is to use READ and DATA statements. The READ statement causes values contained in the DATA statements to be assigned to variables.

• READ and INPUT statements are located where the logic of the program indicates. DATA statements are nonexecutable and may be located anywhere in the program.

• The RESTORE statement causes the next READ statement to begin taking values from the top of the data list.

• Numeric values can be assigned to character variables, but character strings cannot be assigned to numeric variables.

• The INPUT statement is ideally suited for programs in which the data changes often, whereas the READ and DATA statements are particularly useful when it is necessary to read large quantities of data.

• When more than one item is to be printed on a line of output, the spacing can be indicated by the use of commas and semicolons.

• Each line of output can be divided into a predetermined number of print zones. The comma is used to cause results to be printed in the print zones.

• Using a semicolon instead of a comma to separate printed items causes output to be packed more closely on a line.

• Using the TAB function in a PRINT statement permits results to be printed anywhere on an output line.

• The PRINT USING feature provides a flexible method of producing output. The format control characteristics in the image statement define how the output will look.

● Review Questions

1. What are the advantages of the INPUT statement?

2. What is a prompt used for? What two things should a prompt tell the user?

3. Is the following a valid INPUT statement?

    10 INPUT "THE NAME OF YOUR DOG";N

4. Is the following a valid READ statement?

    20 READ N$ B6 A

5. After the following READ/DATA statements were executed, what would be the value of each variable?

    10 DATA 256,49
    20 DATA "TAMPA BAY"
    30 DATA "FLORIDA",40421
    40 READ A,B,C$
    50 READ S$,X

6. What happens when a PRINT statement ends with a comma?

7. What happens when a PRINT statement ends with a semicolon?

8. What will be the output of the following program segment?

    00230 X$ = "MOUNTAIN"
    00240 Y$ = "MOLEHILL"
    00250 PRINT X$;Y$

9. Using the TAB function, what would the PRINT statement look like that prints out NAME starting in column 1, CITY in column 20, and STATE in column 35?

10. How does the PRINT USING statement work?

● Debugging Exercises

Identify the following programs or program segments that contain errors and debug them.

1.
```
00010 INPUT "ENTER CITY AND STATE:";CITY$,ST
00020 INPUT "AND ZIP CODE:";ZIP$
00030 PRINT TAB(5);CITY$;TAB(25),ST;TAB(35);ZIP
```

2. How should these PRINT statements be corrected to match their output if X = 2, Y = 365, Z = 900, R = 52, A$ = YEARS, and B$ = WEEKS"?

Output

Z1	Z2	Z3	Z4	Z5
		TIM TUCKER		
2	365	900	52	
2	365	YEAR		

```
00060 PRINT "TIM";"TUCKER"
00070 PRINT X,Y,Z;R
00080 PRINT X,Y
00090 PRINT A$
```

● Programming Problems

1. Mrs. Mathey wants to know how much it would cost her to fertilize her garden, which measures 15 by 20 feet. The economy fertilizer costs $1.75 per pound, and one pound covers 20 square feet. She also wants to know how much it would cost if she used the deluxe fertilizer, which is $2.00 per pound, and one pound covers 20 square feet. The program should output the cost of using each and the cost difference between the two.

2. Write a program that asks for a person's name and weight in pounds and computes the weight in kilograms (1 pound = 0.453592 kilograms). The program should print the name of the person, his/her weight in pounds, and weight in kilograms, each in a different print zone.

3. Write a program that will provide the user with an arithmetic quiz. The program should ask the user to enter two numbers. Then it should print a message telling the user to press any key when ready to see the sum, difference, product, and quotient of the two numbers. The program should then print the four results mentioned. Your output should be as follows:

```
ENTER ANY TWO NUMBERS
(SEPARATE THE NUMBERS WITH A COMMA) XXX, XXX
PRESS ANY KEY WHEN READY TO SEE THE ANSWERS: X
XXX + XXX = XXXX
XXX − XXX = XXX
XXX*XXX = XXXXXX
XXXX/XXX = XX
```

4. Tod Stiles has friends across the country, and would like to have a computerized address book. Write a program to read the following sample data and print it with the headings NAME, STREET, CITY, and STATE, using the TAB function:

Irene Bulas, 124 Columbia Hts, Brooklyn, NY
Monica Murdock, 778 Riverview Dr., New Orleans, LA
Link Case, 86 Eldorado Dr., Dallas, TX
Karen Milhoan, 799 Royal St. George, Naperville, IL

5. Write a program using READ/DATA statements to tally the cost of grocery list items. The program should calculate the total of the prices, a 6 percent tax on this amount, and the final total. Make use of the PRINT USING statement to print the prices and totals. Use the following data: 12.79, 9.99, 4.57, 3.99. The output should look like this:

```
              12.79
               9.99
               4.57
               3.99
Subtotal      XX.XX
Tax            X.XX
              _____
Total         $XX.XX
```

● Section V
Control Statements

● Introduction

This section introduces the control statement, a powerful programming tool that will be used in all programs from this point on. **Control statements** allow the programmer to control the order in which program statements are executed. The GOTO, IF/THEN/ELSE, and ON/GOTO statements are the control statements introduced here. The section also introduces the technique of looping and two methods of controlling loop execution.

● The GOTO Statement: Unconditional Transfer

All of the programs we have written so far have been executed in a simple sequential manner. That is, the lowest numbered line is executed first, then control passes to the next-lowest numbered line, and so on from the beginning to the end of the program. To solve many programming problems, however, it is necessary to alter the order in which statements are executed. Changing the normal path or flow of program execution is known as **branching,** and a statement that can make such a change is called a branch.

An example of a branch is the GOTO statement. Its general format looks like this:

line# GOTO transfer line#

The transfer line number tells the computer the line number of the next statement to be executed, and control transfers to that program line regardless of its location in the program.

When a GOTO statement is executed, there are three possible actions that may be taken:

● If the statement indicated by the transfer line number is executable, it is executed, and execution continues from that point.
● If the statement indicated by the transfer line number is executable (such as a REM or DATA statement), control passes to the next line after it.
● If the transfer line number is not a line number of the program, an error message is displayed and execution is terminated.

The following is an example of a GOTO statement:

```
00100 GOTO 60
```

This statement causes program execution to branch or "go to" line 60, execute it if possible, and continue execution with the line following line 60.

Because control of the execution path *always* changes when the GOTO statement is encountered, such a statement is known as an **unconditional transfer.** Figures V–1 and V–2 show how execution paths are controlled with GOTO statements.

In Figure V–1, the GOTO statement in line 50 causes control to pass to line 70. Therefore, only the value of Y is printed; line 60 is skipped and left unexecuted.

In Figure V–2, control is transferred to line 50 by the GOTO statement. Line 50 contains a nonexecutable statement, so control passes to line 60. Notice that lines 30 and 40 are skipped and left unexecuted.

At this point a word of caution is in order. Although the GOTO statement gives the programmer increased control over the logical flow of a program, unconditional transfers can produce an execution path so complex and unreadable that the logic is virtually impossible to follow, and debugging becomes a nightmare. Later in this chapter and in other chapters, you will be introduced to control statements that are preferable to the GOTO statement. The GOTO should be used only when it is not feasible to use a different control statement.

● The IF/THEN Statement: Conditional Transfer

The GOTO statement always transfers control. Often, however, it is necessary to transfer control only when a specified condition exists. The IF/THEN statement is used to test for such a condition. If the condition does not exist, the next statement in the program is executed. Such a control transfer is called a **conditional transfer.** The general format of the IF/THEN statement is this:

line# IF condition THEN line#

A condition has the following general format:

expression   relational symbol   expression

● **FIGURE V–1**
GOTO Statement: Example 1

```
   00030 X = 10
   00040 Y = 20
   00050 GOTO 70
   00060 PRINT X
   00070 PRINT Y
   00080 ------
```

● **FIGURE V–2**
GOTO Statement: Example 2

```
   00010 X = 20
   00020 GOTO 50
   00030 -------
   00040 -------
   00050 REM *** THIS ISN'T EXECUTED ***
   00060 PRINT Y
```

For example, in the statement "110 if X < Y + 1 THEN 230," Y < Y + 1 is the condition.

Conditions tested can involve either numeric or character string data. **Relational symbols** that can be used include the following:

Symbol	Meaning	Examples
<	Less than	A < B
< = or ≤	Less than or equal to	X < = Y
>	Greater than	J > 1
> = or ≥	Greater than or equal to	A > = B
=	Equal to	X = T
		N$ = "NONE"
<> or ><	Not equal to	R <>Q
		"APPLE" <> R$

The condition test of the IF/THEN statement is represented in a flowchart by a diamond-shaped decision symbol. The outcome of the test determines which flow line (path of program logic) will be followed. Figure V–3 shows the flowchart of an IF/THEN statement.

Some examples of valid IF/THEN statements follow:

Statement	Computer Execution
| ```
00010 IF X >= 6 THEN 30
00020 A = A + X
00030 PRINT X
``` | If the value contained in X is greater than or equal to 6, the computer branches to line 30. If not, the computer executes the next sequential instruction, line 20. |
| ```
00010 IF K <> N * 40 THEN 50
00020 K = N * 40
``` | If K is not equal to N * 40, the computer transfers to statement 50. Otherwise, it executes the next statement, line 20. |
| ```
00040 IF A$ = "NO" THEN 60
00050 X = X + 1
00060 PRINT X
``` | If the value contained in A$ is NO, control is passed to line 60. If A$ contains anything else, control goes to line 50. |

The program in Figure V–4 checks a student's record and prints the name of that student if he or she made the freshman honor roll. The first condition to be checked is whether the student is a freshman:

```
00120 IF CLASS$ <> "FR" THEN 999
```

If the student is not a freshman, the rest of the student record doesn't need to be checked, and the program ends by branching to line 999. Otherwise, execution continues to line 130, which is skipped because it is nonexecutable.

The second condition to be checked is whether the student's GPA is less than 3.5:

```
00150 IF GPA < 3.5 THEN 999
```

If the student's GPA is too low, control passes to line 999 as with the first condition. If the program execution reaches line 180, the student has survived both tests and his or her name is printed.

● **FIGURE V–3**
Flowchart of an IF/THEN Statement

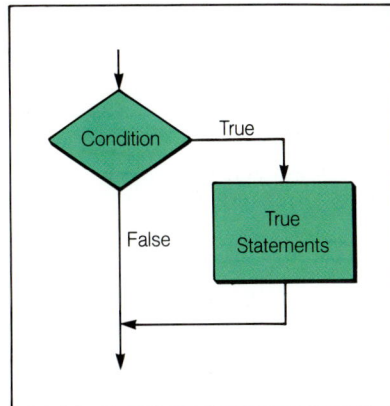
```

```
00010 REM ***              FRESHMAN HONOR ROLL              ***
00020 REM
00030 REM *** PRINT STUDENT NAME IF A FRESHMAN WITH         ***
00040 REM *** A GPA OF 3.5 OR HIGHER.                       ***
00050 REM
00060 REM *** ENTER STUDENT DATA ***
00070 INPUT "ENTER NAME";NME$
00080 INPUT "ENTER CLASS (FR,SO,JR,SR)";CLASS$
00090 INPUT "ENTER GPA";GPA
00100 REM
00110 REM *** REJECT IF NOT FRESHMAN ***
00120 IF CLASS$ <> "FR" THEN 999
00130 REM
00140 REM *** REJECT IF GPA < 3.5 ***
00150 IF GPA < 3.5 THEN 999
00160 REM
00170 REM *** PRINT NAME ***
00180 PRINT
00190 PRINT NME$;" IS ON THE FRESHMAN HONOR ROLL."
00999 END
```

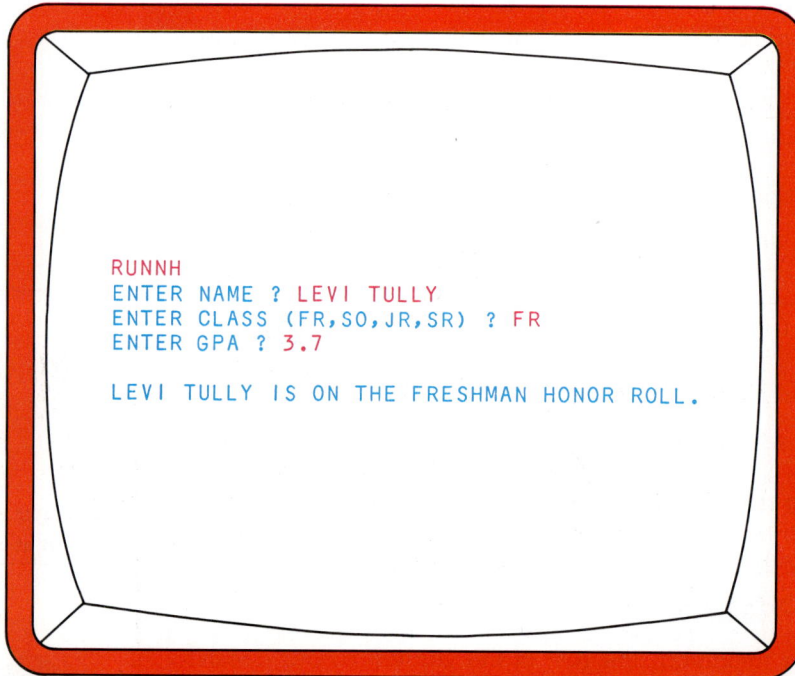

```
RUNNH
ENTER NAME ? LEVI TULLY
ENTER CLASS (FR,SO,JR,SR) ? FR
ENTER GPA ? 3.7

LEVI TULLY IS ON THE FRESHMAN HONOR ROLL.
```

Many BASIC implementations allow other, more general forms of the IF statement. One of these is the following:

line# IF condition THEN statement

The statement following THEN can be a BASIC statement or statements. Some examples follow:

```
00010 IF X < Y THEN A = A + 1 \ PRINT A
00050 IF M = N * P THEN PRINT M
```

IF/THEN/ELSE STATEMENTS

Another useful form of the IF statement is the IF/THEN/ELSE statement. The general format of the IF/THEN/ELSE statement is this:

line# IF condition THEN clause ELSE clause

The clause can be a BASIC statement or statements or a line number to branch to.

If the condition being tested is true, the clause following the THEN statement is executed. If the condition is false, the THEN clause is bypassed, and the clause following ELSE is executed.

The flowchart in Figure V–5 represents the logic of the IF/THEN/ELSE statement.

Some examples of valid IF/THEN/ELSE statements are given here:

```
00010 IF X = Y THEN PRINT "EQUAL" ELSE PRINT "NOT EQUAL"
00020 IF C = A * B THEN X = 1 ELSE X = 0
00030 IF M < R THEN 110 ELSE 150
```

Figure V–6 illustrates the use of an IF/THEN/ELSE statement.

● The ON/GOTO Statement: Conditional Transfer

The ON/GOTO, or computed GOTO, statement transfers control to other statements in the program based on the evaluation of a mathematical expression. The computed GOTO often operates as would multiple IF/ THEN statements; any one of several transfers can occur, depending on the result computed for the expression. Since transfers depend on the expression, the computed GOTO is another conditional transfer statement. Its general format is this:

line# ON expression GOTO line#1,line#2,line#3,…,line#n

The arithmetic expression is always evaluated to an integer, and the line numbers following GOTO must identify statements in the program.

The general execution of the ON/GOTO statement proceeds as follows:

1. The expression is evaluated as an integer.
2. Depending on the value of the expression, control passes to the corresponding line number.

    a. if the value of the expression is 1, control passes to the first line number listed.

● **FIGURE V–5**
Flowchart of an IF/THEN/ELSE Statement

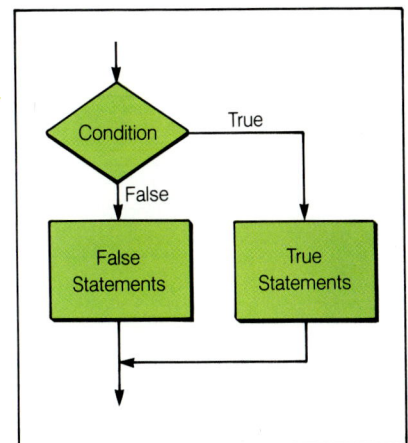

```
00010 REM ***    TEMPERATURE CONVERSION    ***
00020 REM
00030 INPUT "ENTER THE NUMBER OF DEGREES";T1TEMP
00040 PRINT "ENTER '1' FOR FAHRENHEIT TO CELSIUS"
00050 PRINT "      '2' FOR CELSIUS TO FAHRENHEIT"
00060 INPUT CODE
00070 REM
00080 REM *** CALCULATE TEMPERATURE ACCORDING TO CODE ***
00090 IF CODE = 1 THEN T2TEMP = (T1TEMP - 32) * (5 / 9) \ DEG$ = "CELSIUS"
           ELSE T2TEMP = T1TEMP * (9 / 5) + 32 \ DEG$ = "FAHRENHEIT"
00100 REM
00110 PRINT "THE RESULT = ";T2TEMP;" DEGREES ";DEG$
00999 END
```

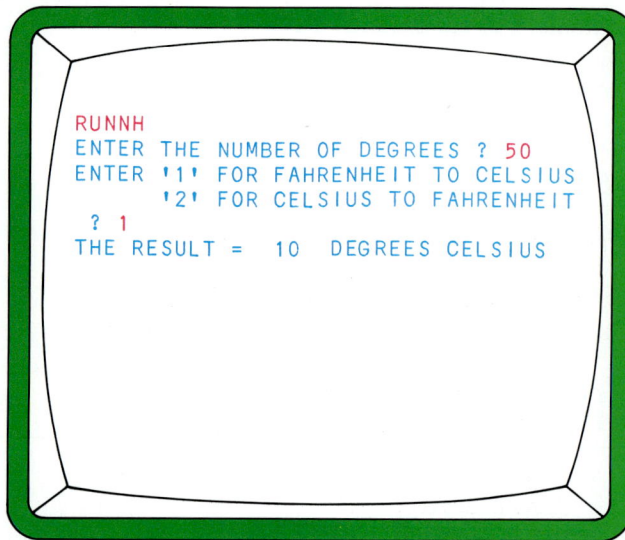

```
RUNNH
ENTER THE NUMBER OF DEGREES ? 50
ENTER '1' FOR FAHRENHEIT TO CELSIUS
         '2' FOR CELSIUS TO FAHRENHEIT
  ? 1
THE RESULT =   10   DEGREES CELSIUS
```

MICROCOMPUTERS	DIFFERENCE
Apple	No IF/THEN/ELSE statements
IBM/Microsoft	None
Macintosh/Microsoft	None
TRS-80	None

b. If the value of the expression is 2, control passes to the second line number listed.

c. If the value of the expression is *n*, control passes to the *n*th line number listed.

Several examples are presented here to illustrate the operation of this statement:

Statement	Computer Execution
00010 ON X GOTO 50,80,100	IF X = 1, control goes to line 50. IF X = 2, control goes to line 80. IF X = 3, control goes to line 100.
00030 ON N / 50 GOTO 90,100	IF N/50 = 1, control goes to line 90. IF N/50 = 2, control goes to line 100.

If the computed expression in an ON/GOTO statement does not evaluate to an integer, the value is either rounded or truncated (digits to the right of the decimal are ignored), depending on the BASIC implementation. For example,

Statement	Value of Variable	Action
00040 ON N / 3 GOTO 60,80	N = 7	$7 \div 3 = 2.33$. The expression is evaluated as 2.33. The remainder is truncated, and the result becomes the integer 2. Control passes to statement 80.

Three additional rules apply to the ON/GOTO statement:

● If the value of the expression is zero, the DECsystem displays an error message. The other systems described in this book ignore the rest of the ON/GOTO statement, and control passes to the next statement.
● If the value of the expression is greater than the number of transfer lines listed (but still within the system's permitted range), the DECsystem displays an error message and execution stops. Other systems merely bypass the ON/GOTO.
● If the value of the expression is negative, or if it exceeds the system's permitted maximum, an error message is displayed and execution stops.

The following table illustrates what happens if the value of the expression is greater than the number of transfer lines listed.

Statement	Value of Variable	Execution
00030 ON COUNT GOTO 70,85,100 00040 COUNT = COUNT - 1	COUNT = 5	**DECsystem:** Execution stops. Error message displayed. **Microcomputers:** Control passes to line 40.

Table V–1 illustrates how various BASIC implementations respond to these conditions.

● Menus

A **menu** is a listing that displays the functions that can be performed by a program. The desired function is chosen by entering a code (typically a simple numeric or alphabetic character) from the terminal keyboard. A computer menu is like a menu in a restaurant. The user (diner) reads a group of possible selections on the screen (menu) and then enters a selection into the computer (describes the desired meal to the waiter or waitress).

● TABLE V–1
ON/GOTO Actions

COMPUTER	EXPRESSION IS	ACTION IF EXPRESSION IS ZERO	ACTION IF EXPRESSION IS NEGATIVE OR GREATER THAN MAXIMUM ALLOWED	ACTION IF EXPRESSION IS GREATER THAN NUMBER OF LINES
DECsystem	truncated	"ON STMT OUT OF RANGE" error	"ON STMT OUT OF RANGE" error	Error message
Apple	truncated	ON/GOTO bypassed	"ILLEGAL QUANTITY" error	ON/GOTO bypassed
IBM/Microsoft	rounded	ON/GOTO bypassed	"ILLEGAL FUNCTION CALL" error	ON/GOTO bypassed
Macintosh/Microsoft	rounded	ON/GOTO bypassed	"ILLEGAL FUNCTION CALL" error	ON/GOTO bypassed
			"?FC" error	ON/GOTO bypassed
TRS-80	rounded	ON/GOTO bypassed	"ILLEGAL FUNCTION CALL" error	ON/GOTO bypassed

The calculator menu program (Figure V–7) illustrates a common use of the ON/GOTO statement in making a menu selection. The user tells the computer whether to add, subtract, multiply, or divide two numbers by entering either 1, 2, 3, or 4. Line 160 transfers the program execution to the appropriate operation.

In the example, after entering the value for A and B, the user indicates that division is the desired operation by typing in the number 3 which is assigned to the variable code. Line 160, an ON/GOTO statement, causes program execution to branch to the third line number, 270. The operation is then performed, and the result is printed.

● Looping Procedures

Often a situation arises in which a single task must be performed several times. For example, a teacher may need a program to find the average test score of all the students in a given class. The job of processing a single student's data is simple enough:

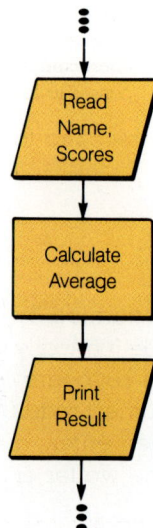

● COMPUTERS AND INFORMATION PROCESSING

● FIGURE V-7
ON/GOTO Example Using a Menu

```
RUNNH
ENTER A,B ? 5,8

      MENU SELECTION
       1 FOR A + B
       2 FOR A - B
       3 FOR A * B
       4 FOR A / B

ENTER A NUMBER 1 - 4 ? 3

THE RESULT =   40
```

```
00010 REM *** CALCULATOR MENU ***
00020 REM
00030 PRINT
00040 INPUT "ENTER A,B";A,B
00050 PRINT
00060 PRINT
00070 PRINT "      MENU SELECTION"
00080 PRINT "       1 FOR A + B"
00090 PRINT "       2 FOR A - B"
00100 PRINT "       3 FOR A * B"
00110 PRINT "       4 FOR A / B"
00120 PRINT
00130 INPUT "ENTER A NUMBER 1 - 4";CODE
00140 REM
00150 REM *** PERFORM SELECTED CALCULATION ***
00160 ON CODE GOTO 190,230,270,310
00170 REM
00180 REM *** ADDITION ***
00190 RESULT = A + B
00200 GOTO 320
00210 REM
00220 REM *** SUBTRACTION ***
00230 RESULT = 1 - B
00240 GOTO 320
00250 REM
00260 REM *** MULTIPLICATIION ***
00270 RESULT = A * B
00280 GOTO 320
00290 REM
00300 REM *** DIVISION ***
00310 RESULT = A / B
00320 PRINT
00330 PRINT
00340 PRINT "THE RESULT = ";RESULT
00999 END
```

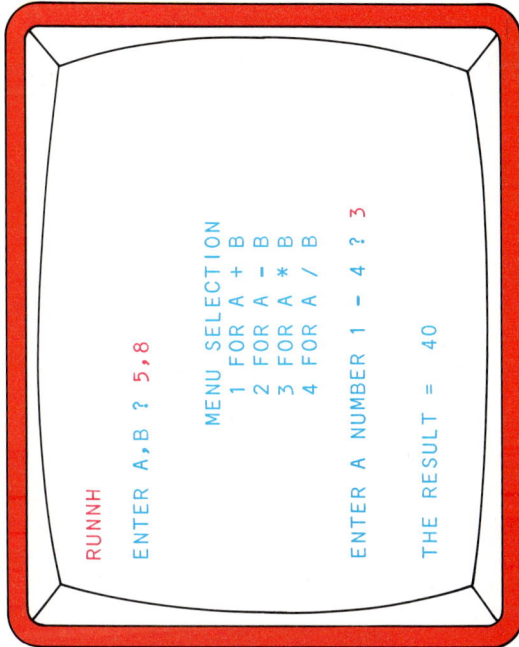

MICROCOMPUTERS	DIFFERENCE
Apple	None
IBM/Microsoft	None
Macintosh/Microsoft	None
TRS-80	None

However, consider the problem of repeating these steps for a class of thirty students:

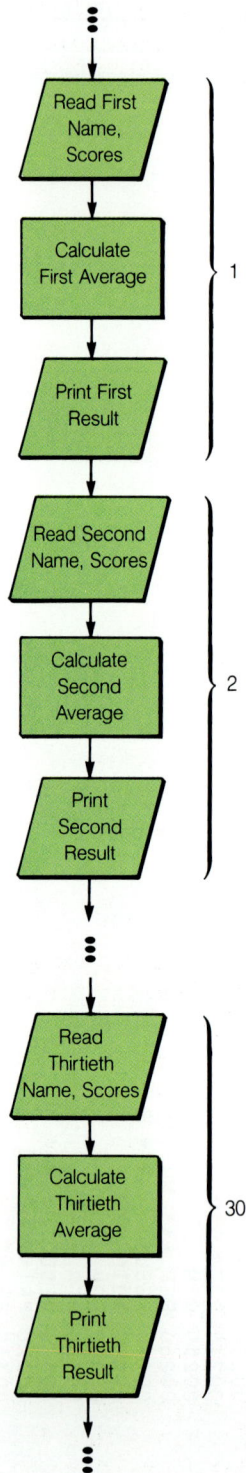

The same three statements to process a single student's data would have to be written thirty times. Although such a solution would be possible, it clearly would be a tedious and taxing job for the programmer. The problem could be greatly simplified by writing the statements to process the data of just one student, then executing those statements as many times as needed. This procedure, called looping, is flowcharted below:

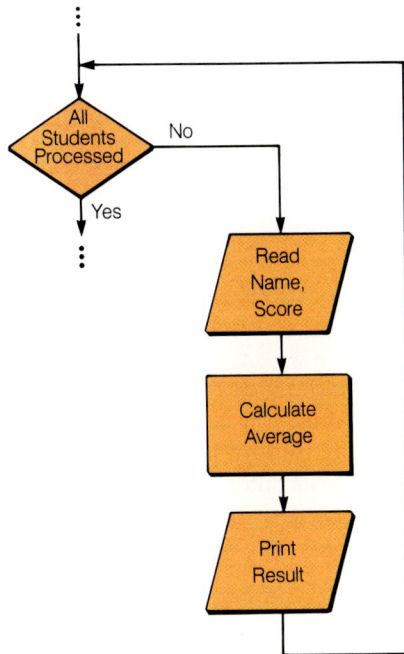

A sequence of steps executed repeatedly in this way constitutes a **loop.** One of the most important uses of control statements is the creation of loops. Control statements can determine which actions are to be repeated and the number of repetitions to be made. Some techniques for loop control include the use of trailer values, counters, and such looping statements as the FOR and NEXT statements. This section presents trailer values and counters; the FOR and NEXT statements are discussed in Section 6.

TRAILER VALUE

A loop controlled by a **trailer value** contains an IF/THEN statement that checks for the end of the data. The last data item is a dummy value that is not part of the data to be processed. Either numeric or alphanumeric data can be used as a trailer value. However, the programmer must always select a trailer value that will not be confused with real data. For example, a customer account number is never 0, which implies that zero may be safely used as a dummy value.

Here is how it works. An IF/THEN statement is placed within the set of instructions to be repeated, usually at the beginning of the loop. One of the variables to which data is entered is tested. If it contains the dummy value, control is transferred out of the loop. If the variable contains valid data (does not equal the trailer value), looping continues.

Figure V–8 contains a loop pattern controlled by a trailer value. The program calculates the commission on sales made by several employees of the Rich Rugs Company. Statement 170 tests the value NME$ for the dummy value:

```
00170 IF NME$ = "LAST" THEN 999
```

If the condition is true, the flow of processing drops out of the loop to line 999. If the condition is false, processing continues to the next line in sequence, line 180. Note that since we used the INPUT statement to enter the data, it is necessary to tell the user how to end the looping process. This is done in lines 140 and 260. The user has to enter two dummy values, LAST and 0, because the INPUT statement expects two values to be entered.

COUNTER

A second method of controlling a loop requires the programmer to create a **counter**—a numeric variable that is incremented each time the loop is executed. Normally, the increment is 1. A counter is effective only if the programmer notifies the computer how many times a loop should be repeated. The following steps are involved in setting up a counter for loop control:

1. Initialize the counter to give it a beginning value.
2. Increment the counter each time the loop is executed.
3. Test the counter to determine if the loop has been executed the desired number of times.

The sales commission program used in Figure V–8 can be modified to use a counter, as shown in Figure V–9. Since there are three salespeople, the loop must be executed three times. The counter in this example is CNTR. It is initialized to 0 in line 150. The IF/THEN statement in line 210 tests the number of times the loop has been executed, as represented by the counter CNTR. Line 280 causes CNTR to be incremented each time the loop is executed. The loop instructions will be executed until CNTR equals 3.

● A Programming Problem

PROBLEM DEFINITION

Ed Hoge, an instructor for Art 101, needs a program that will assign letter grades to students based on their test scores. In addition, he wants to know how many students are in each grade category and how many took the test.

```
00010 REM ***                    RICH RUGS CO.                ***
00020 REM
00030 REM *** THIS PROGRAM CALCULATES THE COMMISSION FOR EACH ***
00040 REM *** SALESPERSON ENTERED.                            ***
00050 REM *** MAJOR VARIABLES:                                ***
00060 REM ***    NME$ - LAST NAME                             ***
00070 REM ***    RTE - RATE OF COMMISSION                     ***
00080 REM ***    SALES - VALUE OF SALES                       ***
00090 REM ***    COMMSN - COMMISSION                          ***
00100 REM
00110 RTE = .15
00120 REM *** ENTER FIRST SALESPERON'S DATA ***
00130 PRINT "ENTER NAME, SALES"
00140 INPUT "TYPE 'LAST,0' TO END";NME$,SALES
00150 REM
00160 REM *** TEST FOR TRAILER VALUE ***
00170 IF NME$ = "LAST" THEN 999
00180 COMMSN = SALES * RTE
00190 PRINT
00200 PRINT "NAME","SALES","COMMISSION"
00210 PRINT NME$,SALES,COMMSN
00220 PRINT
00230 REM
00240 REM *** ENTER NEXT SALESPERSON'S DATA ***
00250 PRINT "ENTER NAME, SALES"
00260 INPUT "TYPE 'LAST,0' TO END";NME$,SALES
00270 GOTO 170
00999 END
```

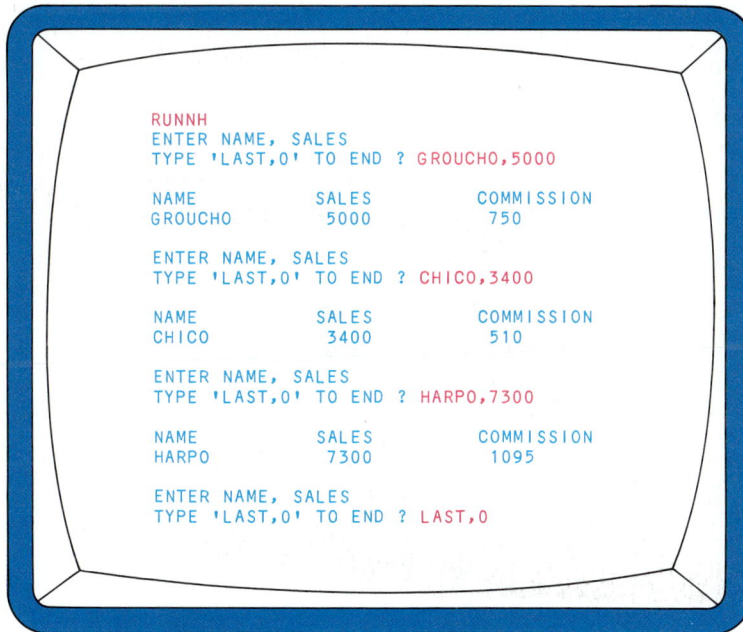

```
RUNNH
ENTER NAME, SALES
TYPE 'LAST,0' TO END ? GROUCHO,5000

NAME            SALES           COMMISSION
GROUCHO         5000            750

ENTER NAME, SALES
TYPE 'LAST,0' TO END ? CHICO,3400

NAME            SALES           COMMISSION
CHICO           3400            510

ENTER NAME, SALES
TYPE 'LAST,0' TO END ? HARPO,7300

NAME            SALES           COMMISSION
HARPO           7300            1095

ENTER NAME, SALES
TYPE 'LAST,0' TO END ? LAST,0
```

MICROCOMPUTERS	DIFFERENCE
Apple	None
IBM/Microsoft	None
Macintosh/Microsoft	None
TRS-80	None

```
00010 REM ***                        RICH RUGS CO.              ***
00020 REM
00030 REM ***  THIS PROGRAM CALCULATES THE COMMISSION FOR       ***
00040 REM ***  EACH SALESPERSON ENTERED.                        ***
00050 REM ***  MAJOR VARIABLES:                                 ***
00060 REM ***     NME$ - LAST NAME                              ***
00070 REM ***     RTE - RATE OF COMMISSION                      ***
00080 REM ***     SALES - VALUE OF SALES                        ***
00090 REM ***     COMMSN - COMMISSION                           ***
00100 REM ***     CNTR - LOOP COUNTER                           ***
00110 REM
00120 RTE = .15
00130 REM
00140 REM *** INITIALIZE COUNTER ***
00150 CNTR = 0
00160 REM
00170 REM *** PRINT HEADINGS ***
00180 PRINT "NAME","SALES","COMMISSION"
00190 REM
00200 REM *** TEST COUNTER VALUES ***
00210 IF CNTR = 3 THEN 999
00220 READ NME$,SALES
00230 COMMSN = SALES * RTE
00240 PRINT
00250 PRINT NME$, SALES, COMMSN
00260 REM
00270 REM *** UPDATE COUNTER VALUE ***
00280 CNTR = CNTR + 1
00290 GOTO 210
00300 REM
00310 REM *** DATA STATEMENTS ***
00320 DATA "GROUCHO",5000,"CHICO",3400,"HARPO",7300
00999 END
```

```
RUNNH
NAME            SALES            COMMISSION

GROUCHO         5000             750

CHICO           3400             510

HARPO           7300             1095
```

MICROCOMPUTERS	DIFFERENCE
Apple	None
IBM/Microsoft	None
Macintosh/Microsoft	None
TRS-80	None

The grading scale is as follows:

Score	Letter Grade
90 or more	A
78 to 89	B
66 to 77	C
54 to 65	D
Less than 54	F

Ed wants the program to print the name, score, and letter grade for each student entered, followed by the total number of grades in each category, and finally the total number of students. The students and their scores follow:

Student	Score
Nan Barnett	96
Bob Szymanski	93
Jim Strong	89
Bob Tynecki	78
Lynn Probst	90
Bill Brandon	51
Denise Siviy	88
Vic Flynn	66
Karen McKee	98
Anne Tate	77

SOLUTION DESIGN

The general problem of producing a grade report can be divided into two subproblems—the repeated task of processing each student, and the task of printing the summary information, which is performed only once.

1. Process each student's data.
2. Report the summary information.

A repeated task suggests a loop. Step A can be further divided into several smaller tasks that must be performed for each student:

1. a. Enter the student's data.
1. b. Determine the grade.
1. c. Update the appropriate counters.
1. d. Print the student's information.

Step B can also be divided into smaller problems:

2. a. Print a heading.
2. b. Print the grade counts.
2. c. Print the total student count.

The structure chart in Figure V–10 diagrams this outline of the problem. Since the number of students is not known, the tasks of Step 1 can be placed in a loop controlled by a trailer value. When each student has been processed, the report of the summary information can be printed. The flowchart in Figure V–11 shows the order of steps necessary to solve the problem.

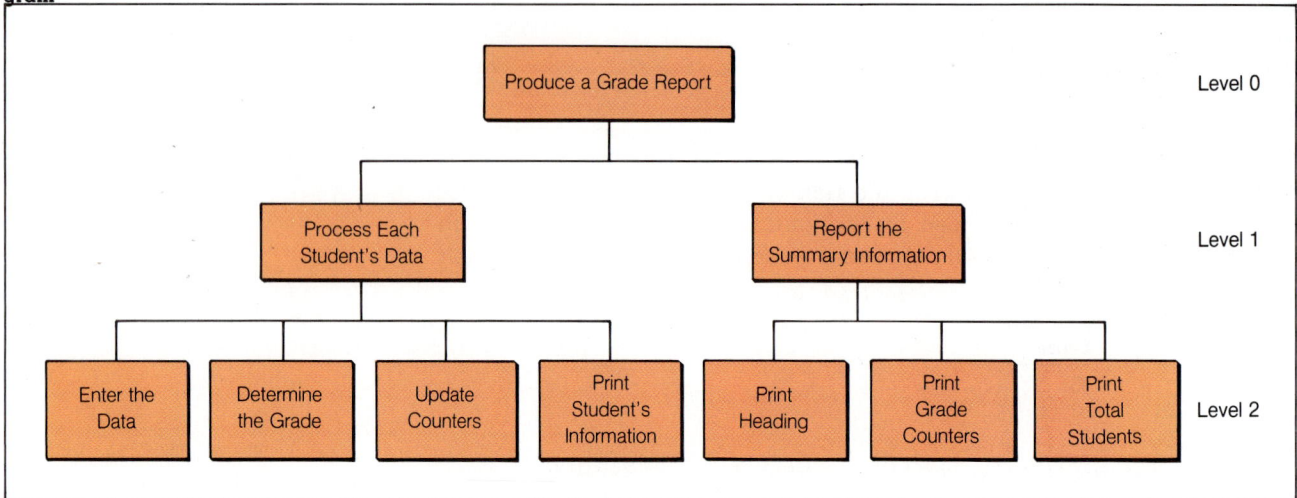

THE PROGRAM

The counter variables are initialized to 0 by the assignment statements in lines 180 through 230 of Figure V–11. The name and score for the first student are entered in line 270. Line 300 tests for the trailer value XXX. As long as the student's name does not equal XXX, the loop is reexecuted. The total number of students is accumulated in line 330. The first test to determine the grade is made in line 340. If the score is less than 90, it is not an A. Control is transferred to line 400, where the score is tested again to see if it is less than 78 (less than that required for a B.) In this fashion, scores less than the lowest number required for a particular grade are passed down to the next lowest level until the correct one is found. Line 600 requires no test; any grade less than 54 is an F. When the trailer value, XXX, is detected, control drops down to line 770, where printing of the totals occurs.

● **Summary Points**

● The GOTO statement is an unconditional transfer of control that allows the computer to bypass or alter the sequence in which instructions are executed.

● The IF/THEN statement permits control to be transferred only when a specified condition is met. If the condition following IF is true, the clause following the word THEN is given control; if it is false, control passes to the next line.

● The IF/THEN/ELSE statement is an extension of the IF/THEN statement. If the condition following IF is true, the clause following THEN is given control. If the condition is false, control is transferred to the clause following ELSE. IF/THEN/ELSE statements may be nested.

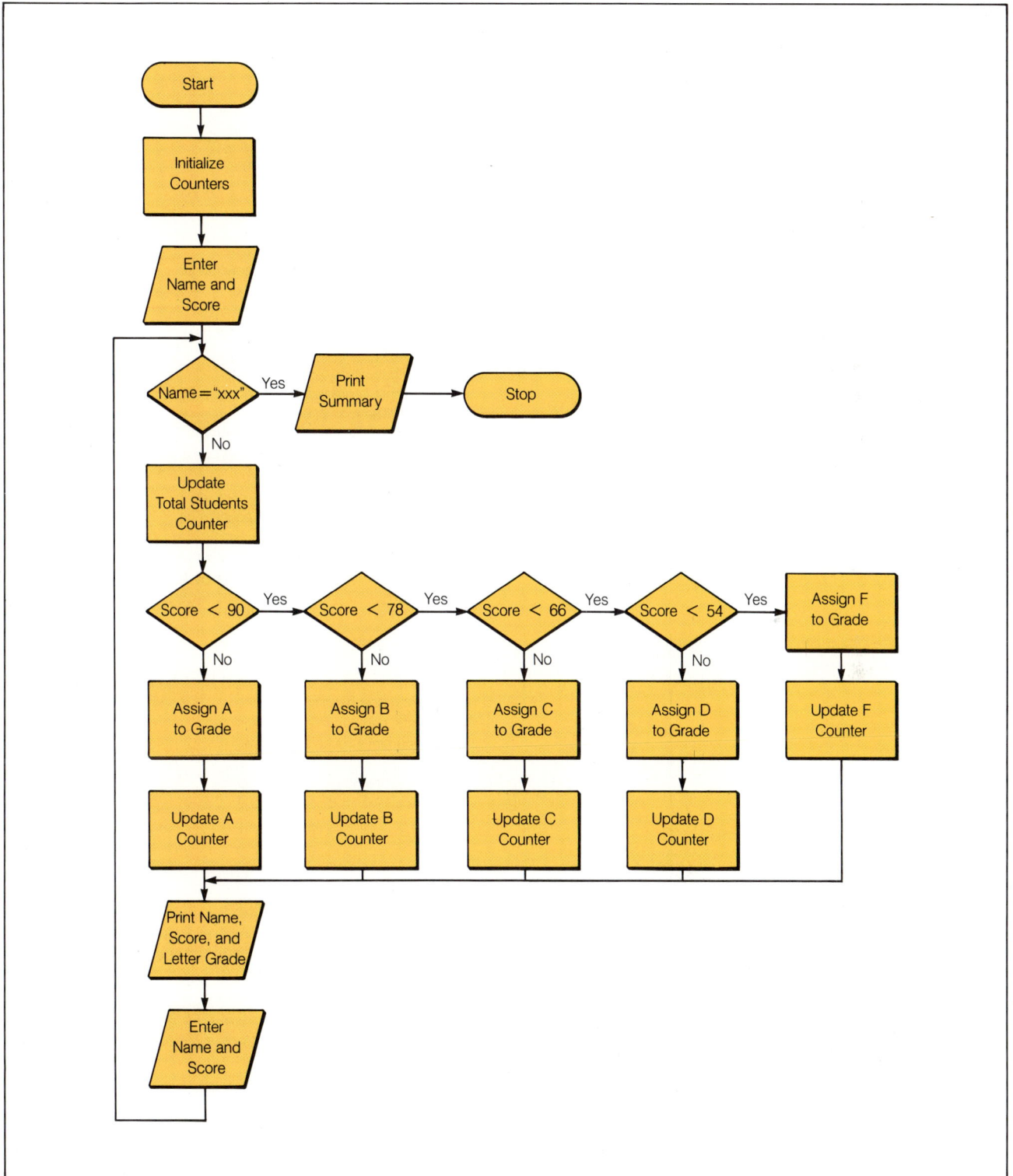

(Continued Next Three Pages)

Pseudocode

Begin

Initialize letter grade counters
Input first student's name and score
Begin loop, do until end of items
    Increment total student counter by 1
    If score is greater than or equal to 90
      Then
        Assign letter grade of "A"
        Increment "A" counter by 1
      Else
        If score is greater than or equal to 78
          Then
            Assign letter grade of "B"
            Increment "B" counter by 1
        End if
      Else
        If score is greater than or equal to 66
          Then
            Assign letter grade of "C"
            Increment "C" counter by 1
        End if
      Else
        If score is greater than or equal to 54
          Then
            Assign letter grade of "D"
            Increment "D" counter by 1
        End if
      Else
        Assign letter grade of "F"
        Increment "F" counter by 1
    End if
    Print student report headings
    Print student's name, score and letter grade
    Input next student's name and score
End loop
Print grade totals and total number of students
End

```
00010 REM ***                    ART 101 GRADES                  ***
00020 REM
00030 REM *** THIS PROGRAM ASSIGNS LETTER GRADES BASED ON ***
00040 REM *** TEST SCORES, THEN TALLIES THE RESULTS. THE  ***
00050 REM *** SCALE USED IS AS FOLLOWS:                   ***
00060 REM ***         >= 90        = A                    ***
00070 REM ***         78 - 89      = B                    ***
00080 REM ***         66 - 77      = C                    ***
00090 REM ***         54 - 65      = D                    ***
00100 REM ***         < 54         = F                    ***
00110 REM *** MAJOR VARIABLES:                            ***
00120 REM ***     NME$ - STUDENT NAME                     ***
00130 REM ***     TESTSCR - STUDENT TEST SCORE            ***
00140 REM ***     TTAL - TOTAL NUMBER OF STUDENTS         ***
00150 REM ***     LETTR$ - LETTER GRADE                   ***
00160 REM
```

```
00170 REM *** INITIALIZE LETTER GRADE COUNTERS ***
00180 A = 0
00190 B = 0
00200 C = 0
00210 D = 0
00220 F = 0
00230 TTAL = 0
00240 REM
00250 REM *** ENTER FIRST STUDENT'S DATA ***
00260 PRINT "ENTER NAME, SCORE"
00270 INPUT "TYPE 'XXX,0' TO END";NME$,TESTSCR
00280 REM
00290 REM *** TEST FOR TRAILER VALUE ***
00300 IF NME$ = "XXX" THEN 770
00310 REM
00320 REM *** UPDATE TOTAL STUDENTS COUNTER ***
00330 TTAL = TTAL + 1
00340 IF TESTSCR < 90 THEN 400
00350 REM
00360 REM *** GRADE = A ***
00370 LETTR$ = "A"
00380 A = A + 1
00390 GOTO 650
00400 IF TESTSCR < 78 THEN 460
00410 REM
00420 REM *** GRADE = B ***
00430 LETTR$ = "B"
00440 B = B + 1
00450 GOTO 650
00460 IF TESTSCR < 66 THEN 520
00470 REM
00480 REM *** GRADE = C ***
00490 LETTR$ = "C"
00500 C = C + 1
00510 GOTO 650
00520 IF TESTSCR < 54 THEN 600
00530 REM
00540 REM *** GRADE = D ***
00550 LETTR$ = "D"
00560 D = D + 1
00570 GOTO 650
00580 REM
00590 REM *** GRADE = F ***
00600 LETTR$ = "F"
00610 F = F + 1
00620 REM
00630 REM *** PRINT STUDENT REPORT ***
00640 PRINT
00650 PRINT "NAME";TAB(25);"SCORE";TAB(35);"GRADE"
00660 PRINT NME$;TAB(27);TESTSCR;TAB(37);LETTR$
00670 PRINT
00680 REM
00690 REM *** ENTER NEXT STUDENT'S DATA ***
00700 PRINT
00710 PRINT "ENTER NAME, SCORE"
00720 INPUT "TYPE 'XXX,0' TO END";NME$,TESTSCR
00730 PRINT
00740 GOTO 300
00750 REM
00760 REM *** PRINT TOTALS ***
00770 PRINT
00780 PRINT "TOTAL # OF A'S = ";A
00790 PRINT "TOTAL # OF B'S = ";B
00800 PRINT "TOTAL # OF C'S = ";C
00810 PRINT "TOTAL # OF D'S = ";D
00820 PRINT "TOTAL # OF F'S = ";F
00830 PRINT
00840 PRINT "TOTAL # OF STUDENTS = ";TTAL
00999 END
```

```
RUNNH
ENTER NAME, SCORE
TYPE 'XXX,0' TO END ? STACEY MATHEY,100
NAME                      SCORE     GRADE
STACEY MATHEY               100       A


ENTER NAME, SCORE
TYPE 'XXX,0' TO END ? JANET LOWRY,95

NAME                      SCORE     GRADE
JANET LOWRY                 95        A


ENTER NAME, SCORE
TYPE 'XXX,0' TO END ? ANN BRESSLER,65

NAME                      SCORE     GRADE
ANN BRESSLER               65        D

ENTER NAME, SCORE
TYPE 'XXX,0' TO END ? MIKE FETTERMAN,82

NAME                      SCORE     GRADE
MIKE FETTERMAN             82        B


ENTER NAME, SCORE
TYPE 'XXX,0' TO END ? PAUL WILLIAMS,71

NAME                      SCORE     GRADE
PAUL WILLIAMS             71        C


ENTER NAME, SCORE
TYPE 'XXX,0' TO END ? XXX,0


TOTAL # OF A'S =  2
TOTAL # OF B'S =  1
TOTAL # OF C'S =  1
TOTAL # OF D'S =  1
TOTAL # OF F'S =  0

TOTAL # OF STUDENTS =  5
```

MICROCOMPUTERS	DIFFERENCE
Apple	None
IBM/Microsoft	None
Macintosh/Microsoft	None
TRS-80	None

- The ON/GOTO statement instructs the computer to evaluate an expression and, based on its value, to branch to one of several points in a program.
- A menu is a listing that displays the functions a program can perform. The user selects the desired function by entering a code from the keyboard.
- The number of times a loop is executed can be controlled by the use of a trailer value or a counter.
- The trailer value is a dummy value entered at the end of all the data.
- A counter can be set up if the programmer knows ahead of time how many times a loop is to be executed.

● Review Questions

1. Why is the GOTO statement an unconditional transfer?
2. Rewrite the following program, using a loop controlled by a trailer value:

```
00010 READ N$,X,Y
00020 Z = X + Y
00030 PRINT N$,Z
00040 READ N$,X,Y
00050 Z = X + Y
00060 PRINT N$,Z
00070 READ N$,X,Y
00080 Z = X + Y
00090 PRINT N$,Z
00100 DATA LARRY,10,5,MOE,25,7,CURLY,17,41
00999 END
```

3. Why is the IF/THEN statement a conditional transfer?
4. In an IF/THEN statement, the THEN clause may be _____.
   a. a line number
   b. a single BASIC statement
   c. multiple BASIC statements
   d. all of the above
   e. a and b only
5. Which of these are valid IF/THEN statements?
   a. 10 IF X <> "NO" THEN 30
   b. 60 IF Y = 2 THEN 100
   c. 100 IF A$ = "APPLE" THEN 150
   d. 200 IF X$ = "YES" THEN 250
6. The statement after ELSE in an IF/THEN/ELSE statement is executed when the condition is _____.
   a. true
   b. false
7. To what line number will control be transferred when this statement is encountered ($N = 51$)?

   100 ON N / 17 GOTO 150, 200, 275
8. What is a menu?
9. What is a trailer value?
10. Rewrite the program in Question 2 using a counter-controlled loop.

● Debugging Exercises

Indentify the following programs or program segments that contain errors, and debug them.

```
1. 00010  PRINT TAB(7);"WORLD CUP STANDINGS"
   00020  PRINT TAB(5);"NAME";TAB(26);"POINTS"
   00030  READ NME$,PTS
   00040  IF NME$ = "DONE" THEN 99
   00050  PRINT TAB(5);NME$;TAB(26);PTS
   00060  READ NME$,PTS
   00070  GOTO 40
   00080  DATA BILL JOHNSON,192,PHIL MAHRE,131
   00090  DATA INGMAR STENMARK,47,DONE
   00999  END
```

```
2. 00010  REM *** CALCULATE SUM OF 20 NUMBERS ***
   00020  Y = 1
   00030  IF Y > 20 THEN 80
   00040  INPUT "ENTER NUMBER";NMBR
   00050  SUM = SUM + NMBR
   00060  GOTO 20
   00070  PRINT "SUM = ";SUM
   00099  END
```

● Programming Problems

1. The Admissions Board of Blighter College conducts three interviews of every prospective student. These interviews are rated and averaged. Based on this average, a report is to be printed recommending the action to be taken by the Board. Each of the three interviews carry a maximum score of fifty points. Your job is to compute the average score for each prospective student and write a report giving the recommended action to be taken. The report also should list the total number of candidates evaluated and the total number of candidates in each category. The test data is as follows:

Name	Interview		
	1	2	3
Buz Murdock	50	45	49
Sam Hunt	35	21	42
Marie Walker	43	32	35
Stacy O'Donnell	19	35	20
Susie McKinniss	41	47	39

2. The Marvel-Vac Company is processing the monthly checks for its door-to-door sales agents. Each agent receives a 35 percent commission on his or her monthly sales. An agent whose sales exceed $1000 receives a $50 bonus, and an agent whose sales are less than $250 must pay a $25 processing charge, which is subtracted from that month's check. Each vacuum sells for $250. Write a program that will calculate each agent's total sales, straight commission, bonus or deduction if necessary, and check total. A report should print each agent's name, straight commission, bonus or deduction adjustment, and total amount to be paid. Use the following data:

Agent	Number of Vacuums Sold
Drake, J.	6
Tully, M.	3
Hendricks, R.	5
Corelli, I.	1
Cross, J.	0

3. Write a program that calculates the value of inventory on hand of each item in stock, and displays the stock number and value on hand. Use a loop controlled by a trailer value, and use the following data:

Stock Number	Price	In Stock
X3308	$13.75	31
X5500	9.50	25
X9611	20.95	14

4. Write a program that will print current weather forecasts. A menu should be used to display the choices. Use the ON/GOTO statement and the following sample data:

Date	Forecast
9/01	Cloudy; 60% chance of afternoon showers; high 70–75°
9/02	Sunny and breezy; high 80–85°
9/03	Partly cloudy; 40% chance of rain; high 65–70°

5. A styling salon manager gives each employee a year-end bonus based on the average value of retail products he or she has sold in the last three months of the year. You are to write a program to find the average of the three values and determine a bonus for each employee. Your output should include the name and bonus of each employee. Use the following data:

Susan Jones	$88	$90	$85
Stacy Matthey	65	73	81
Wendy White	50	46	65
Les Southwyk	44	75	90
Bob Green	35	43	49
Stephanie Miller	68	60	55

Use a loop controlled with a counter. The bonus scale is set up like this:

$90 or more	$50
$80 to 90	$40
$70 to 80	$30
$60 to 70	$20
$59 or less	$10

● Section VI
More About Looping

● Introduction

Section V discussed two methods of controlling loops—counters and trailer values. This section presents another method for loop control—FOR and NEXT statements. In addition, it discusses nested loops (loops within loops).

Let us review what happens when a counter is used to control a loop since the logic of FOR/NEXT loops is very similar. First, the counter variable is set to some initial value. The counter value is compared to the terminal value, and if it does not exceed the terminal value the statements inside the loop are executed once and the counter is incremented. The counter variable then is tested again to see if the loop has been executed the required number of times. When the variable exceeds the designated terminal value, the looping process ends, and the computer proceeds to the rest of the program. For example, assume we want to write a program that will multiply each of the numbers from 1 to 5 by 5 and then add 2. The program in Figure VI–1 does this using a loop controlled by the counter method. We will see later how the FOR/NEXT loop allows us to accomplish the same steps in a more efficient manner.

● The FOR and NEXT Statements

The FOR and NEXT statements allow concise loop definition. The general format of the FOR and NEXT loop is as follows:

line# FOR loop control variable = initial expression TO terminal expression STEP step value

.
.
.

line# NEXT loop control variable

The FOR statement tells the computer how many times to execute the loop. The **loop control variable** is a variable the value of which is used to control loop repetition. When the FOR statement is executed, the loop control variable (also called the **index**) is set to an initial value. This value is tested against the terminal value to determine whether or not the loop

● COMPUTERS AND INFORMATION PROCESSING

```
00010 N = 1
00020 IF N > 5 THEN 99
00030 PRINT N,N * 5 + 2
00040 N = N + 1
00050 GOTO 20
00099 END
```

```
RUNNH
     1              7
     2             12
     3             17
     4             22
     5             27
```

MICROCOMPUTERS	DIFFERENCE
Apple	None
IBM/Microsoft	None
Macintosh/Microsoft	None
TRS-80	None

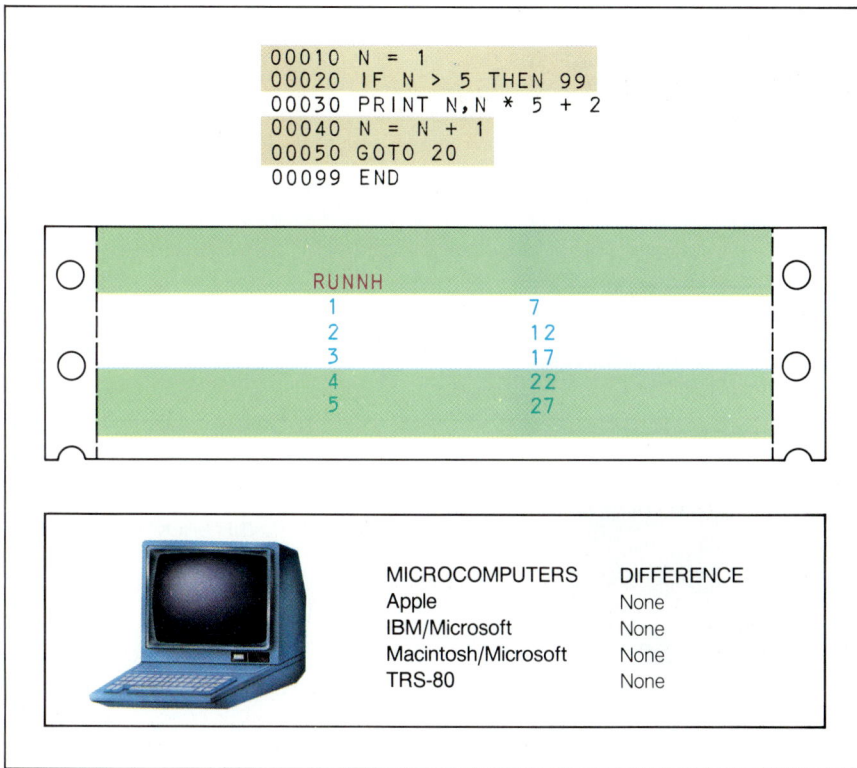

should be executed. The initial and terminal values may be constants, variables, or expressions, all of which must be numeric.

To set the initial value and test the counter took two lines (lines 10 and 20) in Figure VI–1. The FOR statement combines these two steps into one statement:

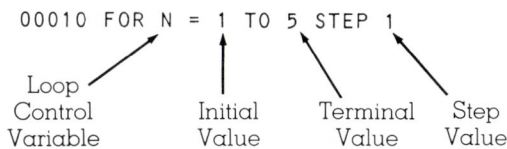

```
00010 FOR N = 1 TO 5 STEP 1
```

Loop
Control   Initial   Terminal   Step
Variable   Value   Value   Value

Lines 40 and 50 in Figure VI–1 increment the loop control variable (the counter) and send control back to line 20. The functions of these two statements are combined in the NEXT statement. In Figure VI–1, after control is transferred back to line 20, the value of the loop control variable is again tested against the terminal value. Once the value is exceeded, control passes to line 99. When FOR and NEXT are used, control goes to the statement immediately following the NEXT statement.

Thus, the loop used in Figure VI–1 can be set up to use FOR and NEXT statements, as shown in Figure VI–2. The FOR statement in line 10 tells the computer to initialize the loop variable, N, to one. Between the FOR and NEXT statements is line 20, the instruction that is to be repeated; it prints N and the result of N * 5 + 2. Line 30, the NEXT statement, increments the loop control variable by the step indicated in the FOR state-

```
00010 FOR N = 1 TO 5 STEP 1
00020     PRINT N,N * 5 + 2
00030 NEXT N
00099 END
```

```
RUNNH
    1              7
    2             12
    3             17
    4             22
    5             27
```

MICROCOMPUTERS	DIFFERENCE
Apple	None
IBM/Microsoft	None
Macintosh/Microsoft	None
TRS-80	None

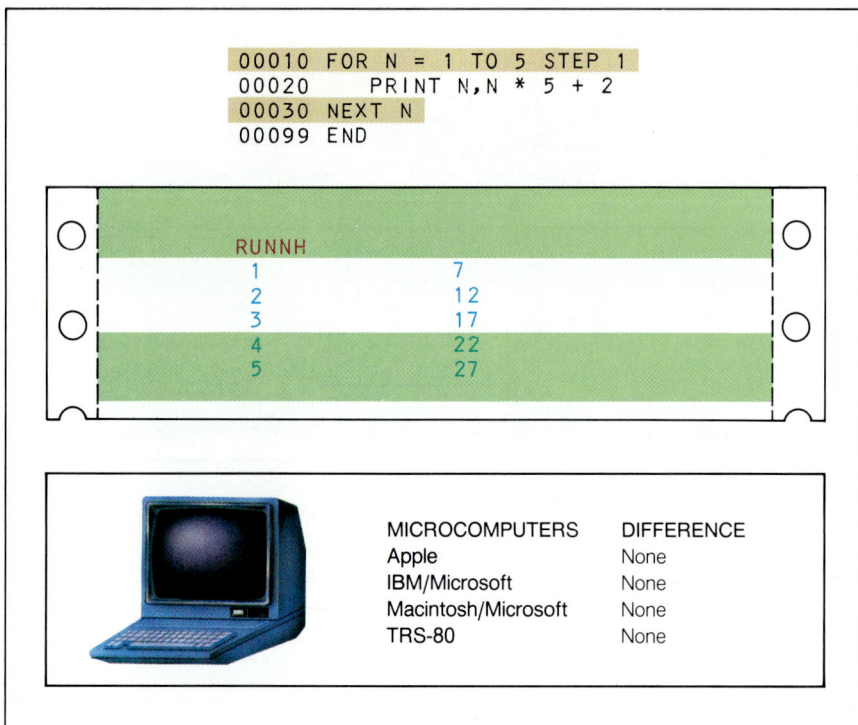

ment. The step value may be a constant, variable, or expression, and it must have a numeric value.

FLOWCHARTING FOR AND NEXT LOOPS

Figure VI-3a illustrates a common method of flowcharting the FOR/NEXT loop. We have developed our own shorthand symbol for FOR/NEXT loops, which is shown in Figure VI-3b. This is very convenient for representing a loop, since it shows the initial, terminal, and step values for the loop control variable in one symbol.

PROCESSING STEPS OF FOR AND NEXT LOOPS

Let us review the steps followed by the computer when it encounters a FOR statement:

1. The step value indicated in the FOR statement is added to the loop control variable. If the step value is omitted, a +1 is added.
2. A check is performed to determine if the value of the loop control
3. The value of the loop control variable is tested against the terminal value.
4. If the loop control variable is less than or equal to the terminal value, then the loop body is executed.
5. If the loop control variable is greater than the terminal value, then the loop body is skipped and control passes to the first statement following the NEXT statement. This means that the loop will not be executed at all.

● **COMPUTERS AND INFORMATION PROCESSING**

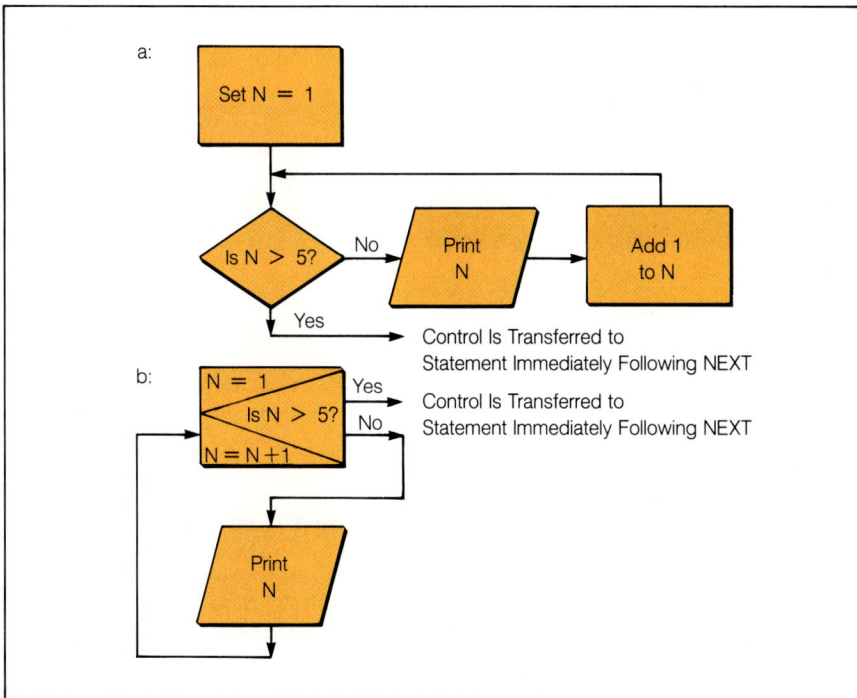

(The Apple is an exception here—it always executes a FOR/NEXT loop at least once.)

Here is what happens when the NEXT statement is found:

1. The step value indicated in the FOR statement is added to the loop control variable. If the step value is omitted, a + 1 is added.
2. A check is performed to determine if the value of the loop control variable exceeds the terminal value.
3. If the loop control variable is less than or equal to the terminal value, then control is transferred back to the statement after the FOR statement and the loop is repeated. Otherwise, the loop is exited and execution continues with the statement following the NEXT statement.

RULES FOR USING FOR AND NEXT STATEMENTS

Some rules to be aware of when you use FOR and NEXT statements follow:

1. The initial value must be less than or equal to the terminal value when using a positive step. Otherwise, the loop will never be executed. For example, a loop containing either of the following statements would not be executed at all:

```
00030 FOR X = 1 TO -10 STEP 2
00020 FOR X = 100 TO 50 STEP 5
```

2. There are times when it is desirable to use a negative step value, for example, to count backward from 10 by 2s (see Figure VI-4). The loop

```
00010 FOR I = 10 TO 2 STEP -2
00020     PRINT I
00030 NEXT I
00099 END
```

```
       RUNNH
        10
         8
         6
         4
         2
```

MICROCOMPUTERS	DIFFERENCE
Apple	None
IBM/Microsoft	None
Macintosh/Microsoft	None
TRS-80	None

is terminated when the value of the loop control variable, I, is less than the specified terminal value, 2. The initial value of the loop variable should be greater than the terminal value when using a negative step; for example,

```
00050 FOR J = 10 TO 1 STEP -2
00100 FOR K -1 TO -10 STEP -2
```

3. The step size in a FOR statement should never be 0. This value would cause the computer to loop endlessly. Such an error condition is known as an **infinite loop:**

```
00070 FOR X = 20 TO 30 STEP 0
```

4. Transfer can be made from one statement to another within a loop. For example, the program in Figure VI–5 reads in four names and the number of hours they worked. It will print out only those people who worked more than 40 hours. Note, however, that a transfer from a statement within the loop to the FOR statement of the loop is poor programming practice. Such a transfer would cause the loop variable to be reset rather than simply continuing the loop process. In the following segment, line 20 is not a proper branch:

```
00010 FOR I = 900 TO 1000
00020    IF I = 950 THEN 10
00030    PRINT I - 50
00040 NEXT I
```

If you want to continue the looping process but want to bypass some inner instruction, branch (transfer control) to the NEXT statement, as was done in Figure VI–5 (line 110).

5. It is possible to modify the loop control variable in the loop body, but

● COMPUTERS AND INFORMATION PROCESSING

this should *never* be done. Note how unpredictable the execution of the following program loop would be. The value of 1 is dependent on the integer entered by the user.

```
00030 FOR I = 1 TO 10
00040    INPUT "ENTER AN INTEGER";X
00050    I = X
00060 NEXT I
```

6. The initial, terminal, and step expressions can be composed of any valid numeric variable, constant, or expression. The following examples are valid where X = 2, Y = 10, and Z = -2:

```
00010 FOR I = X TO (Y + 20) STEP 1
00020    PRINT I + X
00030 NEXT I
```

```
00010 FOR J = Y TO X STEP Z
00020    S = S + J * 3
00030 NEXT J
```

```
00010 FOR K = (X + 1) TO (Y * 2) STEP -Z
00020    PRINT K
00030 NEXT K
```

● FIGURE VI–5
Transferring Control Within a FOR/NEXT Loop

```
00010 REM ***                    WORKER LIST                    ***
00020 REM ***                                                   ***
00030 REM *** THIS PROGRAM PRINTS A LIST OF FULL-TIME WORKERS. ***
00040 REM ***   MAJOR VARIABLES:                                ***
00050 REM ***      NME$ - NAME OF WORKER                        ***
00060 REM ***      HRS - NUMBER OF HOURS WORKED IN ONE WEEK     ***
00070 REM
00080 REM *** LOOP TO CHECK FOUR WORKERS ***
00090 FOR I = 1 TO 4
00100    READ NME$,HRS
00110    IF HRS < 40 THEN 130
00120    PRINT NME$
00130 NEXT I
00140 DATA "SHELLI BECHSTEIN",42,"TONYA KNAUSS",43
00150 DATA "CHARLIE KOLDING",32,"FRANK FURTER",45
00999 END
```

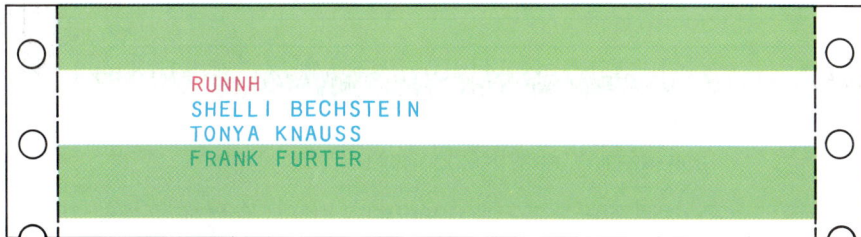

```
RUNNH
SHELLI BECHSTEIN
TONYA KNAUSS
FRANK FURTER
```

MICROCOMPUTERS	DIFFERENCE
Apple	None
IBM/Microsoft	None
Macintosh/Microsoft	None
TRS-80	None

7. Each FOR statement must be accompanied by an associated NEXT statement. In addition, the loop control variable in the FOR statement must be specified in the NEXT statement.

There are some exceptions to Rule 7. Some systems allow nested loops to share a NEXT statement (check your systems manual); for example,

```
00050 NEXT I,J
```

In this case, I is the inner loop control variable, and J is the outer loop control variable and is equivalent to

```
00050 NEXT I
00060 NEXT J
```

Also, on some systems it is not necessary to follow the NEXT statement with a loop control variable. This would be a valid NEXT statement:

```
00050 NEXT
```

When a NEXT statement without a loop control variable is used, it returns control to the closest FOR statement (previous to the NEXT statement) that has not already been paired with a NEXT. The following is an example:

```
00010 FOR I = 1 TO 10
00020    FOR J = 1 TO 5
00030       PRINT I,J
00040    NEXT
00050 NEXT
```

When the computer comes to the NEXT statement on line 50, it pairs it with line 10, FOR I = 1 TO 10, because it is the closest FOR statement without a NEXT statement. Line 20, FOR J = 1 TO 5, has already been paired with the first NEXT statement on line 40.

Figure VI–6 demonstrates the application of a FOR/NEXT loop. The purpose of this program is to find the total number of passengers who ride a roller coaster in a half-hour. There are eight runs each half-hour. The FOR/NEXT loop is set to be executed eight times—once for each run of the roller coaster. Each time through the loop, the user enters the number of passengers on the roller coaster, PASSENGERS, and the computer adds that number to the total, TTAL.

● Nested FOR and NEXT Statements

Section V showed how IF/THEN and IF/THEN/ELSE statements can be nested, so that one statement makes up part of another statement. Similar nesting can be done with loops. A pair of nested FOR/NEXT loops looks like this:

```
FOR I = 1 TO 4
   FOR J = 1 TO 2
      .
      .
      .
   NEXT J
NEXT I
```

Nested loops such as this should be indented as shown to make the structure more readable. In this case, each time the outer loop (loop I) is executed once, the inner loop (loop J) is executed twice since J varies from 1 to 2. When the inner loop has terminated, control passes to the first statement after the NEXT J, which in this case is the statement NEXT I. This statement causes I to be incremented by 1 and tested against the terminal value of 4. If I is still less than or equal to 4, the body of loop I is executed again. The J loop is again encountered, the value of J is reset to 1, and the inner loop is executed until J is greater than 2. Altogether,

● **FIGURE VI–6**
Using the FOR/NEXT Loop to Calculate a Total

```
00010 REM ***                        ROLLER COASTER TALLY                    ***
00020 REM
00030 REM *** THIS PROGRAM COMPUTES THE TOTAL NUMBER OF PASSENGERS ***
00040 REM *** FOR 8 RUNS OF A ROLLER COASTER.                       ***
00050 REM *** MAJOR VARIABLES:                                      ***
00060 REM ***    PASSENGERS - NUMBER OF PASSENGERS ON 1 RUN        ***
00070 REM ***    TTAL - TOTAL NUMBER OF PASSENGERS                 ***
00080 REM
00090 TTAL = 0
00100 FOR I = 1 TO 8
00110    PRINT "ENTER NUMBER OF PASSENGERS ON RUN #";I
00120    INPUT PASSENGERS
00130    TTAL = TTAL + PASSENGERS
00140 NEXT I
00150 PRINT "TOTAL NUMBER OF PASSENGERS = ";TTAL
00999 END
```

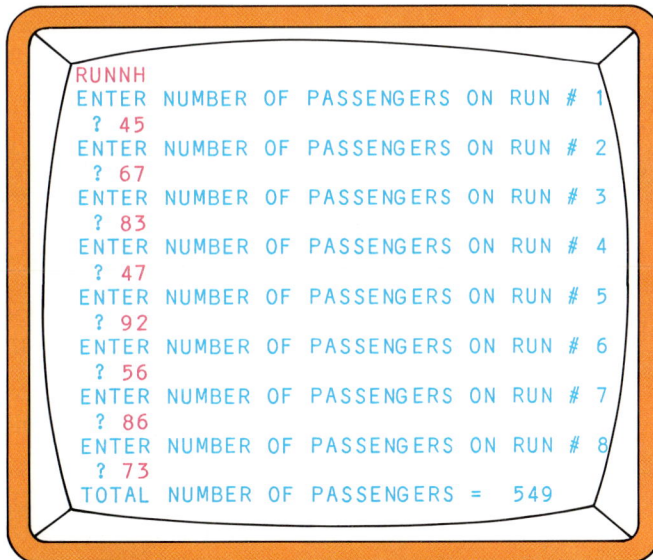

```
RUNNH
ENTER NUMBER OF PASSENGERS ON RUN # 1
? 45
ENTER NUMBER OF PASSENGERS ON RUN # 2
? 67
ENTER NUMBER OF PASSENGERS ON RUN # 3
? 83
ENTER NUMBER OF PASSENGERS ON RUN # 4
? 47
ENTER NUMBER OF PASSENGERS ON RUN # 5
? 92
ENTER NUMBER OF PASSENGERS ON RUN # 6
? 56
ENTER NUMBER OF PASSENGERS ON RUN # 7
? 86
ENTER NUMBER OF PASSENGERS ON RUN # 8
? 73
TOTAL NUMBER OF PASSENGERS =  549
```

MICROCOMPUTERS	DIFFERENCE
Apple	None
IBM/Microsoft	None
Macintosh/Microsoft	None
TRS-80	None

the outer loop is executed I times (4 times in this case) and the inner loop is executed I × J times (4 × 2 = 8 times).

The following rules should be remembered when using nested FOR/NEXT loops.

- Each loop must have a unique loop control variable. The following example is invalid, because execution of the inner loop modifies the value of the outer loop control variable:

```
FOR I = X TO Y STEP 2
    FOR I = Q TO R
        .
        .
        .
    NEXT I
NEXT I
```

These nested loops should be rewritten so that each uses a unique loop control variable:

```
FOR I = X TO Y STEP 2
    FOR J = Q TO R
        .
        .
        .
    NEXT J
NEXT I
```

- The NEXT statement for an inner loop must appear within the body of the outer loop, so that one loop is entirely contained within another.

Invalid
```
FOR I = 1 TO 5
    FOR J = 1 TO 10
        .
        .
        .
NEXT I
    NEXT J
```

Valid
```
FOR I = 1 TO 5
    FOR J = 1 TO 10
        .
        .
        .
    NEXT J
NEXT I
```

In the invalid example, notice that the J loop is not entirely inside the I loop, but extends beyond the NEXT I statement.

- It is possible to nest many loops within one another. (Beware of improper nesting, however, as in the preceding invalid example.) Here is a correct example of multiple nested loops:

```
FOR I = 1 TO 2
    PRINT I

            FOR J = 1 TO 3
                PRINT J;

                        FOR K = 1 TO 3
                            PRINT K
                        NEXT K


            NEXT J

NEXT I
```

● COMPUTERS AND INFORMATION PROCESSING

In this example, each nested loop is completely within its outer loop (the brackets never cross each other). Loop 1 is executed two times, loop 2 is executed six times (2 × 3), and loop 3 is executed eighteen times (2 × 3 × 3).

The following segment illustrates the mechanics of the nested loop. The outer loop will be executed three times, because I varies from 1 to 3. The inner loop will be executed twice each time the outer loop is executed once, so the inner loop will be executed a total of six times (2 × 3):

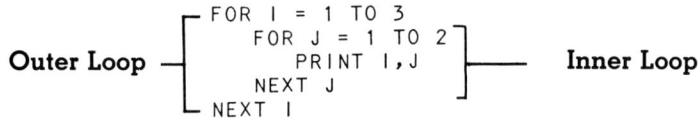

```
              ┌─ FOR I = 1 TO 3
              │      FOR J = 1 TO 2 ┐
Outer Loop ─ │          PRINT I,J  ├──── Inner Loop
              │      NEXT J         ┘
              └─ NEXT I
```

	I	**J**	
a. First time through outer loop; I = 1	1	1	First time through inner loop; J = 1
	1	2	Second time through inner loop; J = 2
b. Second time through outer loop; I = 2	2	1	Inner loop; J = 1
	2	2	Inner loop; J = 2
c. Third time through outer loop; I = 3	3	1	Inner loop; J = 1
	3	2	Inner loop; J = 2

Figure VI–7 illustrates an application of nested loops. The program generates three multiplication tables. The inner loop controls the printing of the columns in each row, and the outer loop controls how many rows will be printed.

First, A is initialized to 1; then execution of the inner loop begins. When B = 1, line 100 tells the computer to print "1 × 1 = 1." The comma at the end of that line tells the computer not to start the output of the next PRINT statement on a new line, but rather to continue in the next print zone of the same line. Line 110 increments B to 2 and returns control to line 90. The variable A has not changed and the terminal value of B has not been exceeded, so "2 × 1 = 2" is printed in the second print zone. The inner loop executes one more time and prints "3 × 1 = 3." After the inner loop has executed the third time, one complete row has been printed:

1 × 1 = 1   2 × 1 = 2   3 × 1 = 3

The PRINT statement in line 120 causes the remainder of the first row to remain blank, and the next output starts on the left margin of the next line. Finally, A is incremented when line 130 is encountered. The process continues until A exceeds its terminal value, 10.

```
00010 REM ***                    MULTIPLICATION TABLES                    ***
00020 REM
00030 REM *** THIS PROGRAM PRINTS A MULTIPLICATION TABLE OF 1 TO 10 ***
00040 REM *** FOR EACH OF THE NUMBERS 1 TO 3.                       ***
00050 REM
00060 REM *** LOOP TO PRINT ROWS ***
00070 FOR A = 1 TO 10
00080     REM *** LOOP TO PRINT COLUMNS ***
00090     FOR B = 1 TO 3
00100        PRINT B;"X";A;"=";B * A,
00110     NEXT B
00120     PRINT
00130 NEXT A
00999 END
```

```
RUNNH
   1 X 1 = 1      2 X 1 = 2      3 X 1 = 3
   1 X 2 = 2      2 X 2 = 4      3 X 2 = 6
   1 X 3 = 3      2 X 3 = 6      3 X 3 = 9
   1 X 4 = 4      2 X 4 = 8      3 X 4 = 12
   1 X 5 = 5      2 X 5 = 10     3 X 5 = 15
   1 X 6 = 6      2 X 6 = 12     3 X 6 = 18
   1 X 7 = 7      2 X 7 = 14     3 X 7 = 21
   1 X 8 = 8      2 X 8 = 16     3 X 8 = 24
   1 X 9 = 9      2 X 9 = 18     3 X 9 = 27
   1 X 10 = 10    2 X 10 = 20    3 X 10 = 30
```

MICROCOMPUTERS	DIFFERENCE
Apple	None
IBM/Microsoft	None
Macintosh/Microsoft	None
TRS-80	None

● **FIGURE VI–7**
Program Using Nested Loops

● The WHILE Loop

An additional set of instructions is used to implement loops: the WHILE/ NEXT. Here is the general format for this loop.

line# WHILE expression

.
.
.
.
.
.

line# NEXT

● **COMPUTERS AND INFORMATION PROCESSING**

Notice that the NEXT statement in this loop is not followed by a variable. Any statements between the WHILE and NEXT statements will be executed each time the loop is repeated. The WHILE loop will be executed as long as the expression in the WHILE statement is true. When the expression is no longer true, control is transferred to the first instruction after the NEXT statement.

In contrast to the FOR/NEXT loop, the WHILE/NEXT loop involves no automatic initialization or incrementing of the loop control variable. A statement before the WHILE statement must initialize the control variable, and another statement within the loop body must at some point change the value of the control variable so that the expression of the WHILE statement can change and end the loop. Otherwise an infinite loop results, as shown here:

```
00010 WHILE CNT < 50
00020     PRINT CNT
00030 NEXT
```

This loop could be correctly written:

```
00010 CNT = 1
00020 WHILE CNT < 50
00030     PRINT CNT
00040     CNT = CNT + 1
00050 NEXT
```

The program in Figure VI–8 uses a WHILE/NEXT loop controlled by a trailer value. The program checks each student score entered to determine the name and score of the highest- and lowest-scoring student. A trailer value of XXX is used for the student name. Lines 220 through 300 set up a WHILE/NEXT loop to process the data. The WHILE statement in line 220 causes the loop to be executed as long as the condition NME$ <> "XXX" evaluates as true. When NME$ equals XXX, the condition becomes false and control passes out of the loop.

Some implementations of BASIC (such as the IBM and Macintosh) create WHILE loops with the WHILE/WEND rather than the WHILE/NEXT statements. The format of the WHILE/WEND follows:

line# WHILE expression

•
•
•

line# WEND

The execution of the WHILE/WEND is identical to that of the WHILE/NEXT.

The WHILE loop can always be used in place of the FOR/NEXT loop, but the reverse is not true. The FOR/NEXT loop executes a prespecified number of times, as given by the initial and terminal values of the loop control variable. The WHILE loop can also execute a given number of times, if the programmer initializes the loop control variable before the loop begins and tests for the given value in the WHILE statement. However, the WHILE loop can also be used when the final number of desired loop executions is not known, such as when a trailer value is used. In such a situation, a properly structured FOR/NEXT loop would not be appropriate.

● Logical Operators

So far in this text, the arithmetic operators ($\hat{},*,/,+,-$) and the relational operators ($=, <>, <, >, <=, >=$) have been covered. Now a third group of operators will be discussed: the **logical** or **Boolean operators.** A logical operator acts on one or more expressions that evaluate as true or false to produce a statement with a true or false value. The three most commonly used logical operators are AND, OR, and NOT.

The operator AND combines two expressions and produces a value of true only when both of these conditions are true. For example, the combined logical expression in the statement.

```
00020 IF (HEIGHT > 72) AND (WEIGHT > 150) THEN PRINT NME$
```

evaluates as true only if the expressions HEIGHT > 72 and WEIGHT > 150 are both true. If one or the other is false, the entire statement is false, and the THEN clause of the statement is ignored. The parentheses in the preceding statement are not necessary, but they improve the readability of the statement.

● **FIGURE VI–8**
Program Using a WHILE/NEXT Loop

```
00010 REM ***                         GRADE RANGE                         ***
00020 REM
00030 REM *** THIS PROGRAM FINDS THE HIGHEST AND THE LOWEST STUDENT ***
00040 REM *** SCORES ENTERED.                                       ***
00050 REM *** MAJOR VARIABLES:                                      ***
00060 REM ***    NME$ - STUDENT'S LAST NAME                         ***
00070 REM ***    SCR - TEST SCORE                                   ***
00080 REM ***    HISCR - HIGHEST SCORE                              ***
00090 REM ***    LOSCR - LOWEST SCORE                               ***
00100 REM ***    HNME$ - NAME OF STUDENT WITH HIGHEST SCORE         ***
00110 REM ***    LNME$ -  "     "      "        "  LOWEST     "     ***
00120 REM
00130 REM *** ENTER FIRST STUDENT SCORE ***
00140 PRINT "ENTER LAST NAME AND SCORE"
00150 INPUT "(TYPE 'XXX,0' TO QUIT)";NME$,SCR
00160 REM
00170 REM *** INITIALIZE HIGH AND LOW SCORES TO FIRST SCORE ***
00180 HISCR = SCR \ HNME$ = NME$
00190 LOSCR = SCR \ LNME$ = NME$
00200 REM
00210 REM *** LOOP TO FIND HIGH AND LOW SCORES ***
00220 WHILE NME$ <> "XXX"
00230    IF SCR > HISCR THEN HISCR = SCR \ HNME$ = NME$
00240    IF SCR < LOSCR THEN LOSCR = SCR \ LNME$ = NME$
00250    REM
00260    REM *** ENTER NEXT SCORE ***
00270    PRINT
00280    PRINT "ENTER LAST NAME, SCORE"
00290    INPUT "(TYPE 'XXX,0' TO QUIT)";NME$,SCR
00300 NEXT
00310 REM
00320 REM *** PRINT RANGE OF SCORES ***
00330 PRINT
00340 PRINT
00350 PRINT HNME$;" RECEIVED THE HIGH SCORE OF";HISCR
00360 PRINT LNME$;" RECEIVED THE LOW SCORE OF";LOSCR
00999 END
```

● COMPUTERS AND INFORMATION PROCESSING

The logical operator OR also combines two expressions, but only one of these expressions needs to evaluate as true for the entire statement to be true. Thus the statement

```
00020 IF (HEIGHT > 72) OR (WEIGHT > 150) THEN PRINT NME$
```

evaluates as true if either HEIGHT > 72 or WEIGHT > 150 is true, or if both are true. The entire condition is false only if the expressions HEIGHT > 72 and WEIGHT > 150 are both false. Table VI–1 shows the results for all possible values of two expressions combined by AND and OR.

The third logical operator, NOT, is a **unary operator** (an operator used with one operand) and therefore is used with a single expression. The effect of NOT is to reverse the logical value of the expression it precedes. For example, if the variable PET$ has the value DOG, the condition of the following statement is false:

```
00020 IF NOT (PET$ = "DOG") THEN 90
```

● **FIGURE VI–8**
Continued

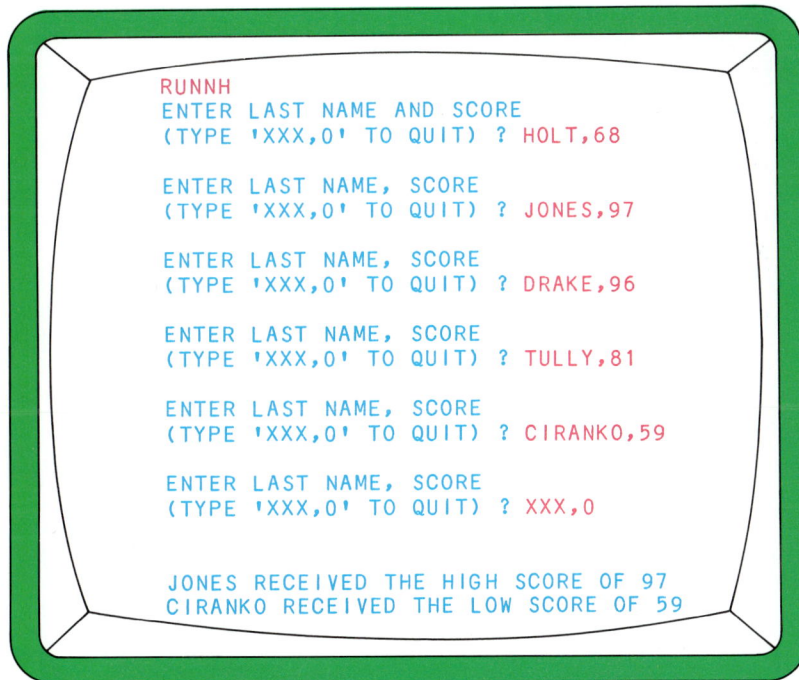

```
RUNNH
ENTER LAST NAME AND SCORE
(TYPE 'XXX,0' TO QUIT) ? HOLT,68

ENTER LAST NAME, SCORE
(TYPE 'XXX,0' TO QUIT) ? JONES,97

ENTER LAST NAME, SCORE
(TYPE 'XXX,0' TO QUIT) ? DRAKE,96

ENTER LAST NAME, SCORE
(TYPE 'XXX,0' TO QUIT) ? TULLY,81

ENTER LAST NAME, SCORE
(TYPE 'XXX,0' TO QUIT) ? CIRANKO,59

ENTER LAST NAME, SCORE
(TYPE 'XXX,0' TO QUIT) ? XXX,0


JONES RECEIVED THE HIGH SCORE OF 97
CIRANKO RECEIVED THE LOW SCORE OF 59
```

MICROCOMPUTERS	DIFFERENCE
Apple	No WHILE/NEXT
IBM/Microsoft	300 WEND
Macintosh/Microsoft	300 WEND
TRS-80	300 WEND

The AND and OR Logical Operators

CONDITION 1	CONDITION 2	CONDITION 1 AND CONDITION 2	CONDITION 1 OR CONDITION 2
true	true	true	true
true	false	false	true
false	true	false	true
false	false	false	false

Because the condition PET$ = "DOG" evaluates as true, the NOT operator reverses this value to false, making the final result of the entire condition false. If PET$ contained any other value, the condition PET$ = "DOG" would evaluate as false, and the NOT would make the value of the entire condition true.

Logical operators can be combined in a single statement, and they are evaluated in the following sequence:

1. NOT
2. AND
3. OR

For example, the following statement combines AND and OR:

```
00050 IF (PET$ = "DOG") OR (AGE = 3) AND (WT = 10) THEN 90
```

Given the predefined order of evaluation, the following diagram shows how the preceding statement would be evaluated if PET$ = "DOG", AGE = 3, and WT = 9:

```
00050   IF (PET$ = "DOG") OR (AGE = 3) AND (WT = 10) THEN 90
```

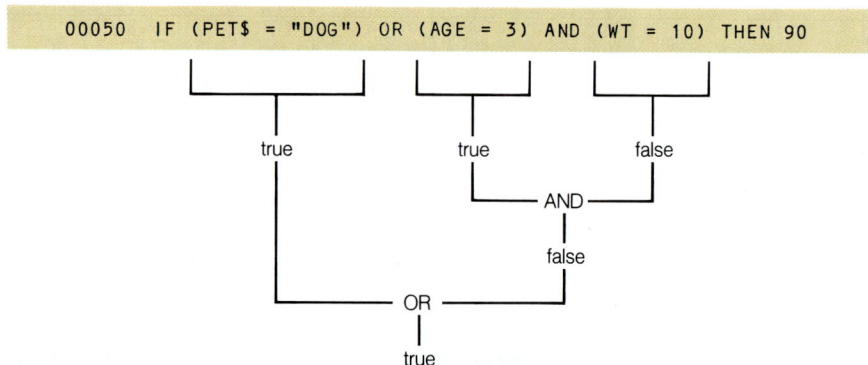

The AND portion of the IF/THEN statement is evaluated first. That result is then combined with the OR portion of the statement to determine the final value of the entire condition. In this case, the statement condition is true, so control is passed to line 90.

The precedence of logical operators (like that of arithmetic operators) can be altered using parentheses. The previous example, using the same variable values as before, could be rewritten as

```
00050 IF ((PET$ = "DOG") OR (AGE = 3)) AND (WT = 10) THEN 90
```

In this example, the OR portion of the expression is evaluated before the AND portion. Thus the parentheses can change the final result of the evaluation, as shown in the following diagram. Compare the evaluation of this statement with the previous diagram.

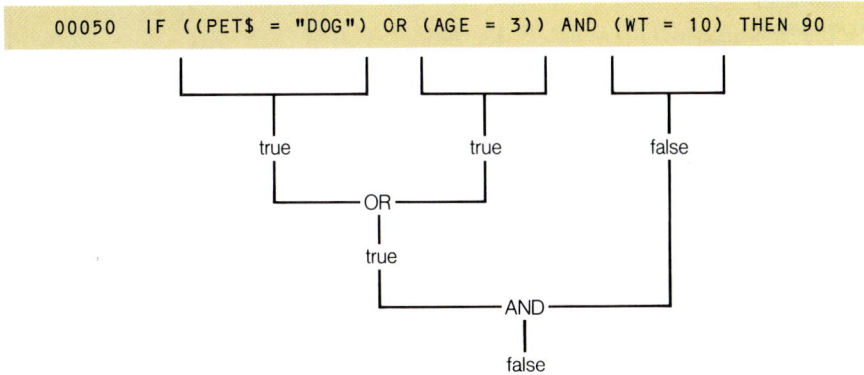

```
00050   IF ((PET$ = "DOG") OR (AGE = 3)) AND (WT = 10) THEN 90
```

```
             true              true            false
              └────OR────┘       │
                   │
                  true
                   └────────────AND────────────┘
                          │
                        false
```

Even if the order of evaluation desired in a condition is the same as the predefined order, it is good programming practice to use parentheses in order to make the logic easier to follow.

NOT can also be combined with AND and OR in a single statement, as shown in the following diagram. Study the evaluation of the condition, making sure that you understand how the use of parentheses and the predefined order of operators has determined the final result of the evaluation. Assume that PET$ = "PIG", AGE = 6, and WT = 1500.

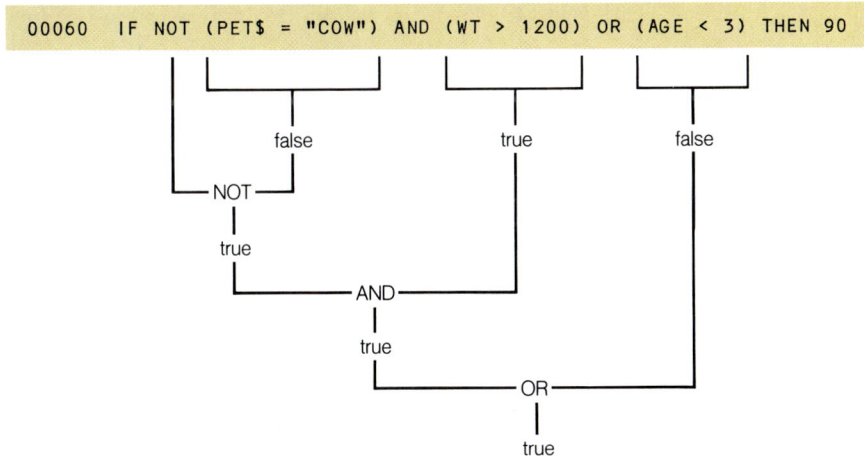

```
00060   IF NOT (PET$ = "COW") AND (WT > 1200) OR (AGE < 3) THEN 90
```

```
                     false            true             false
               └─NOT─┘                  │                 │
                  │
                 true
                  └────────────AND────────────┘           │
                         │
                       true
                        └────────────────────OR───────────┘
                               │
                              true
```

Table VI–2 shows the order in which all types of BASIC operators are evaluated. Further examples involving these operators are shown in Table VI–3.

The program shown in Figure VI–9 demonstrates how logical operators can be used to determine if a triangle is scalene, isosceles, or equilateral.

Order of Precedence

1. Anything in parentheses	6. Relational operators (=, <>, <, >, <=, >=)
2. Exponentiation (*)	7. NOT
3. Unary plus and minus (+, −)	8. AND
4. Multiplication and division (*, /)	9. OR
5. Addition and subtraction (+, −)	

Note: Operators on the same level are evaluated left to right.

Notice that the condition of the first test uses the AND operator to determine if all three sides are equal:

```
00080 IF (S1SIDE = S2SIDE) AND (S1SIDE = S3SIDE) THEN
```

The test for an isosceles triangle is more complex and involves checking for three different conditions. Only one of these conditions needs to be true for the triangle to be isosceles; therefore, this test involves the OR operator. If none of these conditions is true, the triangle must be scalene. As shown by this program, logical operators allow for a variety of conditions to be checked efficiently and simultaneously.

● A Programming Problem

PROBLEM DEFINITION

The computer science department needs a program to display a bar graph that shows the number of students enrolled in each of the computer science classes, sections 100 through 109:

100	37
101	28
102	31
103	34
104	26
105	22
106	30
107	21
108	10
109	18

The output should have appropriate headings, and the horizontal bar should be marked off by 10s.

● TABLE VI–3
Examples of Conditions Using Logical Operators

CONDITION	EVALUATES AS
NOT (1 * 4 = 5)	TRUE
(18 < 16) OR (7 + 2 = 9)	TRUE
(18 < 16) AND (7 + 2 = 9)	FALSE
((2 + 8) <= 11) AND (17 * 2 = 34)	TRUE
NOT (12 > 8 − 2)	FALSE

● COMPUTERS AND INFORMATION PROCESSING

SOLUTION DESIGN

The task of displaying a student enrollment graph can be divided into two basic parts:

1. Display the graph headings.
2. Display a bar for each section.

```
00010 REM *** DETERMINE THE TYPE OF A TRIANGLE:   ***
00020 REM *** SCALENE, ISOSCELES, OR EQUILATERAL. ***
00030 REM
00040 INPUT "ENTER THE THREE SIDES: "S1SIDE,S2SIDE,S3SIDE
00050 PRINT "TRIANGLE IS ";
00060 REM
00070 REM *** CHECK FOR EQUILATERAL ***
00080 IF (S1SIDE = S2SIDE) AND (S2SIDE = S3SIDE) THEN PRINT "EQUILATERAL"
          \ GOTO 999
00090 REM
00100 REM *** CHECK FOR ISOSCELES; IF NOT, THEN IT'S SCALENE ***
00110 IF (S1SIDE = S2SIDE) OR (S1SIDE = S3SIDE) OR (S2SIDE = S3SIDE) THEN PRINT
          "ISOSCELES" ELSE PRINT "SCALENE"
00999 END
```

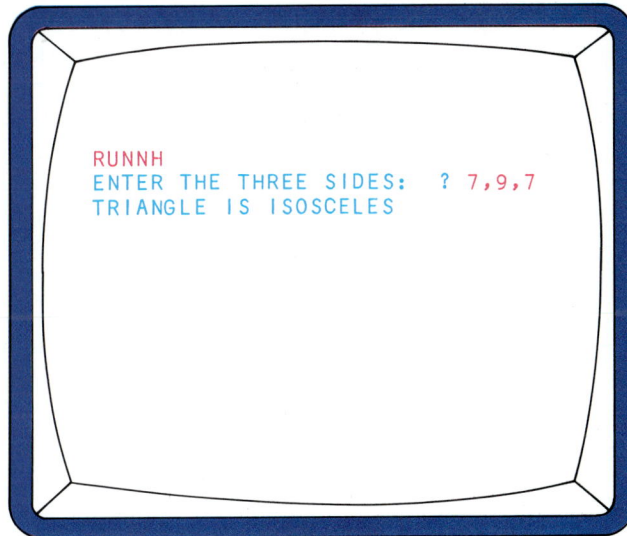

```
RUNNH
ENTER THE THREE SIDES:  ? 7,9,7
TRIANGLE IS ISOSCELES
```

MICROCOMPUTERS	DIFFERENCE
Apple	None
IBM/Microsoft	None
Macintosh/Microsoft	None
TRS-80	None

The graph headings consist of the graph title, the labels for the section numbers and student numbers, and the horizontal scale of multiples of ten.

The bar to be displayed for each class section is made up of two parts: the section number and the row of asterisks showing the number of students. Step 2 described above can therefore be further divided:

2. a. Display the section number.
2. b. Display the row of asterisks.

Figure VI–10 shows this analysis of the problem solution.

The steps, 2.a and 2.b, must be repeated for each class section, and thus should be placed in a loop. Since the second of these steps, displaying the asterisks, itself calls for a loop, this program will use a nested loop. Figure VI–11 shows the steps needed for this solution.

THE PROGRAM

Figure VI–11 is a good illustration of nested FOR/NEXT loops. Lines 90 through 150 print the headings with appropriate spacing. The outer loop (lines 180 through 250) is set to run from 100 to 109, so the variable I represents the section number. Line 190 prints the section number and tabs the printer to column 9. Line 200 reads the number of students; then the inner loop (lines 210 through 230) is set to repeat the PRINT statement (line 220) as many times as there are students. Because lines 190 and 220 end with a semicolon, the printer will print the section number and all of the asterisks on one line. After the row of asterisks has been printed and the inner loop is finished, the printer must be advanced to the next line; this is done in line 240. Because line 240 does not end with a comma or semicolon, the printer moves to the next line.

Many variations can be made to this bar graph display. The asterisk can be replaced by any other character. Also, the limitations placed by

● **FIGURE VI–10**
Structure Chart for Enrollment Program

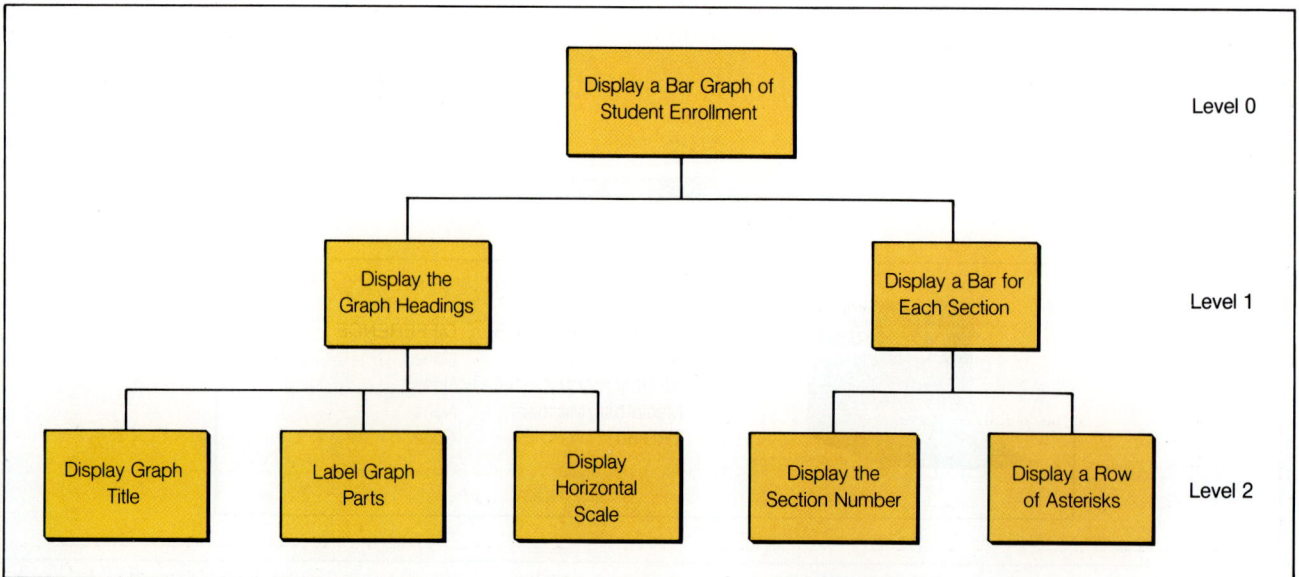

● **COMPUTERS AND INFORMATION PROCESSING**

the width of the terminal can be overcome by using appropriate scales. For example, each asterisk could represent two students.

● Summary Points

● The FOR/NEXT loop executes the number of times specified in the FOR statement. The NEXT statement increments the loop control variable, tests it against the terminal value, and returns control to the statement immediately following the FOR statement if another loop execution is required.

● **FIGURE VI–11**
Enrollment Program and Flowchart

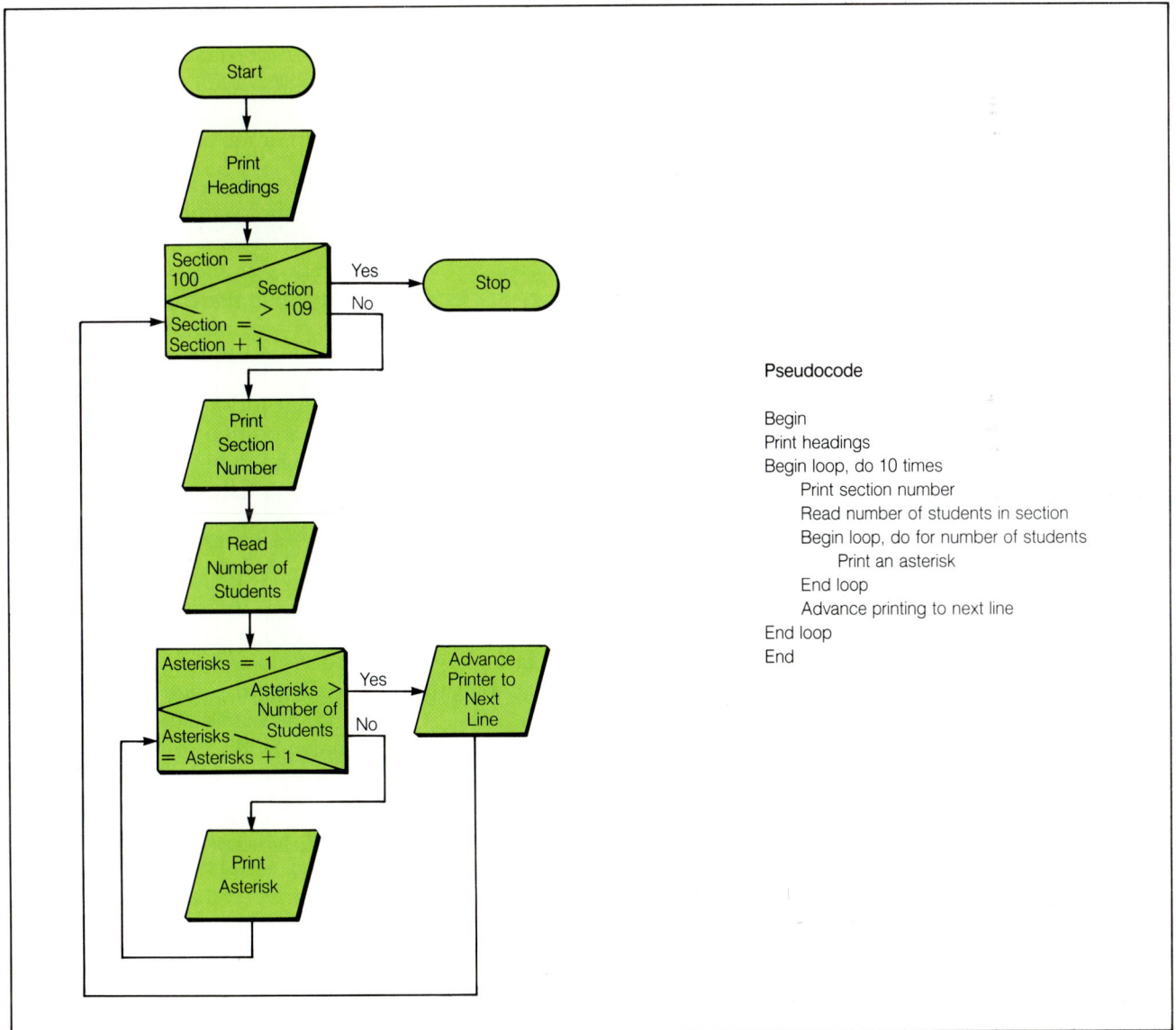

Pseudocode

Begin
Print headings
Begin loop, do 10 times
    Print section number
    Read number of students in section
    Begin loop, do for number of students
        Print an asterisk
    End loop
    Advance printing to next line
End loop
End

(Continued Next Page)

```
00010 REM ***                        ENROLLMENT GRAPH                        ***
00020 REM
00030 REM *** THIS PROGRAM DISPLAYS A BAR GRAPH THAT SHOWS THE NUMBER ***
00040 REM *** OF STUDENTS ENROLLED IN EACH COMPUTER SCIENCE SECTION.  ***
00050 REM *** MAJOR VARIABLES:                                        ***
00060 REM ***    STUDENTS - NUMBER OF STUDENTS IN ONE SECTION         ***
00070 REM
00080 REM *** PRINT HEADINGS ***
00090 PRINT
00100 PRINT
00110 PRINT TAB(16);"CLASS ENROLLMENT"
00120 PRINT
00130 PRINT "SEC. #";TAB(16);"STUDENTS"
00140 PRINT TAB(8);1;TAB(17);10;TAB(27);20;TAB(37);30
00150 PRINT
00160 REM
00170 REM *** PRINT GRAPH ***
00180 FOR I = 100 TO 109
00190    PRINT I;TAB(9);
00200    READ STUDENTS
00210    FOR J = 1 TO STUDENTS
00220       PRINT "*";
00230    NEXT J
00240    PRINT
00250 NEXT I
00260 REM
00270 REM *** DATA STATEMENTS ***
00280 DATA 37,28,31,34,26,22,30,21,10,18
00999 END
```

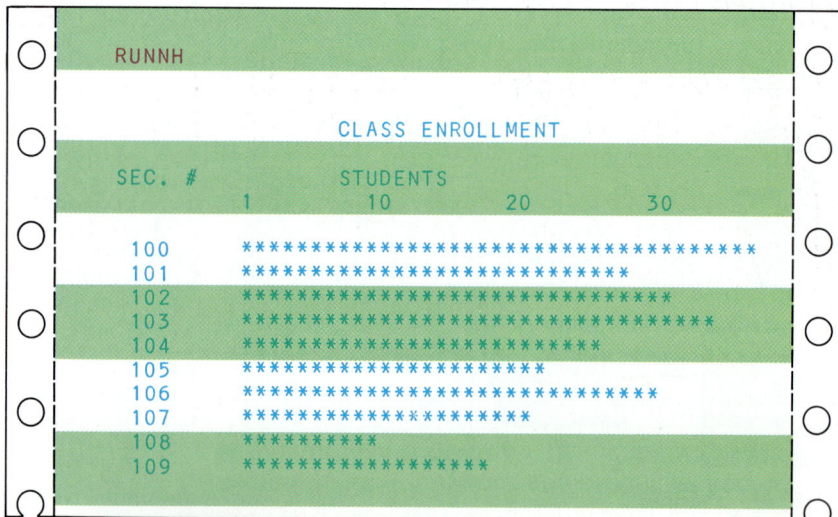

```
RUNNH


                    CLASS ENROLLMENT

       SEC. #            STUDENTS
                    1          10          20          30

        100     *************************************
        101     ****************************
        102     *******************************
        103     **********************************
        104     **************************
        105     **********************
        106     ******************************
        107     *********************
        108     **********
        109     ******************
```

MICROCOMPUTERS	DIFFERENCE
Apple	None
IBM/Microsoft	None
Macintosh/Microsoft	None
TRS-80	None

- Some rules to remember when using FOR and NEXT loops follow:
  —The initial value must be less than or equal to the terminal value when using a positive step value. Otherwise, the loop will never be executed.
  —The step value can be negative. If it is, the initial value must be greater than or equal to the terminal value in order for the loop to execute at least once.
  —The step value should never be 0; this creates an infinite loop.
  —The loop control variable in the NEXT statement must be the same loop control variable that was used in the corresponding FOR statement.
  —Transfer can be made from one statement to another within a loop. However, transfer from a statement in the loop body to the FOR statement is poor programming practice.
  —The value of the loop control variable should not be modified by program statements within the loop.
  —The initial, terminal, and step expressions can be composed of any valid numeric variable, constant, or mathematical formula.
  —Each FOR statement must be accompanied by a NEXT statement.
  —FOR/NEXT loops can be nested.
  —The NEXT statement of the nested inner loop must come before the NEXT statement of the outer loop.
- The WHILE statement repeats execution of its loop body as long as the given condition is true.
- The logical operators NOT, AND, and OR are used with conditions. NOT is a unary operator that negates a condition. An expression containing AND evaluates as true when both conditions joined by the AND are true. A condition containing OR is true if at least one of the joined conditions is true.

○ Review Questions

1. Is this a valid FOR statement?

```
00020 FOR C$ = 1 TO 10 STEP 2
```

2. When is a WHILE loop a more appropriate choice than a FOR/NEXT loop?

3. What is the output from the following statements?

```
00030 L = 10
00040 FOR L = 1 TO 6
00050    PRINT L
00060 NEXT L
```

4. Can arithmetic expressions be used as initial and terminal values?

5. If the step value is negative, will the loop be terminated when the initial value is less than or greater than the terminal value?

6. Can control be transferred from one statement to another within a loop? From a statement within a loop to the FOR statement?

7. Is this a valid FOR/NEXT loop?

```
00010 FOR I = 1 TO 10
00020    READ X
00030    IF X > 20 THEN 50
00040    S = S + W
00050 NEXT I
```

8. Which of the following is a valid WHILE loop?

```
00050 WHILE X < 10          00100 WHILE Q + 6 < R
00060    PRINT X            00110    S = S + 1
00070    X = X + 1          00120    PRINT S
00080 NEXT                  00130 NEXT
```

9. Is this a valid nested loop?

```
00090 FOR I = 10 TO 1 STEP -1
00100    PRINT I
00110    FOR J = 2 TO 6 STEP 2
00120       S = I + J
00130       FOR K = 1 TO 3
00140          S = S + K
00150          PRINT S
00160       NEXT J
00170       PRINT J
00180    NEXT J
00190 NEXT I
```

10. How many times is the following inner loop executed? How many times is the outer loop executed?

```
00060 FOR I = 1 TO (3 * 4) STEP 2
00070    FOR J = 1 TO 2 STEP .5
00080       PRINT I,J
00090    NEXT J
00100 NEXT I
```

● Debugging Exercises

Identify the following programs or program segments that contain errors, and debug them.

```
1. 00010 FOR I = 1 TO 10
   00020    READ C
   00030    IF C = 1 THEN 10
   00040    READ N
   00050 NEXT I
2. 00010 K = 1
   00020 WHILE K < 5
   00030    PRINT K
   00040    INPUT N$,AMT
   00050    IF AMT < 20.0 THEN 70
   00060    PRINT N$,AMT
   00070 NEXT
```

● Programming Problems

1. Your landlord is considering a raise in rent of 5 percent, 7 percent, or 10 percent. To determine how much additional money you and your fellow tenants cannot afford to pay, write a program to show sample rents of $200 to $600 (by increments of $50) and the three proposed increased rents for each. Create a table like the following:

RENT	+5%	+7%	+10%
200	XXX	XXX	XXX
250	XXX	XXX	XXX
•	•	•	•
•	•	•	•

2. Write a program to display a multiplication table. Allow the user to enter the upper and lower limits of the table, then print the appropriate values. Use the following format for the table:

X	3	4	5	6
3	9	12	15	18
4	12	16	20	24
5	15	20	25	30
6	18	24	30	36

3. The high school tennis team is holding its annual tryouts. The coach selects the team members on the basis of the results of a series of matches. Each player is placed on a first, second, or third string team depending on his or her number of wins:

Number of Wins	Team
10 or more	First string
4 to 9	Second string
3 or less	Third string

You are to write a program using a WHILE loop that indicates on which team a player belongs. Use the following data:

Name	Wins
Sanders, S.	7
Crosby, D.	5
Casey, E.	9
Case, L.	12
Sandoval, V.	10
Coles, S.	3
Schnur, R.	2

4. Write a program to calculate X^N. This value should be found by multiplying X times itself N number of times (e.g. $X^4 = X * X * X * X$). Use the following values for X and N to test your program:

X	N
1	2
6	3
5	4
2	6

The output should have the following format:

X raised to the N = R.

A trailer value should be used to determine the end of the data.

5. The Happy Hedonist Health Spa has asked you to write a payroll program that will calculate the weekly net pay for each of its employees. The employees have the option of participating in a medical insurance plan that deducts $10 per week. The income tax rate is 25 percent. Use a FOR/NEXT loop in your program.

The following is the company pay code key:

Code	Wage Rate
1	$5.00
2	6.75
3	9.50

Use the following data:

Name	Medical Plan	Hours	Wage Code
Cochran, K.	Yes	40	2
Batdorf, D.	Yes	45	1
Jones, S.	No	38	3
Goolsby, L.	Yes	30	2
Halas, G.	No	35	1

The output should appear as follows:

NAME	NET PAY
XXXXXXXXX	$XXX.XX

● Section VII
Modularizing Programs

● Introduction

We have previously discussed the two main characteristics of structured programs: (1) they incorporate easy-to-follow logic (which is achieved mainly by using decision and looping structures whenever possible, instead of using GOTO statements), and (2) they are divided into subprograms, each of which is designed to perform a specific task.

Decision and looping structures were introduced in the two previous sections. This section will explain how programs are divided into subprograms or modules, which in BASIC are called **subroutines.** The GOSUB and ON/GOSUB statements are the two methods of executing a subroutine in BASIC, and both will be covered here.

● The Importance of Modularizing Programs

Dividing a program into modules is useful for two reasons: (1) the logic of a program that is divided into modules, each performing a distinct task, is easier to follow, and (2) the same module can be executed any number of times. For example, if the program needs to do the same task at two different points, the subroutine that performs this task may simply be executed twice. Without the subroutine, the programmer would have to write the same program segment twice.

● Writing Subroutines

A subroutine is a sequence of statements, typically located after the main body of the program. Two statements in BASIC can be used to **call** a subroutine, that is, to cause it to be executed. These two statements are the GOSUB and the ON/GOSUB statements.

THE GOSUB STATEMENT

The GOSUB statement transfers the flow of program control from the calling program to a subroutine. A subroutine can be called either from the main program or from another subroutine. The format of the GOSUB statement is:

line# GOSUB transfer line#

The transfer line number must be the first line number of the subroutine to be executed. This is very important, because the computer will not detect an error if it is instructed to branch to an incorrect line. It will detect an error only if the transfer line number does not exist in the program. The GOSUB statement causes an unconditional branch to this specified line number. For example, the following statement will always cause a branch to the subroutine starting at line 1000:

```
00100 GOSUB 1000
```

THE RETURN STATEMENT

After a subroutine is executed, the RETURN statement causes program control to return to the line following the one that contained the GOSUB statement. The format of the RETURN statement is as follows:

line# RETURN

Note that no transfer line number is needed in the RETURN statement. The computer automatically returns control to the statement immediately following the GOSUB statement that called the subroutine. If the line returned to is a nonexecutable statement, such as a REM statement, the computer simply skips it. Each subroutine must contain a RETURN statement; otherwise, the program cannot branch back to the point from which the subroutine was called.

A PROGRAM CONTAINING MULTIPLE CALLS TO THE SAME SUBROUTINE

Look at the program in Figure VII–1. This program prints a simple multiplication table. It contains a subroutine that prints a row of asterisks to divide the multiplication table into sections to make it more readable. The subroutine is called from three places in the main program: line 70, line 90, and line 190. Each time this subroutine is called, program control transfers to line 1000. Because lines 1000 through 1050 are nonexecutable statements, execution skips down to line 1060. Lines 1060 through 1080 contain a FOR/NEXT loop that is used to print a line of 80 asterisks. Then program control returns to the line following the statement that called the subroutine. In Figure VII–1, both the main program and the subroutine are labeled. Arrows are drawn to show the flow of execution of the program.

In this example, the subroutine is very short, so it would be easy to repeat the necessary series of statements each time they are needed. If the subroutine were 10, 20, or more lines long, however, it would be tedious and wasteful to type it three times. Using the subroutine simplifies the program logic by organizing specific tasks into neat, orderly subsections.

Notice that the subroutine in Figure VII–1 begins at line 1000. To make programs more readable, programmers often start subroutines at readily

● COMPUTERS AND INFORMATION PROCESSING

Program Demonstrating Multiple Calls to a Subroutine

```
00010 REM ***              MULTIPLICATION PROGRAM              ***
00020 REM
00030 REM ***      THE PURPOSE OF THIS PROGRAM IS TO           ***
00040 REM *** ILLUSTRATE MULTIPLE CALLS TO A SINGLE SUBROUTINE. ***
00050 REM
00060 PRINT TAB(30);"MULTIPLICATION TABLE"
00070 GOSUB 1000
00080 PRINT TAB(5);"ONE";TAB(33);"TWO";TAB(59);"THREE"
00090 GOSUB 1000
00100 REM
00110 REM *** PRINT TABLES ***
00120 FOR OUTER = 1 TO 10
00130    FOR IN = 1 TO 3
00140       PRINT OUTER;" * ";IN;" = ";OUTER * IN,
00150    NEXT IN
00160    PRINT
00170 NEXT OUTER
00180 PRINT
00190 GOSUB 1000
00200 GOTO 9999
01000 REM
01010 REM ***********************************
01020 REM ***            SUBROUTINE          ***
01030 REM ***********************************
01040 REM ***  ASTERISK TO OUTLINE OUTPUT  ***
01050 REM ***********************************
01060 FOR I = 1 TO 80
01070    PRINT "*";
01080 NEXT I
01090 PRINT
01100 RETURN
09999 END
```

Main Program

Subroutine

```
RUNNH
                        MULTIPLICATION TABLE
********************************************************************************
     ONE                      TWO                      THREE
********************************************************************************
 1  *  1  =  1           1  *  2  =  2           1  *  3  =  3
 2  *  1  =  2           2  *  2  =  4           2  *  3  =  6
 3  *  1  =  3           3  *  2  =  6           3  *  3  =  9
 4  *  1  =  4           4  *  2  =  8           4  *  3  =  12
 5  *  1  =  5           5  *  2  =  10          5  *  3  =  15
 6  *  1  =  6           6  *  2  =  12          6  *  3  =  18
 7  *  1  =  7           7  *  2  =  14          7  *  3  =  21
 8  *  1  =  8           8  *  2  =  16          8  *  3  =  24
 9  *  1  =  9           9  *  2  =  18          9  *  3  =  27
10  *  1  =  10         10  *  2  =  20         10  *  3  =  30
********************************************************************************
```

identifiable line numbers, such as multiples of 1000. For example, the first subroutine might start at line 1000, the second at line 2000, and so on. This practice of starting at readily identifiable line numbers will be followed in this textbook.

In Figure VII–1, when program execution reaches the last line of the main program (line 200) it is ready to stop. We do not want to execute the subroutine again at this point, because it has already been called where it was needed in the program. Therefore, it is necessary to branch to the END statement, which has a line number of 09999. This branch statement will skip over any subroutines that have been placed between the end of the main program and the END statement.

On the DECsystem, the END statement must be at the end of the entire program and must also have the highest line number. Not all BASIC implementations have these requirements. On many systems, the END statement may be placed immediately after the last statement of the main program and before the subroutines. If this is possible on your system, it is recommended that you use this method because it avoids the use of a GOTO statement.

THE ON/GOSUB STATEMENT

Because the GOSUB statement is an unconditional transfer statement, it always transfers program control to the subroutine starting at the indicated line number. Sometimes, however, it is necessary to branch to one of several subroutines depending on existing conditions. The ON/GOSUB statement is useful for this purpose.

The ON/GOSUB statement allows for the conditional transfer of program control to one of several subroutines. The format of the ON/GOSUB statement is:

line# ON expression GOSUB transfer line#1[,transfer line#2,...]

The ON/GOSUB is similar to the ON/GOTO statement (Section 5) in that it uses an expression to determine the line number to which program control will transfer. This expression must be arithmetic. The transfer line numbers in the ON/GOSUB statement, however, are not within the calling program. Each transfer line number indicates the beginning of a subroutine.

The general execution of the ON/GOSUB proceeds as follows:

1. The expression is evaluated as an integer. On the DECsystem, this value is truncated if it is a real number. See Table VII–1 for system differences in this respect.

2. Depending on the value of the expression, control passes to the subroutine starting at the corresponding line number. If the value of the expression is n, control passes to the subroutine starting at the nth line number listed. (For example, if the expression evaluates as 1, control transfers to the first line number in the list.)

3. After the specified subroutine is executed, control is transferred back

COMPUTER	ACTION TAKEN IF EXPRESSION IS GREATER THAN NUMBER OF LINE NUMBERS	EXPRESSION TRUNCATED OR ROUNDED?
DECsystem	"ON statement out of range at line 00120"	Truncated
Apple	Control is passed to next executable statement	Truncated
IBM/Microsoft	Control is passed to next executable statement	Rounded
Macintosh/Microsoft	Control is passed to next executable statement	Rounded
TRS-80	Control is passed to next executable statement	Rounded

to the line following the ON/GOSUB statement by a RETURN statement at the end of the subroutine.

The ON/GOSUB statement provides a more structured approach to programming than the ON/GOTO statement because the location of the return of control is determined by the BASIC system and not by the programmer. This eliminates the chance of the programmer stating the incorrect line number in the GOTO statement.

On the DECsystem, if the expression in an ON/GOSUB statement evaluates as a number larger than the number of transfer line numbers indicated, an error message is printed and program execution terminates. Table VII–1 explains how different systems handle this situation.

Figure VII–2 demonstrates a simple use of the ON/GOSUB statement. The user enters an integer value representing his or her year in college (1, 2, 3, or 4). This integer value is assigned to the variable YR, which is then used to determine which subroutine will be executed. If YR = 1, the subroutine starting at line 1000 will be executed; if YR = 2, the subroutine starting at line 2000 will be executed; if YR = 3, the subroutine starting at line 3000 will be executed; and if YR = 4, the subroutine starting at line 4000 will be executed. After the appropriate subroutine is executed, control is returned to the main program, which then stops executing.

USING THE STRUCTURE CHART TO MODULARIZE A PROGRAM

So far in this textbook, we have been using structure charts to help analyze the steps necessary to solve programming problems. Structure charts enable us to visualize the specific tasks a program must perform to achieve the desired overall result. Because structure charts represent the subtasks involved in solving a problem, they are very helpful in developing modularized programs. Once the tasks of a program are identified, each of these can be implemented in the program as a separate subroutine.

We will illustrate the use of structure charts with a simple problem. We are going to write a program that will calculate the cost of a long distance phone call based on the following table (note that the user should enter the number of miles as an integer value):

Distance of Call	Cost Per Minute
Within 99 miles	12¢ per minute for first 5 minutes, 10¢ per minute thereafter
Between 100 and 199 miles	15¢ per minute for first 5 minutes, 13¢ per minute thereafter
Between 200 and 299 miles	18¢ per minute, regardless of length of the call

● **FIGURE VII-2**
Program Using the ON/GOSUB Statement

```
00010 REM ***              GRADUATION PROGRAM              ***
00020 REM
00030 REM ***    THIS PROGRAM PRINTS THE CLASS A STUDENT ***
00040 REM *** BELONGS TO (FRESHMAN, SOPHOMORE, JUNIOR,    ***
00050 REM *** SENIOR) AND THE YEAR OF GRADUATION WHEN     ***
00060 REM *** THE CORRESPONDING INTEGER (1, 2, 3, OR 4)   ***
00070 REM *** IS ENTERED.                                 ***
00080 REM *** MAJOR VARIABLES:                            ***
00090 REM *** STUDENT$          STUDENT'S NAME            ***
00100 REM *** YR                YEAR                      ***
00110 REM
00120 REM *** ENTER THE NECESSARY DATA ***
00130 INPUT "ENTER THE STUDENT'S NAME ";STUDENT$
00140 INPUT "ENTER THE STUDENT'S YEAR (1,2,3, OR 4) ";YR
00150 REM
00160 REM *** BRANCH TO SUBROUTINE THAT WILL PRINT MESSAGE ***
00170 ON YR GOSUB 1000,2000,3000,4000
00180 GOTO 9999
01000 REM
01010 REM *****************************************
01020 REM ***          SUBROUTINE FRESHMAN       ***
01030 REM *****************************************
01040 REM
01050 PRINT STUDENT$;" IS A FRESHMAN"
01060 PRINT "AND WILL GRADUATE IN 1991"
01070 RETURN
02000 REM
02010 REM *****************************************
02020 REM ***          SUBROUTINE SOPHOMORE      ***
02030 REM *****************************************
02040 REM
02050 PRINT STUDENT$;" IS A SOPHOMORE"
02060 PRINT "AND WILL GRADUATE IN 1990"
02070 RETURN
03000 REM
03010 REM *****************************************
03020 REM ***          SUBROUTINE JUNIOR        ***
03030 REM *****************************************
03040 REM
03050 PRINT STUDENT$;" IS A JUNIOR"
03060 PRINT "AND WILL GRADUATE IN 1989"
03070 RETURN
04000 REM
04010 REM *****************************************
04020 REM ***          SUBROUTINE SENIOR        ***
04030 REM *****************************************
04040 REM
04050 PRINT STUDENT$;" IS A SENIOR"
04060 PRINT "AND WILL GRADUATE IN 1988"
04070 RETURN
09999 END
```

● **COMPUTERS AND INFORMATION PROCESSING**

```
RUNNH
ENTER THE STUDENT'S NAME  ? TOM JONES
ENTER THE STUDENT'S YEAR (1,2,3, OR 4)  ? 3
TOM JONES IS A JUNIOR
AND WILL GRADUATE IN 1989
```

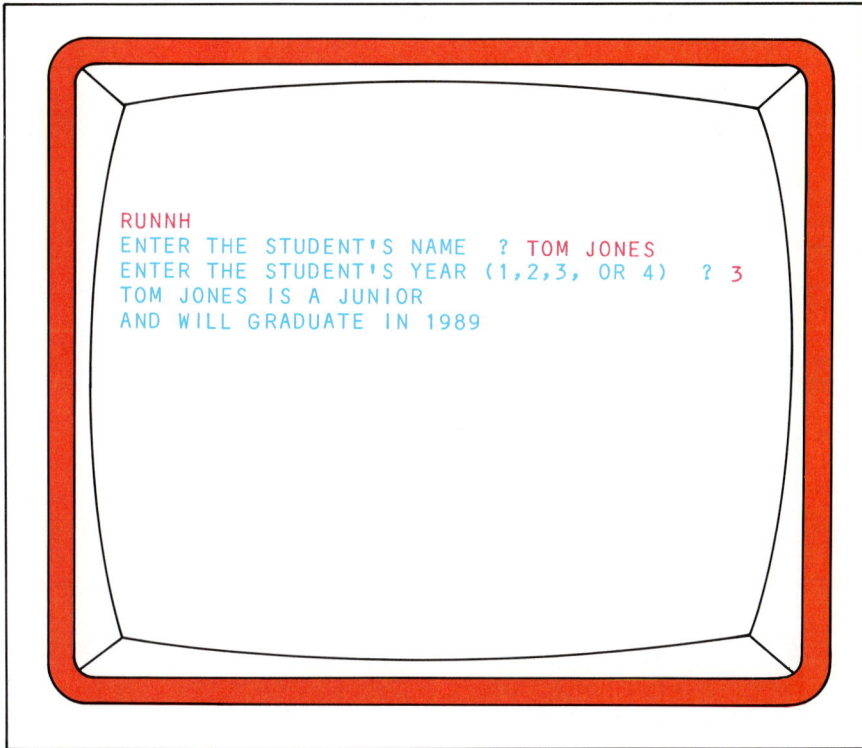

No phone calls can be placed outside the 299-mile radius.

First we need to develop an algorithm for this problem. The steps needed to solve this problem could be listed like this:

1. Enter the distance and length of time of the call.
2. Calculate the cost of the call based on the distance.
3. Print the cost of the call.

A structure chart for this problem is shown at the top of Figure VII–3. Steps 1 and 3 are simple enough to implement: Step 1 can be written as a subroutine that allows the user to enter the distance and length of time of the call, and Step 3 can be written as a subroutine that prints the final cost with an appropriate label. Because these are such simple steps, they could be included within the main program itself. In this example, however, we are including them as subroutines to demonstrate how every task in the program can be modularized.

Step 2 is more complex. We want the program to use one of three rates in determining the cost, depending on the distance. This is a situation that is well suited to the ON/GOSUB statement; three subroutines can be used to perform these calculations, as shown in Figure VII–3. The following ON/GOSUB statement will cause program control to be transferred to the needed subroutine, if the computer system being used is one that truncates the value of the ON/GOSUB expression, as the DEC-system does:

```
00120 ON (DIST + 100) / 100 GOSUB 2000,3000,4000
```

Program Using a Calculated Value in the ON/GOSUB Statement

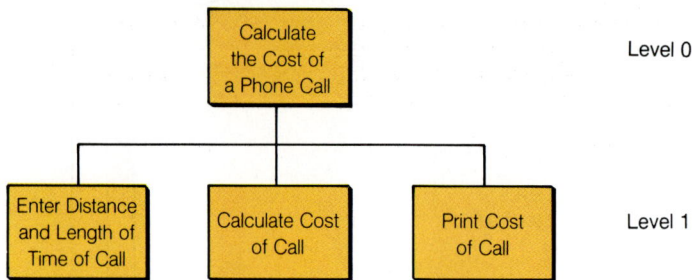

```
00010 REM *** THIS PROGRAM CALCULATES THE COST ***
00020 REM *** OF A LONG DISTANCE PHONE CALL     ***
00030 REM *** DEPENDING ON THE LENGTH OF TIME   ***
00040 REM *** AND THE DISTANCE OF THE CALL.     ***
00050 REM *** MAJOR VARIABLES:                  ***
00060 REM *** DIST      DISTANCE OF THE CALL    ***
00070 REM *** TME       TIME LENGTH OF THE CALL ***
00080 REM *** AMT       COST OF THE CALL        ***
00090 REM
00100 REM *** CALL SUBROUTINE TO ENTER DATA ***
00110 GOSUB 1000
00120 ON (DIST +100) / 100 GOSUB 2000,3000,4000
00130 REM
00140 REM *** CALL SUBROUTINE TO PRINT COST ***
00150 GOSUB 5000
00160 GOTO 9999
01000 REM
01010 REM ************************************************
01020 REM ***          SUBROUTINE ENTER DATA          ***
01030 REM ************************************************
01040 REM *** INPUT OF DATA FOR PROCESSING ***
01050 REM
01060 INPUT "WHAT IS THE DISTANCE OF THE CALL";DIST
01070 INPUT "HOW LONG WAS THE CALL";TME
01080 RETURN
02000 REM
02010 REM ************************************************
02020 REM ***         SUBROUTINE WITHIN 99 MILES      ***
02030 REM ************************************************
02040 REM *** CALCULATE COST OF CALL WITHIN 99 MILES ***
02050 REM
02060 IF TME < 5 THEN AMT = TME * .12 ELSE AMT = 5 * .12 + (TME - 5) * .10
02070 RETURN
03000 REM
03010 REM ************************************************
03020 REM ***          SUBROUTINE 100 - 199 MILES     ***
03030 REM ************************************************
03040 REM *** CALCULATE COST OF CALL IN 100 - 199 MILE RANGE ***
03050 REM
03060 IF TME < 5 THEN AMT = TME * ,15 ELSE AMT = 5 * .15 + (TME - 5) * .13
03070 RETURN
04000 REM
04010 REM ************************************************
04020 REM ***          SUBROUTINE 200 - 299 MILES     ***
04030 REM ************************************************
04040 REM *** CALCULATE COST OF CALL IN 200 - 299 MILE RANGE ***
04050 REM
```

● **FIGURE VII–3**
Continued

```
04060 AMT = TME * .18
04070 RETURN
05000 REM
05010 REM *********************************************
05020 REM ***           SUBROUTINE PRINT COST        ***
05030 REM *********************************************
05040 REM *** PRINT THE COST OF THE TELEPHONE CALL    **
05050 REM
05060 PRINT "THE COST OF THIS PHONE CALL IS ";AMT
05070 RETURN
09999 END
```

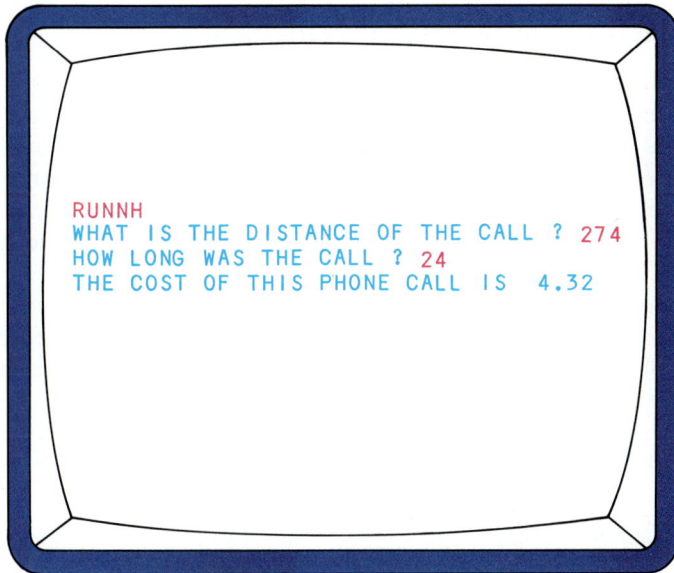

```
RUNNH
WHAT IS THE DISTANCE OF THE CALL ? 274
HOW LONG WAS THE CALL ? 24
THE COST OF THIS PHONE CALL IS  4.32
```

Let's test this expression by assuming that the number of miles entered is 199. With this value substituted, the statement would look like this:

```
00120 ON (199 + 100) / 100 GOSUB 2000,3000,4000
```

The expression (199 + 100) / 100 is equal to 2.99. This number is truncated to 2, so the program will branch to the second subroutine, which starts at line 3000. This is the subroutine used to calculate phone bills in the 100- to 199-mile radius.

Test this program yourself, using different values for the distance. If your BASIC system rounds the expression rather than truncating it, however, the expression must be written differently:

```
00120 ON (DIST + 50) / 100 GOSUB 2000,3000,4000
```

To check this statement, let's again assume that 199 has been entered as the value for DIST:

```
00120 ON (199 + 50) / 100 GOSUB 2000,3000,4000
```

The expression evaluates as 2.49, which rounds to 2. This value will cause the program to branch to the subroutine starting at line 3000, which is exactly what we want it to do.

It is often possible to use expressions similar to the preceding one in ON/GOSUB statements. They can often simplify the programming process, but they must be thoroughly tested to make certain that they will always evaluate as expected.

The complete program is shown in Figure VII–3. Note that this main program contains only four executable statements, three of which are used to call subroutines; the fourth statement branches to the end of the program. This is an example of a **driver program,** that is, a program the main purpose of which is to call the subprograms. These subprograms then perform the actual processing.

SINGLE-ENTRY, SINGLE-EXIT SUBROUTINES

Chapter 6 discussed the fact that program structures such as loops, decisions, and subroutines should have only one entry point and one exit point. This is an important principle of structured programming.

A subroutine may be called any number of times in a given program, but it should always be entered at the first line of the subroutine. Branching to the middle of a subroutine makes program logic virtually impossible to follow and often leads to errors.

Figure VII–4 illustrates two program segments, both of which perform the same task. The top segment is incorrectly written, because the IF/THEN/ELSE statement in line 110 can allow control to be passed either to the first line of the subroutine (line 1000) or to the middle of the sub-

● **FIGURE VII–4**
Demonstration of Single-Entry Subroutine Principle

```
00100 INPUT "ENTER YOUR SCORE";PTS
00110 IF PTS > 80 THEN GOSUB 1000 ELSE GOSUB 1060
00120 GOTO 9999
01000 REM
01010 REM ****************************************
01020 REM ***              SUBROUTINE         ***
01030 REM ****************************************
01040 REM
01050 PRINT "YOU DID VERY WELL!"
01060 PRINT "YOU PASSED THE COURSE."
01080 RETURN
09999 END
```
Incorrectly Written Program Segment With Branch to the Middle of Subroutine

```
00100 INPUT "ENTER YOUR SCORE";PTS
00110 GOSUB 1000
00120 GOTO 9999
01000 REM
01010 REM **********************************************
01020 REM ***              SUBROUTINE              ***
01030 REM **********************************************
01040 REM
01050 IF PTS > 0 THEN PRINT "YOU DID VERY WELL!"
01060 PRINT "YOU PASSED THE COURSE."
01070 RETURN
09999 END
```

Correctly Written Program Segment With a Single-Entry Point to Subroutine

routine (line 1060). The bottom example shows how this segment can be correctly written. Note that an IF/THEN statement within the subroutine is used to control execution.

Likewise, a subroutine should contain only one RETURN statement, which should be the last statement of the subroutine. This rule is referred to as the single-exit point principle. At the top of Figure VII–5 is a program segment that is incorrectly written because it contains two RETURN statements, one in line 1050 and one in line 1080. The bottom program segment accomplishes the same task by using an IF/THEN statement (line 1050) to branch to the RETURN statement at the end of the subroutine.

MENUS

Many programming applications require that the user be presented with a list of tasks that the program is able to perform. The use of menus for this purpose has already been discussed in connection with the ON/GOTO statement. The ON/GOSUB statement is also well suited for use with menus. The user can enter a value based on the choices offered in the menu, and the correct subroutine can be executed to perform the desired task.

Figure VII–6 contains a program that uses the ON/GOSUB statement with a menu. When this program is executed, the user is asked to enter

● **FIGURE VII–5**
Demonstration of Single-Exit Subroutine Principle

```
00100  INPUT "ENTER YOUR SCORE";PTS
00110  GOSUB 1010
00120  GOTO 9999
01000  REM
01010  REM ******************************************
01020  REM ***              SUBROUTINE           ***
01030  REM ******************************************
01040  REM
01050  IF PTS < 80 THEN PRINT "YOU FAILED" \ RETURN ELSE PRINT "YOU PASSED"
01060  CREDITHR = CREDITHR + 4
01070  ST$ = "OK"
01080  RETURN
09999  END
```

Incorrectly Written Program Segment With Multiple RETURNs

```
00100  INPUT "ENTER YOUR SCORE";PTS
00110  GOSUB 1000
00120  GOTO 9999
01000  REM
01010  REM ******************************************
01020  REM ***              SUBROUTINE           ***
01030  REM ******************************************
01040  REM
01050  IF PTS < 80 THEN PRINT "YOU FAILED" \ GOTO 1080 ELSE PRINT "YOU PASSED"
01060  CREDITHR = CREDITHR + 4
01070  ST$ = "OK"
01080  RETURN
09999  END
```

Correctly Written Program Segment With a Single RETURN

```
00010 REM ***                        PROGRAM MEAL COST                      ***
00020 REM
00030 REM *** THIS PROGRAM CALCULATES THE COST OF A PURCHASE AT A           ***
00040 REM *** FAST FOOD RESTAURANT.  THE USER ENTERS AN INTEGER AT          ***
00050 REM *** THE KEYBOARD WHICH REPRESENTS THE COST OF A SPECIFIC          ***
00060 REM *** ITEM.  THE USER THEN ENTERS HOW MANY OF THAT ITEM ARE         ***
00070 REM *** DESIRED.  THE COST OF THE ITEM IS THEN CALCULATED.            ***
00080 REM *** THE USER IS THEN ALLOWED TO ENTER ANOTHER ITEM. AFTER         ***
00090 REM *** THE USER HAS ENTERED AN ORDER, THE TOTAL COST OF THE          ***
00100 REM *** ORDER IS PRINTED.                                             ***
00110 REM *** MAJOR VARIABLES:                                              ***
00120 REM *** FOOD              CODE NUMBER TO INDICATE ITEM                 ***
00130 REM *** CST               COST OF AN ITEM                             ***
00140 REM *** NUMBER            HOW MANY OF THE CHOSEN ITEM                  ***
00150 REM *** TTCST             TOTAL COST OF THE ORDER                     ***
00160 REM
00170 REM *** INITIALIZE TOTAL COST TO ZERO   ***
00180 TTCST = 0
00190 REM
00200 REM *** PRINT THE MENU   ***
00210 PRINT
00220 PRINT "CODE NUMBER";TAB(25);"ITEM";TAB(52);"COST OF ITEM"
00230 PRINT
00240 FOR I = 1 TO 80
00250     PRINT "-";
00260 NEXT I
00270 PRINT
00280 PRINT USING 6020,1,"HAMBURGER",0.75
00290 PRINT USING 6020,2,"CHEESEBURGER",0.90
00300 PRINT USING 6020,3,"DRINK",0.50
00310 PRINT USING 6020,4,"FRENCH FRIES",0.55
00320 PRINT
00330 PRINT TAB(6);"5      USED TO INDICATE END OF THE ORDER"
00340 PRINT
00350 FOR I = 1 TO 80
00360     PRINT "-";
00370 NEXT I
00380 PRINT
00390 PRINT
00400 INPUT "ENTER CODE FOR FOOD ITEM (5 TO FINISH) ";FOOD
00410 ON FOOD GOSUB 1000,2000,3000,4000,5000
00420 IF FOOD <> 5 GOTO 200 ELSE GOTO 9999
01000 REM
01010 REM ***********************************************************
01020 REM ***             SUBROUTINE HAMBURGERS                   ***
01030 REM ***********************************************************
01040 REM ***                  HAMBURGERS ORDERED                 ***
01050 REM
01060 CST = 0.75
01070 INPUT "HOW MANY HAMBURGERS DO YOU DESIRE ";NUMBER
01080 TTCST = TTCST + (CST * NUMBER)
01090 RETURN
02000 REM
02010 REM ***********************************************************
02020 REM ***            SUBROUTINE CHEESEBURGERS                 ***
02030 REM ***********************************************************
02040 REM ***                CHEESEBURGERS ORDERED                ***
02050 REM
02060 CST = 0.90
02070 INPUT "HOW MANY CHEESEBURGERS DO YOU DESIRE ";NUMBER
```

a code number depending on the food item desired. Then the statement in line 410 causes the correct subroutine to be executed depending on the item chosen. Each subroutine prompts the user for the desired quantity of that particular item, calculates the cost, and then adds it to the total cost of the food purchased. If the user enters code number 5, the total bill is printed and the program stops executing. Otherwise, the menu is displayed again so that the user can enter another choice.

USING STUBS TO ENTER PROGRAMS

So far, considerable attention has been given to top-down development of programming problem solutions. It is also possible to use a top-down method when entering a program to the computer. When writing a large program that contains many subroutines, it is poor programming practice to enter the entire program at one time. A far wiser approach is to start by entering the main program (the driver) and one or two subroutines.

● FIGURE VII-6
Continued

```
02080 TTCST = TTCST + (CST * NUMBER)
02090 RETURN
03000 REM
03010 REM ************************************************
03020 REM ***            SUBROUTINE DRINKS            ***
03030 REM ************************************************
03040 REM ***              DRINKS ORDERED             ***
03050 REM
03060 CST = 0.50
03070 INPUT "HOW MANY DRINKS DO YOU DESIRE ";NUMBER
03080 TTCST = TTCST + (CST * NUMBER)
03090 RETURN
04000 REM
04010 REM ************************************************
04020 REM ***          SUBROUTINE FRENCH FRIES        ***
04030 REM ************************************************
04040 REM ***           FRENCH FRIES ORDERED          ***
04050 REM
04060 CST = 0.55
04070 INPUT "HOW MANY FRENCH FRIES DO YOU DESIRE ";NUMBER
04080 TTCST = TTCST + (CST * NUMBER)
04090 RETURN
05000 REM
05010 REM ************************************************
05020 REM ***          SUBROUTINE PRINT COST          ***
05030 REM ************************************************
05040 REM ***        PRINT TOTAL COST OF ORDER        ***
05050 REM
05070 PRINT
05080 PRINT USING 6030,"THE TOTAL COST OF THIS ORDER IS",TTCST
05090 RETURN
06000 REM
06010 REM *** IMAGE STATEMENTS ***
06020 :        #                'LLLLLLLLLLL        $#.##
06030 :'LLLLLLLLLLLLLLLLLLLLLLLLLLLLLLLLLLL  $$##.##
09999 END
```

(Continued Next Two Pages)

```
RUNNH

CODE NUMBER              ITEM                    COST OF ITEM

    ------------------------------------------------------------
        1           HAMBURGER                   $0.75
        2           CHEESEBURGER                $0.90
        3           DRINK                       $0.50
        4           FRENCH FRIES                $0.55

        5       USED TO INDICATE END OF THE ORDER

    ------------------------------------------------------------

ENTER CODE FOR FOOD ITEM (5 TO FINISH) ? 2
HOW MANY CHEESEBURGERS DO YOU DESIRE   ? 4

CODE NUMBER              ITEM                    COST OF ITEM

    ------------------------------------------------------------
        1           HAMBURGER                   $0.75
        2           CHEESEBURGER                $0.90
        3           DRINK                       $0.50
        4           FRENCH FRIES                $0.55

        5       USED TO INDICATE END OF THE ORDER

    ------------------------------------------------------------

ENTER CODE FOR FOOD ITEM (5 TO FINISH) ? 3
HOW MANY DRINKS DO YOU DESIRE  ? 2

CODE NUMBER              ITEM                    COST OF ITEM

    ------------------------------------------------------------
        1           HAMBURGER                   $0.75
        2           CHEESEBURGER                $0.90
        3           DRINK                       $0.50
        4           FRENCH FRIES                $0.55

        5       USED TO INDICATE END OF THE ORDER

    ------------------------------------------------------------

ENTER CODE FOR FOOD ITEM (5 TO FINISH)  ? 4
HOW MANY FRENCH FRIES DO YOU DESIRE ? 2

CODE NUMBER              ITEM                    COST OF ITEM

    ------------------------------------------------------------
        1           HAMBURGER                   $0.75
        2           CHEESEBURGER                $0.90
        3           DRINK                       $0.50
        4           FRENCH FRIES                $0.55

        5       USED TO INDICATE END OF THE ORDER

    ------------------------------------------------------------

ENTER CODE FOR FOOD ITEM (5 TO FINISH) ? 5

THE TOTAL COST OF THIS ORDER IS    $5.70
```

MICROCOMPUTERS	DIFFERENCE
Apple	No IF/THEN/ELSE; no PRINT USING; output needs reformatting.
IBM/Microsoft	No separate image statement with PRINT USING.
Macintosh/Microsoft	No separate image statement with PRINT USING.
TRS-80	No separate image statement with PRINT USING.

Subroutines that are not yet implemented are called, but each of these nonimplemented subroutines consists merely of a **stub.** A stub contains a PRINT statement that indicates a given subroutine has been called but is not yet implemented. The stub must also contain a RETURN statement to return control to the main program. The idea is to enter the program in manageable segments, which can then be executed and tested for errors in an orderly way. As segments of the program work properly, more can gradually be added and tested.

Let's see how the program in Figure VII–6 might have been developed in this manner. First, the main program would be typed into the computer. At this point the programmer might also want to enter subroutines 1 and 5. The number of subroutines entered at one time is entirely dependent upon the judgment of the programmer. We have chosen to enter a subroutine that calculates the cost of one of the food items (in this case, hamburgers), and also the subroutine that prints the total bill so that we can check to see if the results obtained by the program are accurate.

Let's assume that lines 10 through 1090 and lines 5000 through 09999 are entered exactly as they appear in Figure VII–6. The rest of the program could be entered like this:

```
02000  PRINT "SUBROUTINE 2 NOT YET IMPLEMENTED"
02010  RETURN
03000  PRINT "SUBROUTINE 3 NOT YET IMPLEMENTED"
03010  RETURN
04000  PRINT "SUBROUTINE 4 NOT YET IMPLEMENTED"
04010  RETURN
```

Therefore, it is possible for the user to order hamburgers and have the total cost of the hamburgers printed. If the user attempts to order cheeseburgers, the following message will appear on the screen.

SUBROUTINE 2 NOT YET IMPLEMENTED

Control will then return to line 420 of the main program. The user will not be prompted to enter the number of cheeseburgers desired, nor will any value be added to the variable containing the total cost of the order. This same thing will happen if the user attempts to order drinks or french fries.

The programmer is now able to determine if the main program, the hamburger subroutine, and the final printing subroutine are working properly. If the total cost printed is incorrect, or if there is some other error, it is much easier to pinpoint the problem than if the entire program had been entered at once. When the programmer is certain that the program is working properly, more subroutines can be gradually added and tested. This method of entering and testing programs greatly simplifies the debugging process, particularly for large programs.

● Checking for Invalid Data

Interactive programs should check to make certain that data entered by the user is valid. If the data is invalid, the program should ask the user to reenter it. For example, in the program in Figure VII–6, the user is asked to enter an integer between 1 and 5. If the user entered a number that was less than 1 or more than 5, the program would not be able to execute properly. In order to protect the program from such an occurrence, the program should check the data entered and make certain that it falls within the allowable range.

The following subroutine shows how this checking can be accomplished. A WHILE/NEXT loop (lines 7050–7090) is used to determine if the value of FOOD is within the valid range. This condition is checked using the logical operator OR:

```
00430 WHILE FOOD < 1 OR FOOD > 5
```

This loop will be executed only if the value of FOOD is less than 1 or greater than 5. Otherwise, the loop will be skipped. If the loop is executed, the user is instructed to reenter a code number, making certain that the number is between 1 and 5.

```
07000 REM ****************************************
07010 REM ***          SUBROUTINE CODE CHECK        ***
07020 REM ****************************************
07030 REM ***          CHECK FOR CODE OF 1 - 5      ***
07040 REM
07050 WHILE FOOD < 1 OR FOOD > 5
07060     PRINT "CODE MUST BE AN INTEGER"
07070     PRINT "BETWEEN 1 AND 5."
07080     INPUT "PLEASE REENTER CODE";FOOD
07090 NEXT
07100 RETURN
```

In programs that are not interactive, invalid data must be handled in a different manner. Suppose that the program in Figure VII–6 had been written using READ/DATA statements instead of INPUT statements. How could the programmer handle data outside the allowable range?

One method is to ignore the invalid data item and go on to the next item. An error message could be printed, stating that an invalid data item was encountered and ignored. Another method is to print an error message and stop program execution prematurely. For example, if the value 7 was entered in this example, a message such as INVALID VALUE ENTERED TO VARIABLE FOOD could be printed. Program execution could then be terminated by the STOP statement, which has the following format:

line# STOP

The STOP statement differs from the END statement in that STOP can appear as often as necessary in a program, whereas the END statement can appear only once. Also, on the DECsystem, the END statement must have the highest line number, whereas the STOP statement can have any line number. When the STOP statement is executed, the computer prints a message similar to the following:

```
STOP at line 00310 of MAIN PROGRAM
```

This type of error checking is a feature of any well-written program. From this point on, you should attempt to write programs that are protected as much as possible from invalid input.

● A Programming Problem

PROBLEM DEFINITION

The public library needs a program to calculate the total cost of the books it adds to its collection. This cost includes not only the purchase price of the book but also the cost of processing the book. The program should be interactive, allowing the librarians to enter the data at the keyboard. The total book cost should then be printed on the terminal screen.

Processing costs are dependent upon two factors: (1) the type of book (reference, circulating, or paperback), and (2) whether or not the book is a duplicate of one already in the library. It is cheaper to process books that are duplicates of those already in the library's collection, because cards for these books are already in the card catalog and the cost of card production is saved. Processing costs are as follows:

Reference book
not a duplicate	$8.50
duplicate	$7.40

Circulating book
not a duplicate	$7.82
duplicate	$6.60
bestseller	$1.75 additional

Paperback
not a duplicate	$4.60
duplicate	$3.10

The type of book should be entered using an integer code:

1—Reference
2—Circulating
3—Paperback

Note the additional $1.75 cost for processing circulating books that are also bestsellers. This cost is for a plastic cover to give the book extra protection. The necessary input and output for this program are shown in the following example:

Input:

Price	Type of Book	Duplicate	Bestseller
			(applies to code 2 only)
25.39	2	N	N

Needed Output:

TOTAL COST: $33.21

SOLUTION DESIGN

Each time this program is executed, it will calculate the total cost (purchase price plus processing cost) of one book. The program needs four input variables. These input variables are one numeric variable for the price of the book, another numeric variable to represent the book code, a character string variable to store a Y if the book is a duplicate and an N if it is not, and, if the book code entered is a 2, a character string variable to indicate whether the book is a bestseller. The output variable will be a numeric variable containing the total cost. The needed variables are summarized in the following table:

Input Variables

price of book	(PRICE)
code for type of book	(CODE)
duplicate indicator	(DUP$)
best seller indicator	(SELLER$)

Program Variables

processing cost	(PRCST)

Output Variables

total cost	(TTCST)

Three basic steps are necessary to determine the total book costs:

1. Enter the data for the book.
2. Calculate the correct processing cost.
3. Determine the total cost.

Step 1 can be divided into three substeps that ask the user to enter the price of the book, the code for the type of book, and the duplicate indicator. This step should also include checking to make certain that the values entered for the book code and the duplicate indicator are valid. If an invalid value has been entered, the user should be prompted to reenter that value. Since each of these substeps is relatively simple, when we write the program we will include them all in a single subroutine.

Step 2 is the most difficult part of this problem. It involves performing one of three options, depending on whether a reference, circulating, or paper book is being processed. Because only one of these options will be executed, this is an ideal situation for a conditional branch to one of three subroutines, each of which will calculate the cost for a particular type of book. The book type code can be used as the controlling expression in an ON/GOSUB statement to transfer program control from the main program to the appropriate subroutine.

Step 3 involves adding the processing cost to the purchase price of the book and printing this total.

The basic steps to solve the problem can be further divided as follows:

1. a. Enter the price of the book.
1. b. Enter the code for the type of book.
1. c. Enter the duplicate indicator.
3. a. Add processing cost to book price.
3. b. Print the total cost.

The structure chart for this solution is shown in Figure VII–7.

THE PROGRAM

Study the complete program as shown in Figure VII–8. Note that the main body of the program is a driver program and is therefore quite short.

The first subroutine enables the user to enter the necessary data. This subroutine contains two WHILE/NEXT loops that check for invalid data. The first loop (lines 1150–1180) allows the user to reenter the value of the type code if an invalid code has been entered. The second loop (lines 1220–1250) makes certain that the user has entered either a Y or an N as the duplicate book indicator. If a different value has been entered, the user is asked to reenter the data.

The value entered for the book type code must be a 1, 2, or 3. This value is then used in the ON/GOSUB statement in line 310 to determine which one of the three subroutines will be executed. Each of the subroutines calculates the processing cost for one type of book. The circulating book subroutine is a little more complicated than the other two, because it must ask the user if the book is a bestseller and include an additional charge if it is. After the processing cost of the book has been determined, control returns to the main program, where the final subroutine is called to add the processing cost to the purchase price and print the total cost.

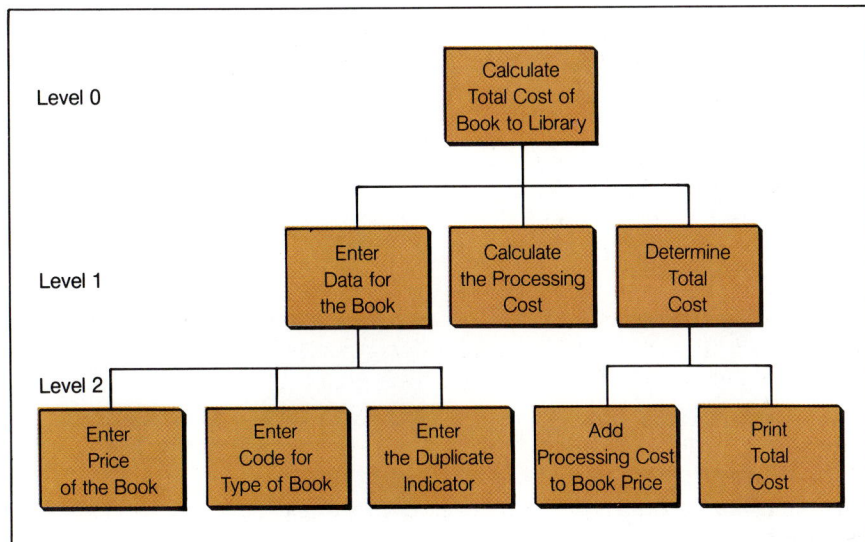

● **FIGURE VII–7**
Structure Chart for Book Processing Cost Problem

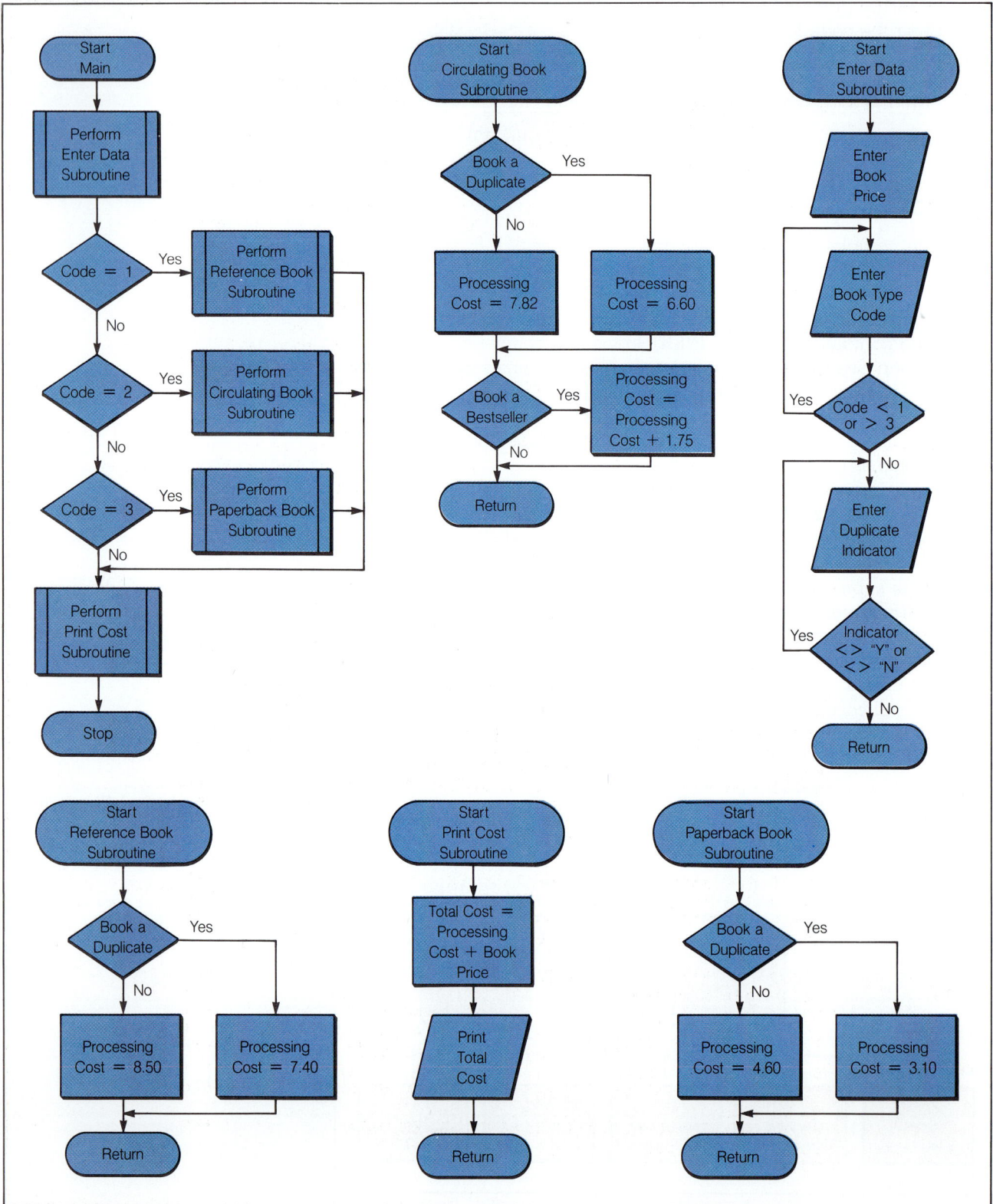

● FIGURE VII-8
Book Processing Cost Program

● COMPUTERS AND INFORMATION PROCESSING

Pseudocode

Begin main program
Perform enter data subroutine
If type code = 1 perform reference book subroutine
If type code = 2 perform circulating book subroutine
If type code = 3 perform paperback book subroutine
Perform print cost subroutine
End main program

Begin enter data subroutine
Prompt user to enter price
Prompt user to enter type code
Begin loop, do until code >= 1 and <= 3
   Prompt user to reenter type code
End loop
Prompt user to enter duplicate indicator
Begin loop, do until indicator is equal to "Y" or "N"
   Prompt user to reenter duplicate code
End loop
End enter data subroutine

Begin reference book subroutine
If book is duplicate
   Then processing cost = 7.40
   Else processing cost = 8.50
End if
End reference book subroutine

Begin circulating book subroutine
If book is duplicate
   Then processing cost = 6.60
   Else processing cost = 7.82
End if
Prompt user to enter bestseller indicator
If book is a bestseller
   Then add 1.75 to processing cost
End if
End circulating book subroutine

Begin paperback book subroutine
If book is duplicate
   The processing cost = 3.10
   Else processing cost = 4.60
End if
End paperback book subroutine

Begin print cost subroutine
Total cost = processing cost + book price
Print total cost
End print cost subroutine

```
00010 REM ***                    PROGRAM BOOKCOST              ***
00020 REM
00030 REM ***   THIS PROGRAM CALCULATES THE TOTAL COST    ***
00040 REM *** OF A BOOK. THE TOTAL COST IS OBTAINED BY ***
00050 REM *** ADDING THE PRICE OF THE BOOK TO THE PRO-  ***
00060 REM *** CESSING COST, WHICH IS BASED ON THE TYPE.***
00070 REM ***         1.   REFERENCE BOOK                     ***
00080 REM ***                   NOT A DUPLICATE     $8.50     ***
00090 REM ***                   DUPLICATE           $7.40     ***
00100 REM ***         2.   CIRCULATING BOOK                   ***
00110 REM ***                   NOT A DUPLICATE     $7.82     ***
00120 REM ***                   DUPLICATE           $6.60     ***
00130 REM ***                   BESTSELLER          $1.75     ***
00140 REM ***         3.   PAPERBACK                          ***
00150 REM ***                   NOT A DUPLICATE     $4.60     ***
00160 REM ***                   DUPLICATE           $3.10     ***
00170 REM
00180 REM ***   MAJOR VARIABLES:                              ***
00190 REM ***   PRICE          PRICE OF THE BOOK              ***
00200 REM ***   CODE           TYPE OF BOOK AS ABOVE          ***
00210 REM ***   DUP$           IS BOOK A DUPLICATE(Y/N)?      ***
00220 REM ***   PRCST          PROCESSING COST                ***
00230 REM ***   SELLER$        IS BOOK A BESTSELLER(Y/N)?     ***
00240 REM ***   TTCST          TOTAL COST OF BOOK             ***
00250 REM
00260 REM *** CALL SUBROUTINE TO ENTER DATA                   ***
00270 GOSUB 1000
00280 REM
```

```
00290 REM *** CALL APPROPRIATE SUBROUTINE TO CALCULATE ***
00300 REM *** THE PROCESSING COST                       ***
00310 ON CODE GOSUB 2000,3000,4000
00320 REM
00330 REM *** CALL SUBROUTINE TO ADD PROCESSING COST   ***
00340 REM *** TO BOOK PRICE AND PRINT TOTAL COST       ***
00350 GOSUB 5000
00360 GOTO 9999
01000 REM
01010 REM ***********************************************
01020 REM ***           SUBROUTINE ENTER DATA          ***
01030 REM ***********************************************
01040 REM *** SUBROUTINE TO ALLOW USER TO ENTER DATA   ***
01050 REM
01060 INPUT "ENTER PRICE OF THE BOOK";PRICE
01070 PRINT
01080 PRINT
01090 PRINT
01100 PRINT "1 - REFERENCE BOOK"
01110 PRINT "2 - CIRCULATING BOOK"
01120 PRINT "3 - PAPERBACK"
01130 INPUT "ENTER TYPE CODE FOR THE BOOK, USING THE CODES LISTED ABOVE";CODE
01140 REM
01150 REM ** LOOP TO ALLOW CODE TO BE REENTERED IF CURRENT ENTRY IS INVALID ***
01160 WHILE CODE < 1 OR CODE > 3
01170    INPUT "TYPE CODE MUST BE A 1, 2, OR 3.  PLEASE REENTER CODE";CODE
01180 NEXT
01190 PRINT
01200 INPUT "IS BOOK A DUPLICATE (Y/N)";DUP$
01210 REM
01220 REM *** LOOP TO ALLOW DUPLICATE INDICATOR TO BE REENTERED, IF INVALID ***
01230 WHILE DUP$ <> "Y" AND DUP$ <> "N"
01240    INPUT "IS BOOK A DUPLICATE?  PLEASE ENTER A 'Y' OR AN 'N'";DUP$
01250 NEXT
01260 RETURN
02000 REM
02010 REM ***********************************************
02020 REM ***          SUBROUTINE REFERENCE BOOK       ***
02030 REM ***********************************************
02040 REM *** SUBROUTINE TO CALCULATE PROCESSING COST  ***
02050 REM *** OF REFERENCE BOOK                         ***
02060 REM
02070 IF DUP$ = "Y" THEN PRCST = 7.40 ELSE PRCST = 8.50
02080 RETURN
03000 REM
03010 REM ***********************************************
03020 REM ***          SUBROUTINE CIRCULATING BOOK     ***
03030 REM ***********************************************
03040 REM *** SUBROUTINE TO CALCULATE PROCESSING COST  ***
03050 REM *** OF CIRCULATING BOOK                       ***
03060 REM
03070 IF DUP$ = "Y" THEN PRCST = 6.60 ELSE PRCST = 7.82
03080 INPUT "IS THE BOOK A BESTSELLER (Y/N)?";SELLER$
03090 IF SELLER$ = "Y" THEN PRCST = PRCST + 1.75
03100 RETURN
04000 REM
04010 REM ***********************************************
04020 REM ***            SUBROUTINE PAPERBACK BOOK     ***
04030 REM ***********************************************
04040 REM *** SUBROUTINE TO CALCULATE PROCESSING COST  ***
```

```
04050 REM *** OF PAPERBACK BOOK                              ***
04060 REM
04070 IF DUP$ = "Y" THEN PRCST = 3.10 ELSE PRCST = 4.60
04080 RETURN
05000 REM
05010 REM *****************************************************
05020 REM ***                SUBROUTINE PRINT COST           ***
05030 REM *****************************************************
05040 REM *** SUBROUTINE TO CALCULATE AND PRINT TOTAL   ***
05050 REM *** COST                                       ***
05060 REM
05070 TTCST = PRCST + PRICE
05080 PRINT
05090 PRINT USING 5120,"***     TOTAL COST:",TTCST
05100 RETURN
05110 REM *** IMAGE STATEMENT ***
05120 : 'LLLLLLLLLLLLLLLLLLL    $$##.##
09999 END
```

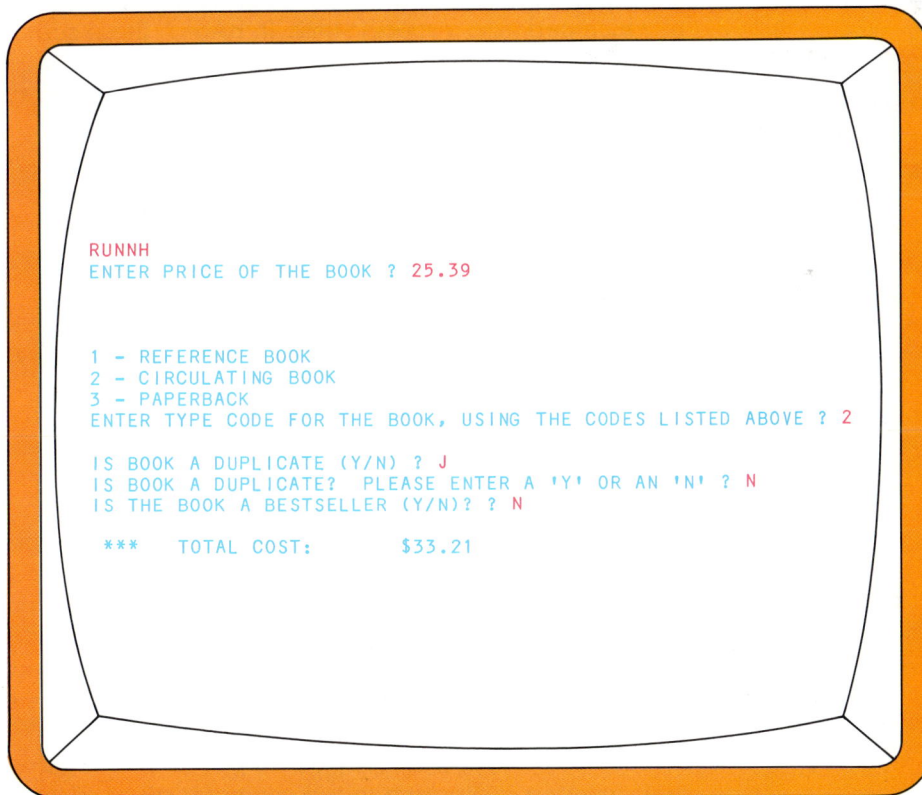

```
RUNNH
ENTER PRICE OF THE BOOK ? 25.39


1 - REFERENCE BOOK
2 - CIRCULATING BOOK
3 - PAPERBACK
ENTER TYPE CODE FOR THE BOOK, USING THE CODES LISTED ABOVE ? 2

IS BOOK A DUPLICATE (Y/N) ? J
IS BOOK A DUPLICATE?  PLEASE ENTER A 'Y' OR AN 'N' ? N
IS THE BOOK A BESTSELLER (Y/N)? ? N

 ***    TOTAL COST:      $33.21
```

MICROCOMPUTERS	DIFFERENCE
Apple	No IF/THEN/ELSE, no PRINT USING
IBM/Microsoft	No separate image statement with PRINT USING
Macintosh/Microsoft	No separate image statement with PRINT USING
TRS-80	No separate image statement with PRINT USING

● Summary Points

● Modularizing programs involves dividing them into subprograms, each of which performs a specific task. In BASIC, these subprograms or modules are referred to as subroutines.

● The use of subroutines makes program logic easier to follow. Also, a given subroutine can be called any number of times.

● Two BASIC statements can be used to call subroutines: GOSUB and ON/GOSUB.

● The GOSUB statement is an unconditional branch that causes the flow of execution to be passed to the line number contained in the GOSUB statement.

● The RETURN statement causes control to be transferred back to the statement after the one that called the subroutine.

● The ON/GOSUB statement allows for a conditional branch to one of several stated subroutines, depending on the evaluation of the expression in the ON/GOSUB statement. If the value of the expression is n, control passes to the subroutine starting at the nth line number listed.

● An important rule in structured programming is that all subroutines should have a single entry point and a single exit point. Otherwise, the possibility of an error in the program is greatly increased. Also, entering or exiting from the middle of a subroutine makes the logic of the program convoluted and difficult to follow.

● Menus often use the ON/GOSUB statement, which provides a simple way for the program to branch to the correct subroutine depending on the code number entered by the user.

● Stubs allow a program to be developed in a methodical fashion. Rather than entering a program to the computer all at once, the programmer can add and test subroutines gradually. Once the parts already entered work properly, more of the program can be entered. This procedure makes it easier to locate program errors.

● All programs should check for invalid data and print an error message if any is found. In interactive programs, the user can be prompted to reenter the data.

Review Questions

1. Name two advantages of modularizing programs.
2. How can a structure chart help in modularizing a program?
3. Why doesn't the RETURN statement contain a transfer line number? That is, how is it possible that program control can be transferred back to the correct statement even though no transfer line number is specified in the RETURN statement?
4. Where are RETURN statements placed in programs?
5. Why is the GOSUB statement referred to as an unconditional branching statement?
6. What happens if the transfer line number in a GOSUB statement is a nonexecutable statement?
7. Why is it important that a subroutine have only one entry point and one exit point?
8. Explain how the ON/GOSUB statement works. How is it different from the GOSUB statement?
9. What is a driver program?
10. How can stubs be used when entering programs to the computer?

Debugging Exercises

Identify the following programs and program segments that contain errors and debug them.

1.
```
00100 INPUT "ENTER THE STUDENT'S GRADE";PTS$
00110 ON PTS$ GOSUB 2000,3000,4000,5000
```

2.
```
00010 INPUT "ENTER THE INTEGER VALUE OF THE MONTH";MNTH
00020 WHILE (MNTH > 1) OR (MNTH > 12)
00030    PRINT "PLEASE ENTER THE INTEGER"
00040    PRINT "BETWEEN 1 AND 12 THAT"
00050    INPUT "REPRESENTS THE MONTH";MNTH
00060 NEXT
00070 PRINT MNTH
```

Programming Problems

1. World Travel wants a program that displays a menu with a list of countries to which the agency can send a customer with special discount rates. After the user enters the name of a particular country, the program should print all cities in that country in which the special rates are available. Use the following data:

Country	Cities
France	Nice
	Cannes
	Nantes
	Chamonix
Italy	Milan
	Verona
	Venice
	Naples
U.S.A.	Chicago
	San Francisco
	New York
	Miami

2. Budget Balloons provides hot-air balloon rides for fairs, parties, and other special occasions. The basic fee is $65.00 for the first hour and $45.00 for every additional hour. The company needs a program to help calculate its clients' bills. The program should call a subroutine to do the actual calculating, and use a loop to allow as many bills to be calculated as desired. The output of the program should include the name of the client and his or her total bill.

3. The R & R Railways wants a program to determine the cost for passengers to various cities. The cost per person for the following cities is as follows:

Columbus	$ 39.00
Denver	142.00
New York	108.00
New Orleans	158.00

A menu should display the names of the cities and ask how many people would like to purchase tickets. If a customer wants first-class tickets, there is an additional $30.00 flat fee. The cost of the needed tickets should be calculated in subroutines. Develop your own data to test the program.

4. As the manager of an apartment building, you need a program to help you keep track of the various apartments for rent. Write a program using subroutines which will give the user a choice of a studio, one-bedroom, or two-bedroom apartment. The monthly rent depends on the size of the apartment and whether it is to be furnished or unfurnished (this data should also be entered by the user). Use the following data:

Type	Rent Deposit	Furnished	Unfurnished
Studio	$ 75	$150	$135
One-bedroom	150	275	250
Two-bedroom	200	325	315

The program should print the apartment description, required deposit, and monthly rent according to the choices entered, using the following format:

Description: One-bedroom furnished
Deposit $150
Rent: $275

5. Dan's yard care business needs a program to help with the billing of its customers. The user should be able to enter the due date for all bills to be processed. For each customer, enter a name, address, and the applicable charges selected from the following list:

Lawn mow	$15.00
Tree trim	12.00
Hedge/bush trim	10.00
Edging	7.00

All customers receive the standard service of a lawn mow. The program should print an itemized bill showing the total amount due and the amount owed for late payment, which is the total plus 5 percent. Use your own test data. Your output should resemble the following:

Name: Cummings, E.   Due Date: 09/17/87
Address: 445 Cherry St.

Services:

Lawn mow	$15.00
Hedge/bush trim	10.00
Edging	7.00
Total amount due:	$32.00
After due date:	$33.60

● Section VIII
Functions

● Introduction

A useful feature of BASIC is the **function,** a subprogram designed to perform a specific task and return a single value. BASIC has numerous **library functions,** or built-in functions, which perform common mathematical operations, such as finding the square root of a number or its absolute value. Other library functions operate on character strings, performing tasks such as finding the length of a string. These functions are also called **intrinsic** or **predefined functions.** They are useful to the programmer, who is spared the necessity of writing the sequence of statements otherwise needed to perform these operations. In some cases, however, it is useful for the programmer to write a function to meet a particular need. Functions that are written by the programmer are called **user-defined functions.** This section discusses both library functions and user-defined functions.

● Library Functions

Library functions are those that have been built into the BASIC language and included in the BASIC language library, where the programmer can easily reference them. In order to use a library function in a program, the programmer must call or reference the function, just as a subroutine must be called by the main program. The general format of a function call is as follows:

function name (argument)

The **argument** required within the parentheses is the value needed by the function to obtain a result, and can consist of the following:

- A constant
- A variable
- Another function
- Expressions involving any of the preceding

The type of argument depends on the function used. The function performs its specific task, using the argument value, and returns a single value to the calling program.

A function call can be used in a BASIC statement in the place of a constant, a variable, or an expression. A function call evaluates as a single value and cannot be used to the left of an equal sign. For example, the function that finds the square root of a number, SQR, could be used in the following statement that assigns the value 5 to the variable SUM:

```
00060 SUM = SQR(4) = 3
```

The following statement would be invalid, however, because it attempts to assign the value of SUM plus 3 to the value 2 (the square root of 4):

```
00060 SQR(4) = SUM + 3
```

When a function call occurs in a statement, it is evaluated before any other operations in the statement are evaluated. Therefore, a function call has a higher priority than arithmetic, relational, and logical operators.

There are two categories of BASIC library functions: numeric functions and string functions. Some of the numeric functions available on most systems will be discussed first.

NUMERIC FUNCTIONS

Table VIII–1 shows eleven common numeric functions that are available on most systems and used by all of the systems discussed in this text.

The Trigonometric Functions

Four of these functions—SIN, COS, TAN, and ATN—are trigonometric functions used in mathematical, engineering, and scientific applications. The argument for these functions is an angle measure given in radians; however, often a trigonometric problem is more easily understood using degrees. You may convert from one unit to the other as follows.

Radians to degrees:
1 radian = 57.29578 degrees
N radians = N * 57.29578 degrees

● **TABLE VIII–1**
Numeric Functions

FUNCTION	OPERATION
ABS (X)	Absolute value of X
ATN (X)	Trigonometric arc tangent of X radians
COS (X)	Trigonometric cosine of X radians
EXP (X)	e^x
INT (X)	Greatest integer less than or equal to X
LOG (X)	Natural logarithm (if $x = e^y$, LOG (X) = Y)
RND	Random number between 0 and 1
SGN (X)	Sign of X: $+1$ if $X > 0$, 0 if $X = 0$, -1 if $X < 0$
SIN (X)	Trigonometric sine of X radians
SQR (X)	Square root of X
TAN (X)	Trigonometric tangent of X radians

To convert 2.5 radians to degrees, for example, multiply 2.5 by 57.29578. The product is approximately 143 degrees.

Degrees to radians:
1 degree = 0.01745 radians
N degrees = N * 0.01745 radians

To convert 180 degrees to radians, multiply 180 by 0.01745. The result is equal to π (approximately 3.14 radians).

The Exponential Function

The exponential or EXP function performs the calculation EXP (X) = e^x. The constant e is equal to approximately 2.718. For example, the following statement assigns the value e^x to Y:

```
00050 Y = EXP(X)
```

The Natural Logarithm Function

The natural logarithm or LOG function is the reverse of the EXP function. For example, if $X = e^y$, then LOG (X) = Y. In other words, Y (the natural logarithm of X) is the power that e is raised to in order to find X. If we know X but need to know the value of Y, we can use the following statement to assign the natural logarithm of X to Y:

```
00030 Y = LOG(X)
```

The argument of the LOG function must be a positive real number.

The Square Root Function

The square root or SQR function determines the positive square root of its argument. In most BASIC implementations, the argument must be a nonnegative number (the Apple, which requires that the argument be greater than zero, is the only exception among the systems discussed in this book). The following examples illustrate the SQR function:

Statement	Result
00020 Y = SQR(X)	$Y = \sqrt{X}$
00050 Z = SQR(SQR(16))	$Z = 2$
00030 T = SQR((A * B) / (A - C))	$T = \sqrt{\dfrac{AB}{A - C}}$

The Integer Function

The integer, or INT, function computes the largest integer less than or equal to the argument value. For example:

X	INT (X)
8	8
5.34	5
16.9	16
-2.75	-3
-0.5	-1

If the argument is a positive value with a fractional part, the digits to the right of the decimal point are truncated (cut off). Notice from the preceding examples that truncation does not occur when the argument is negative. For instance, when the argument equals -2.75, the INT function returns -3, the largest integer *less than* or *equal to* that value. This fact can be seen on the number line, where the farther to the left a number lies, the less value it has:

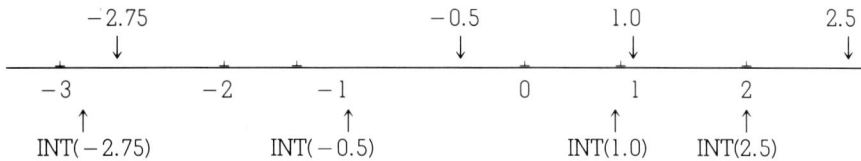

Although the INT function alone does not round its argument, it can be used in an expression that rounds to the nearest integer, nearest tenth, or nearest hundredth, or to any other degree of accuracy desired. The program in Figure VIII–1 rounds a number to the nearest integer, as shown in line 50. Line 60 rounds the same number to the nearest tenth, by adding 0.05 to the number and multiplying the result by 10. Then the INT function is applied and the result is divided by 10. The steps to round the number to the nearest hundredth follow the same pattern in line 70, but instead add 0.005 and multiply and divide by 100.

The Sign Function

The sign or SGN function determines the sign of a number. If $X > 0$, then SGN $(X) = 1$; if $X = 0$, then SGN $(X) = 0$; and if $X < 0$, then SGN $(X) = -1$. For example:

X	SGN (X)
8.5	1
0	0
-5.02	-1
-1005	-1

The Absolute Value Function

The absolute value or ABS function returns the absolute value of its argument. Remember that the absolute value is always positive or zero; if the argument has a negative value, the ABS function serves to remove the negative sign. For example:

X	ABS (X)
-2	2
0	0
3.54	3.54
-2.75	2.75

This function is often used to identify significant differences between given values. For example, the Internal Revenue Service may want to know which individuals owe the government a substantial sum or are owed a substantial sum by the government. The program in Figure

VIII–2 demonstrates how the absolute value function might be used to identify such individuals. Line 50 tests for persons who either owe or are being refunded at least $1,000.00.

The Random Number Function

The random number or RND function produces a random number between 0 and 1. The term **random** means that any value in a given set of values is equally likely to occur. The function is useful for any situation requiring an input quantity of which the exact value is unpredictable.

● FIGURE VIII–1
Rounding with the INT Function

```
00010 REM *** ROUND A NUMBER TO THE NEAREST INTEGER, ***
00020 REM *** TENTH, AND HUNDREDTH.                  ***
00030 REM
00040 INPUT "PLEASE ENTER A NUMBER ";NMBR
00050 R1 = INT(NMBR + 0.5)
00060 R2 = INT((NMBR + 0.05) * 10) / 10
00070 R3 = INT((NMBR + 0.005) * 100) / 100
00080 PRINT
00090 PRINT "NEAREST";TAB(12);"NEAREST";TAB(23);"NEAREST"
00100 PRINT "INTEGER";TAB(13);"TENTH";TAB(23);"HUNDREDTH"
00110 PRINT R1;TAB(13);R2;TAB(24);R3
00999 END
```

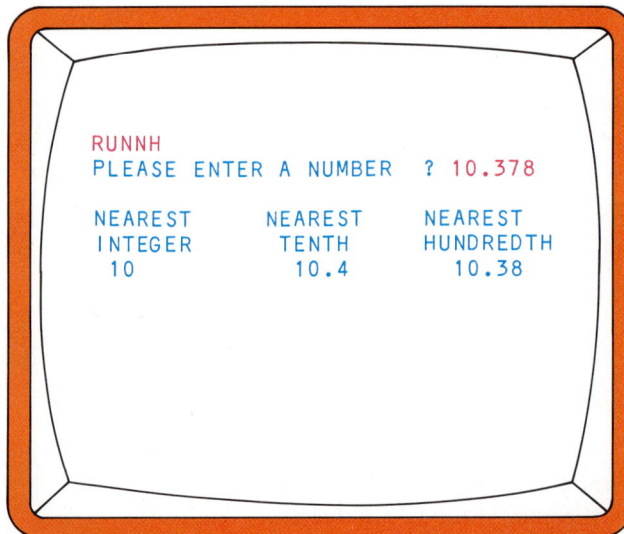

```
RUNNH
PLEASE ENTER A NUMBER  ? 10.378

NEAREST      NEAREST      NEAREST
INTEGER      TENTH        HUNDREDTH
 10           10.4         10.38
```

MICROCOMPUTERS	DIFFERENCE
Apple	None
IBM/Microsoft	None
Macintosh/Microsoft	None
TRS-80	None

● **COMPUTERS AND INFORMATION PROCESSING**

The RND function is particularly important in applications involving statistics, computer simulations, and games.

At first it might not seem hard to produce random values. This task is difficult, however, for machines of very precise structure and logic (such as computers). The numbers produced by a computer are not truly random, such as those resulting from a throw of dice, but are more accurately described as pseudorandom. In order to produce a sequence of seemingly unrelated numbers, the RND function uses a special algorithm that differs among the various computer manufacturers. The particular sequence of numbers generated by this algorithm depends on a value

● **FIGURE VIII–2**
Program Demonstrating the ABS Function

```
00010 REM *** IDENTIFY AUDIT CANDIDATES ***
00020 REM
00030 READ NME$,AMT
00040 WHILE NME$ <> "XXX"
00050     IF ABS(AMT) >= 1000 THEN PRINT NME$;" TO BE AUDITED"
00060     READ NME$,AMT
00070 NEXT
00080 REM *** DATA STATEMENTS ***
00090 DATA S.MANDELL,-1090,F.SINATRA,4150,I.ROSTOV,-8070
00100 DATA A.KURAGIN,999,XXX,0
00999 END
```

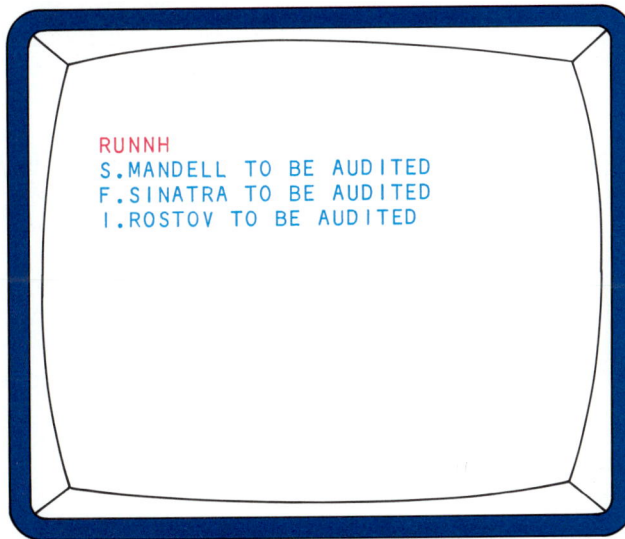

```
RUNNH
S.MANDELL TO BE AUDITED
F.SINATRA TO BE AUDITED
I.ROSTOV TO BE AUDITED
```

MICROCOMPUTERS	DIFFERENCE
Apple	No WHILE loop
IBM/Microsoft	70 WEND
Macintosh/Microsoft	70 WEND
TRS-80	70 WEND

known as a seed. When a new seed value is supplied to the algorithm, a new sequence of numbers is produced. If the seed is never changed, however, a program containing the RND function produces the same series of "random" numbers each time it is run.

The method used to reseed the random number generator varies among different computers. Often the seed is obtained from the computer's internal clock (e.g., the number of seconds after midnight) or is supplied by the program user. Some systems require that the RND function be used with an argument; other systems do not. The box "Random Numbers" shows how you can obtain random numbers between 0 and 1 on the systems considered in this text.

Random numbers greater than 1 can be produced by combining the RND function with other mathematical operations. The following formula generates a real random number R between L (low limit) and H (high limit):

$$R = RND * (H - L) + L$$

A formula to generate a random integer 1 between L and H is:

$$1 = INT (RND * (H - L) + L)$$

If the range of the random integer should include L and H, the value 1 is added to H − L as follows:

$$1 = INT (RND * (H - L + 1) + L)$$

● Random Numbers

Random numbers between 0 and 1 can be obtained as follows.

DECSYSTEM

The RND function needs no argument with the DECsystem. The function gives the same numbers each time the program is run unless it is reseeded: therefore, these numbers are not truly random. Once a program is working correctly, the RANDOMIZE statement can be inserted before the statement containing RND. The RANDOMIZE statement automatically reseeds the random number generator, thus causing the RND function to produce different numbers each time the program is run. An example follows:

```
00030 RANDOMIZE
        .
        .
        .
00060 X = RND
```

APPLE

Only one statement is needed with the Apple computer to produce different numbers each time the program runs. The RND function requires one argument; the sign and value of the argument affect the result. A positive argument, as in the following example, returns a random real number greater than or equal to 0 and less than 1:

```
10 X = RND(3)
```

If the argument is 0, as in the following example, the most recently generated random number is returned.

```
10 X = RND(0)
```

If the argument is negative, a particular random number sequence is started that is the same every time RND is used with that negative argument:

```
10 X = RND(-4)
```

If a RND call with a positive argument follows a RND call with a negative argument, it will generate the particular, repeatable sequence of numbers peculiar to the negative argument. Each different negative argument starts a different repeatable sequence.

IBM

As with the DECsystem, the RND function used alone on the IBM produces the same sequence of numbers each time the program runs. Used without an argument or with an optional positive argument, the RND function generates a random number between 0 and 1.

As with the Apple, an argument of 0 gives the last random number generated, and a negative argument begins a particular sequence that is the same every time that negative argument is used.

The RANDOMIZE statement is needed to provide a new random number seed and therefore give a truly random result. The format of this statement with the IBM is as follows:

RANDOMIZE [integer]
    or
RANDOMIZE TIMER

The integer, if used, must be changed each time the program runs to produce new numbers. If the integer is omitted, the prompt message

Random Number Seed (−32768 to 32767)?

asks the user to enter a number within this range.

If the function name TIMER is specified, a new number seed determined by the computer's clock is generated for each program run and no prompt appears. For example:

```
10 RANDOMIZE TIMER
20 PRINT RND
```

MACINTOSH

The RND function on the Macintosh works in the same manner as described for the IBM.

TRS-80

The RND function requires an argument of 0 to obtain a number between 0 and 1. The RANDOM statement serves to reseed the random number generator, and must precede the RND to give a truly random result. An example follows:

```
20 RANDOM
     .
     .
     .
60 X = RND(0)
```

The program in Figure VIII–3 shows how these formulas can be used to generate random numbers in any given range.

STRING FUNCTIONS

Up to this point, we have manipulated numbers but have done little with strings except print them out or compare them in IF and THEN tests. Many business applications require more sophisticated manipulations of strings.

● COMPUTERS AND INFORMATION PROCESSING

A string is simply a series of alphanumeric characters such as #OJQ$P or HORNBLOWER, H. Usually, BASIC requires that quotation marks be placed around strings.

BASIC string functions allow programmers to modify, **concatenate** (join together), compare, and analyze the composition of strings. These functions are useful for sorting lists of names, finding out subject matter in text, printing mailing lists, and so forth. For example, we can help the computer understand that John J. Simmons is the same as Simmons, John J. The most common string functions are listed in Table VIII–2.

Concatenation

It is possible to join strings together using the concatenation function. In business this is often desirable when working with names or addresses. The plus sign (+) serves as the concatenation operator. For example, the statement

```
00020 A$ = "NIGHT" + "MARE"
```

● FIGURE VIII–3
Random Number Program

```
00010 REM *** GENERATE RANDOM NUMBERS FOR A GIVEN RANGE. ***
00020 REM
00030 RANDOMIZE
00040 INPUT "ENTER LOW LIMIT, HIGH LIMIT";LO,HI
00050 PRINT
00060 PRINT
00070 R1 = RND * (HI - LO) + LO
00080 R2 = INT(R1)
00090 PRINT "BETWEEN ";LO;" AND ";HI;":"," REAL"," INTEGER"
00100 PRINT ,,R1,R2
00999 END
```

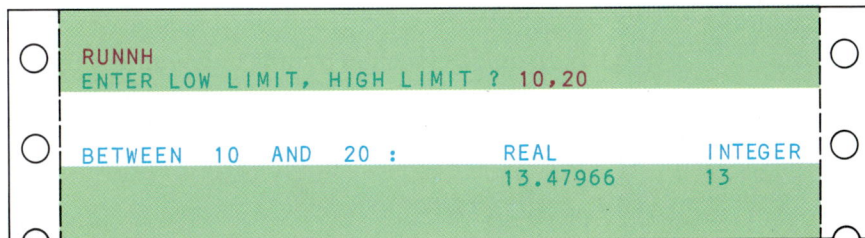

```
RUNNH
ENTER LOW LIMIT, HIGH LIMIT ? 10,20


BETWEEN   10   AND   20 :          REAL              INTEGER
                                   13.47966          13
```

MICROCOMPUTERS	DIFFERENCE
Apple	The RND function requires an argument.
IBM/Microsoft	10 20 13.70857 13
Macintosh/Microsoft	The RND function requires an argument.
TRS-80	10 20 13.70857 13

FUNCTION	OPERATION	EXAMPLE
string1 + string2	Concatenation; joins two strings	"KUNG" + "FU" is "KUNG FU"
ASCII (string) or ASC (string)	Returns the ASCII code for the first character in the string	IF A$ = "DOG", THEN ASCII (A$) is 68
CHR$ (integer expression)	Returns the string representation of the ASCII code of the expression	CHR$(68) is "D"
LEFT$ (string, integer expression)	Returns the number of leftmost characters of a string specified by the expression	LEFT$("ABCD",2) is "AB"
LEN (string)	Returns the length of a string	IF N$ = "HI THERE", THEN LEN(N$) is 8
MID$ (string, expression1, expression2)	Starting with the character at expression1, returns the number of characters specified by expression2	MID$("MARIE",2,3) is "ARI"
RIGHT$(string, expression)	*DEC:* Returns the rightmost characters of a string, starting with character specified by the expression	RIGHT$("ABCDE",2) is "BCDE"
	Micros: Returns the number of rightmost characters specified by the expression	RIGHT$("ABCDE",2) is "DE"
STR$(expression)	Converts a number to its string equivalent	STR$(123) is "123"
VAL(string)	Returns the numeric value of a number string	IF N$ = "352 63" THEN VAL(N$) is 35263

assigns the string NIGHTMARE to the variable A$. Similarly, the following segment results in X$ containing the value SAN FRANCISCO:

```
00020 A$ = "SAN"
00030 B$ = " FRAN"
00030 C$ = "CISCO"
00040 X$ = A$ + B$ + C$
```

The LEN Function

The length or LEN function returns the number of characters in the single string that is its argument. (Remember that blanks in quoted strings are counted as characters.) The following statement assigns the value 9 to NMBR:

```
00080 NMBR = LEN("YOUR NAME")
```

An example of how the LEN function might be used is given in the statements that follow, which print a centered heading for an 80-column screen:

```
00090 INPUT "ENTER HEADING";HEAD$
00100 X = LEN(HEAD$)
00110 CNTR = (80 - X) / 2
00120 PRINT TAB(CNTR);HEAD$
```

The LEFT$ and RIGHT$ Functions

The LEFT$ function returns a string that consists of the leftmost portion of the string argument, from the first character to the character position specified by the expression. For instance, the following statement assigns to X$ the value BE SEEING:

```
00030 X$ = LEFT$("BE SEEING YOU!",9)
```

The program in Figure VIII–4 demonstrates the LEFT$ function. Notice that the length of the string, which controls the number of times the FOR loop is executed, is determined in line 50 by the LEN function.

The microcomputer discussed in this book handle the RIGHT$ function differently than the DECsystem does. On the DECsystem, the RIGHT$ function returns the rightmost part of the string, from the *character po-*

● **FIGURE VIII–4**
The LEFT$ Function

```
00010 REM *** PRINT A PATTERN WITH THE LEFT$ FUNCTION ***
00020 REM
00030 INPUT "ENTER A STRING ";BLURB$
00040 PRINT
00050 LNG = LEN(BLURB$)
00060 FOR I = 1 TO LNG
00070   X$ = LEFT$(BLURB$,I)
00080   PRINT X$
00090 NEXT I
00099 END
```

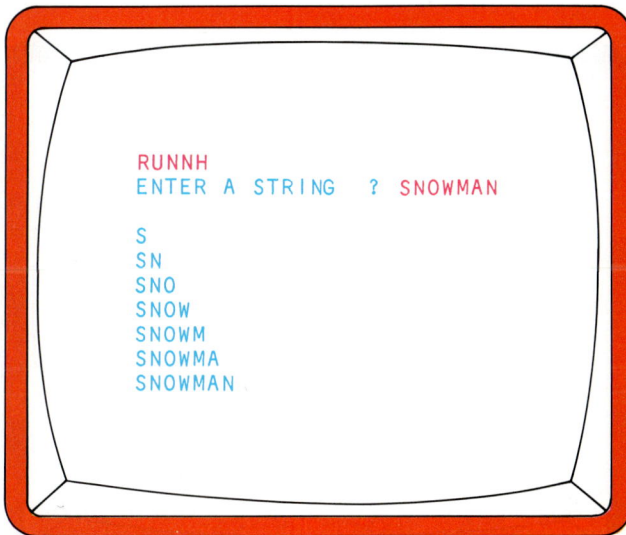

```
RUNNH
ENTER A STRING   ?  SNOWMAN

S
SN
SNO
SNOW
SNOWM
SNOWMA
SNOWMAN
```

MICROCOMPUTERS	DIFFERENCE
Apple	None
IBM/Microsoft	None
Macintosh/Microsoft	None
TRS-80	None

sition given by the expression to the end of the string. Thus the following statement assigns the value SEEING YOU! to X$:

```
00030 X$ = RIGHT$("BE SEEING YOU!",4)
```

With the microcomputers, however, this function returns the *number of characters* specified by the expression from the right end of the string. On these systems, the following instruction would assign to X$ the last nine characters of the string. In this case the value EING YOU!:

```
30 X$ = RIGHT$("BE SEEING YOU!",9)
```

The programs in Figures VIII–5 and VIII–6 demonstrate the RIGHT$ func-

● **FIGURE VIII–5**
The RIGHT$ Function on the DECsystem

```
00010 REM *** PRINT A PATTERN WITH THE RIGHT$ FUNCTION ***
00020 REM
00030 INPUT "ENTER ANY STRING ";BLURB$
00040 PRINT
00050 LNG = LEN(BLURB$)
00060 FOR I = 1 TO LNG
00070    X$ = RIGHT$(BLURB$,I)
00080    PRINT X$
00090 NEXT I
00099 END
```

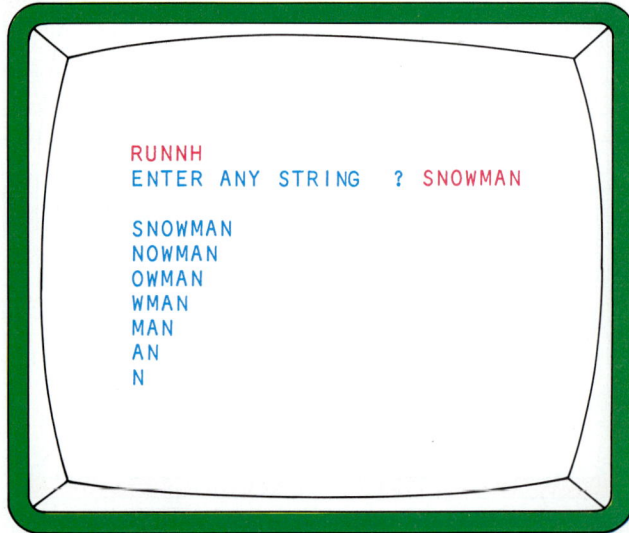

```
RUNNH
ENTER ANY STRING   ? SNOWMAN

SNOWMAN
NOWMAN
OWMAN
WMAN
MAN
AN
N
```

MICROCOMPUTERS	DIFFERENCE
Apple	Refer to Figure VIII-9.
IBM/Microsoft	Refer to Figure VIII-9.
Macintosh/Microsoft	Refer to Figure VIII-9.
TRS-80	Refer to Figure VIII-9.

● COMPUTERS AND INFORMATION PROCESSING

tion as used on the DECsystem and the IBM respectively. Notice how line 60 differs between the two programs to produce the same output.

The LEFT$ function is often useful when comparing character strings. Suppose a program asks the user to answer a yes or no question but does not specify whether the question should be answered by typing the entire word YES or NO or just the first letter Y or N. We can use the LEFT$ function to compare just the first character of the user's response, allowing the user to type either YES/NO or Y/N. The example that follows illustrates this:

```
00010  INPUT "ARE YOU MARRIED ";A$
00020  A$ = LEFT$(A$,1)
00030  IF A$ = "Y" THEN PRINT "YES" ELSE PRINT "NO"
```

```
10 REM *** PRINT A PATTERN WITH THE RIGHT$ FUNCTION ***
20 REM
30 INPUT "ENTER ANY STRING ";BLURB$
40 PRINT
50 LNG = LEN(BLURB$)
60 FOR I = LNG TO 1 STEP -1
70    X$ = RIGHT$(BLURB$,I)
80    PRINT X$
90 NEXT I
99 END
```

```
RUN
ENTER ANY STRING ? SNOWMAN

SNOWMAN
NOWMAN
OWMAN
WMAN
MAN
AN
N
```

MICROCOMPUTERS	DIFFERENCE
Apple	None
IBM/Microsoft	None
Macintosh/Microsoft	None
TRS-80	None

The MID$ Function

The MID$ function is more complicated. Here is the general format:

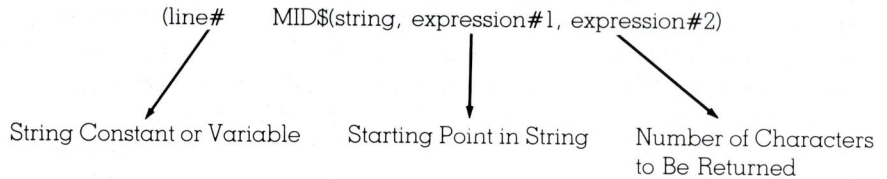

(line#   MID$(string, expression#1, expression#2)

String Constant or Variable   Starting Point in String   Number of Characters to Be Returned

Sometimes expression 2 is omitted; in that case, the characters—from the starting point to the end of the string—are returned. The following statement assigns to X$ a string four characters long, starting at the fifth character: NDIP.

```
00020 X$ = MID$("SERENDIPITY",5,4)
```

The MID$ function is useful when you want to look at some middle characters of a string. For instance, assume you have a file of telephone numbers, and you want to print out only those with an exchange of 352. Here are the telephone numbers:

```
491-354-1070
491-353-0011
491-352-3520
491-352-1910
491-352-7350
491-353-9822
```

The program in Figure VIII–7 will compare the exchange of "352" and print the telephone numbers that qualify.

The ASCII and CHR$ Functions

The ASCII function returns the ASCII value of the first character of its string argument, which can be a string constant, variable, or expression.

On the DECsystem, the function name is ASCII; the same function on the microcomputers discussed in this book is called ASC, and its format is the same as for the DEC. Table VIII–3 lists characters and their corresponding ASCII values. For example, the following statement examines the first character of the argument, R, and assigns its ASCII value of 82 to the variable RVALUE:

```
00030 RVALUE = ASCII("RETURN A VALUE")
```

The CHR$ function performs the reverse operation of the ASCII function: It returns the single character that corresponds to a given ASCII value. The following statement assigns to MES$ the value III!

```
00070 MES$ = CHR$(72) + CHR$(73) + CHR$(33)
```

The ASCII and CHR$ functions are demonstrated in the program in Figure VIII–8, which prints a listing of the alphabet with its corresponding ASCII codes.

The ASCII and CHR$ functions are helpful in allowing programs to respond to both lowercase and uppercase input. Using these functions, a program can allow the user to answer a yes or no question with y, Y, n, or N. Table VIII–3 shows that the codes for the lower case letters range from 97 through 122, and those for uppercase letters range from 65 through 90. An IF/THEN statement can be used to compare the ASCII value of the user response to 96. If the value is greater than 96, a lowercase letter has been typed; if the value is less than 96, the letter is uppercase.

Once the program has determined the type of letter, it can convert the letter to either uppercase or lowercase for comparison. An uppercase letter can be changed to lowercase by adding 32 to the ASCII value, and a lowercase letter can be made uppercase by subtracting 32. The fol-

● **FIGURE VIII–7**
The MID$ Function

```
00010 REM *** PRINT NUMBERS WITH A 352 EXCHANGE ***
00020 REM
00030 FOR I = 1 TO 6
00040     READ TNUM$
00050     IF MID$(TNUM$,5,3) = "352" THEN PRINT TNUM$
00060 NEXT I
00070 REM
00080 REM *** DATA STATEMENTS ***
00090 DATA 491-354-1070,491-353-0011,491-352-3520
00100 DATA 491-352-1910,491-352-7350,491-353-9822
00999 END
```

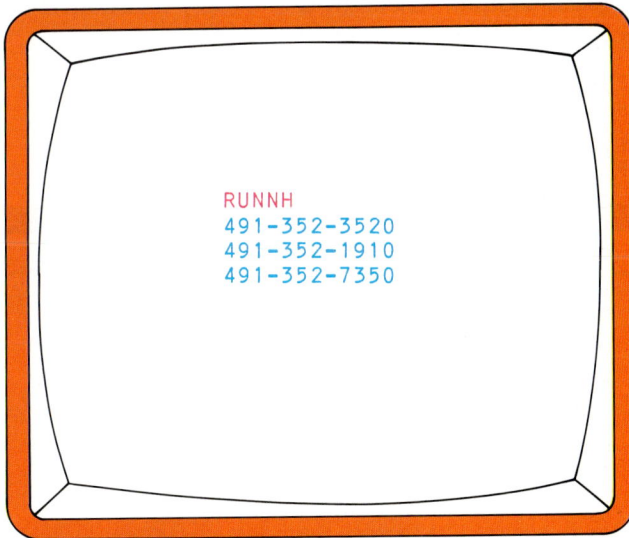

```
RUNNH
491-352-3520
491-352-1910
491-352-7350
```

MICROCOMPUTERS	DIFFERENCE
Apple	None
IBM/Microsoft	None
Macintosh/Microsoft	None
TRS-80	None

	32	!	33	"	34	#	35
$	36	%	37	&	38	'	39
(	40	)	41	*	42	+	43
,	44	–	45	.	46	/	47
0	48	1	49	2	50	3	51
4	52	5	53	6	54	7	55
8	56	9	57	:	58	;	59
<	60	=	61	>	62	?	63
ə	64	A	65	B	66	C	67
D	68	E	69	F	70	G	71
H	72	I	73	J	74	K	75
L	76	M	77	N	78	O	79
P	80	Q	81	R	82	S	83
T	84	U	85	V	86	W	87
X	88	Y	89	Z	90	[	91
\	92	]	93	^	94	_	95
`	96	a	97	b	98	c	99
d	100	e	101	f	102	g	103
h	104	i	105	j	106	k	107
l	108	m	109	n	110	o	111
p	112	q	113	r	114	s	115
t	116	u	117	v	118	w	119
x	120	y	121	z	122	{	123
l	124						

lowing program segment checks a user's reply and converts it to upper-case if necessary in order to compare it.

```
00030 INPUT "ARE YOU ALLERGIC TO ANY MEDICATIONS? (Y/N) ";AN$
00040 X = ASCII(AN$)
00050 IF X > 96 THEN AN$ = CHR$(X - 32)
00060 IF AN$ <> "Y" THEN PRINT "NO ALLERGIES"
```

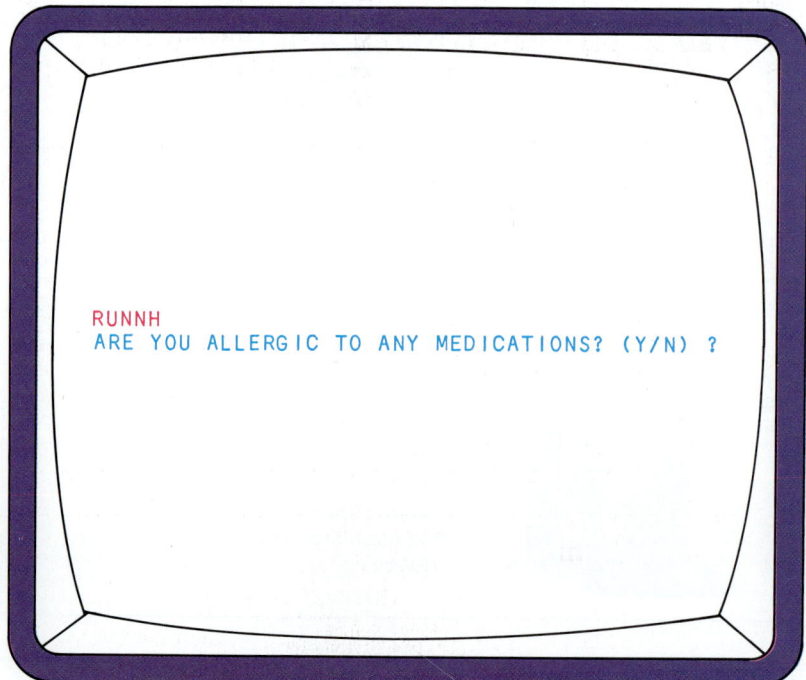

```
RUNNH
ARE YOU ALLERGIC TO ANY MEDICATIONS? (Y/N) ?
```

```
00010 REM *** ASCII ALPHABET TABLE ***
00020 REM
00030 PRINT "CHARACTER","ASCII CODE"
00040 PRINT
00050 INDX = ASCII("A")
00060 FOR I = 1 TO 26
00070    PRINT CHR$(INDX),INDX
00080    INDX = INDX + 1
00090 NEXT I
00099 END
```

```
RUNNH
CHARACTER        ASCII CODE

A                65
B                66
C                67
D                68
E                69
F                70
G                71
H                72
I                73
J                74
K                75
L                76
M                77
N                78
O                79
P                80
Q                81
R                82
S                83
T                84
U                85
V                86
W                87
X                88
Y                89
Z                90
```

MICROCOMPUTERS	DIFFERENCE
Apple	50 X = ASC("A")
IBM/Microsoft	50 X = ASC("A")
Macintosh/Microsoft	50 X = ASC("A")
TRS-80	50 X = ASC("A")

The VAL and STR$ Functions

The VAL function converts a numeric string expression (such as "12.34") into its equivalent numeric value.

The characters of the argument string can include the digits 0 through 9, the plus and minus signs, and the decimal point. Any leading blanks in the string are ignored. The microcomputers discussed in this book also allow the string argument to contain nonnumeric characters; see the box "VAL Function Differences."

By using the VAL function, it is possible to change a number in a character string to a number that can be used in mathematical computations. The program in Figure VIII–9 reads an integer value to a string variable and uses the VAL function to compute the sum of its digits.

The STR$ function performs the reverse of the VAL function operation: it converts a real number to a string. Its general format is as follows, where the expression evaluates as a numeric value:

STR$ (expression)

The program in Figure VIII–10 demonstrates the STR$ function. Remember that once a number has been converted to a string, it can no longer be used in mathematical computations unless it is converted back to a numeric value.

● VAL Function Differences

If the string argument of the VAL function contains nonnumeric characters (other than leading blanks), the DECsystem gives an error message. Such a string is handled differently on the Apple, IBM, Macintosh, and TRS-80: If the first nonblank character of the string is nonnumeric, the function returns a value of zero. For example, the following statement would output 0:

```
00070 PRINT VAL(" BG, OH  43402")
```

Otherwise, the function examines the string one character at a time until an unacceptable character is encountered. On all of the systems mentioned above, a blank is acceptable within a numeric string; it is simply ignored. The following statement would be valid and would assign to N1 the value 1084:

```
00070 N1 = VAL(" 1084 WELSH VIEW DR.")
```

● User-Defined Functions

The DEF, or definition, statement can be used by the programmer to define a function not already included in the BASIC language. Once a function has been defined, the programmer can use it as many times as necessary in the program. The DEF statement can be placed anywhere in the program before the function is first called, but in the interests of

● COMPUTERS AND INFORMATION PROCESSING

clarity and organization, all DEF statements should appear near the beginning of the program. The general format of the DEF statement is as follows:

line# DEF function name (argument list) = expression

The function name consists of the letters FN followed by a valid variable name (e.g., FNROUND, FNAREA, or FNX). The arguments are one or

```
00010 REM *** FIND THE SUM OF THE DIGITS OF AN INTEGER ***
00020 REM *** MAJOR VARIABLES:                          ***
00030 REM ***    NSTR$    -    NUMBER STRING            ***
00040 REM ***    DIG$     -    SINGLE DIGIT CHARACTER   ***
00050 REM ***    NDIG     -    NUMERIC VALUE OF DIGIT   ***
00060 REM
00070 SUM = 0
00080 INPUT "ENTER A NON-NEGATIVE INTEGER ";NSTR$
00090 LONG = LEN(NSTR$)
00100 FOR I = 1 TO LONG
00110    DIG$ = MID$(NSTR$,I,1)
00120    NDIG = VAL(DIG$)
00130    SUM = SUM + NDIG
00140 NEXT I
00150 PRINT "SUM = ";SUM
00999 END
```

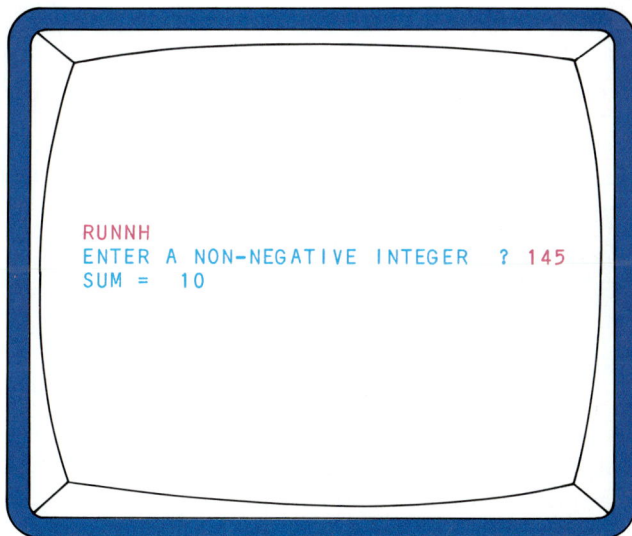

```
RUNNH
ENTER A NON-NEGATIVE INTEGER  ? 145
SUM =  10
```

MICROCOMPUTERS	DIFFERENCE
Apple	None
IBM/Microsoft	None
Macintosh/Microsoft	None
TRS-80	None

```
00010 REM *** LOCAL MAILING ADDRESS ***
00020 REM
00030 INPUT "ENTER HOUSE NUMBER";NMBR
00040 INPUT "ENTER STREET";ROAD$
00050 REM
00060 REM *** CONVERT NUMBER TO STRING ***
00070 NMB$ = STR$(NMBR)
00080 PRINT
00090 PRINT NMB$ + " " + ROAD$
00099 END
```

```
RUNNH
ENTER HOUSE NUMBER ? 1084
ENTER STREET ? WELSH VIEW DRIVE

1084 WELSH VIEW DRIVE
```

MICROCOMPUTERS	DIFFERENCE
Apple	None
IBM/Microsoft	None
Macintosh/Microsoft	None
TRS-80	None

more variables that are replaced by values given when the function is called (the Apple allows only one argument). The expression contains the operations performed by the function; it evaluates as a single value, which is returned by the function. The entire DEF statement cannot exceed one logical line. (The DECsystem also limits it to 33 characters.)

A call to a user-defined function has the following format:

function name (expression list)

The function name matches a function name appearing in a previous DEF statement. The one or more expressions are evaluated, and the results are used to replace the arguments of the DEF statement on a one-to-one basis.

The following segment demonstrates the use of a simple user-defined function. When the computer encounters line 10, it stores in memory the definition for the function FNR. Line 20 initializes PRICE to 5.50. When the computer encounters line 30, it evaluates the expression in parentheses at 5.50; then, using the definition for FNR, it substitutes this value for X. Therefore the expression (X + 20)/2 evaluates as 12.75. This value becomes the function value, which is printed by line 30.

```
00010 DEF FNR(X) = (X + 20) / 2
00020 PRICE = 5.50
00030 PRINT FNR(PRICE)
```

```
RUNNH
  12.75
```

The arguments in the DEF statement are sometimes called dummy arguments because they have no real values; they only show how the input values of the function will be used. A dummy argument can have the same name as a regular program variable without affecting the value of the regular variable, as shown in the following example.

```
00010 N = 3
00020 DEF FNCUBE(N) = N * N * N
00030 PRINT N
00040 Y = 4
00050 PRINT FNCUBE(Y)
00060 PRINT N
```

```
RUNNH
  3
  64
  3
```

The expression of the function definition can contain variables that do not appear in the argument list. When the function is called, the most current values of these variables are used, as demonstrated in Figure VIII–11.

The expression of the function definition can also contain calls to previously defined functions or library functions. For example, the definition of line 60 is valid:

```
00050 DEF FNMULT(X,Y) = X * Y
00060 DEF FNCALC(X,Y) = SGN(X) + FNMULT(X,Y)
```

However, a function definition cannot call itself. The following statement is invalid:

```
00060 DEF FNMULT(X,Y) = FNMULT(X,Y) + X + Y
```

Many systems (including those discussed in this book, with the exception of the Apple) also allow the programmer to define string functions. The type of a function, like that of a variable, is indicated by its name. For example, the function FNA$ specifies a string function, while FNA is a real value function. Figure VIII–12 demonstrates a user-defined string function that prints a name in the format of last name, first initial.

● A Programming Problem

PROBLEM DEFINITION

Create an interactive program that generates a mathematical sequence and allows a player to guess the next number in the sequence. The program should show the player the first three numbers of the sequence and offer him or her the option of seeing the next number. If so desired, it should print the next number in the sequence; the player may see as many numbers as he or she requests. The player should then be asked for a guess as to the next number, and the program should print appropriate messages in response to the guess. If the guess is correct, the game is over; otherwise, the player is again given the option of seeing more numbers.

The program should allow for upper- or lowercase responses of either

```
00010 REM *** CALCULATE TOTAL COST ***
00020 REM
00030 DEF FNCALC(X,Z) = (X * Z) + ((X * Z) * TAX)
00040 TAX = 0.10
00050 INPUT "ENTER QUANTITY, PRICE ";QUANT,PRICE
00060 TPRICE = FNCALC(QUANT,PRICE)
00070 PRINT "TOTAL COST = ";TPRICE
00099 END
```

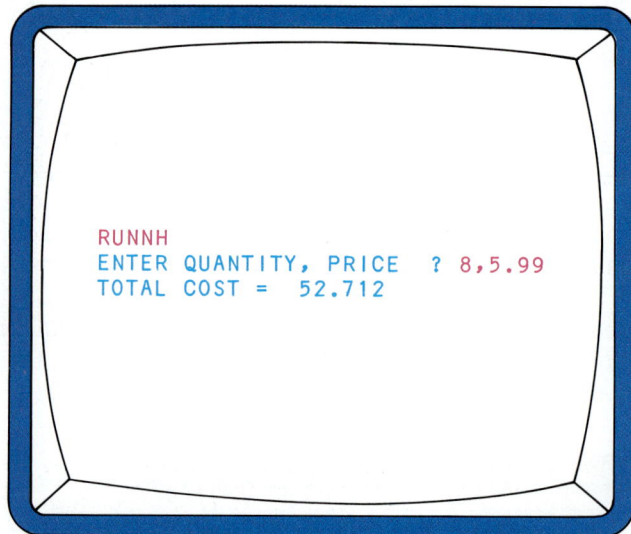

```
RUNNH
ENTER QUANTITY, PRICE  ? 8,5.99
TOTAL COST =  52.712
```

MICROCOMPUTERS	DIFFERENCE
Apple	Only 1 argument allowed for user defined functions.
IBM/Microsoft	None
Macintosh/Microsoft	None
TRS-80	None

● COMPUTERS AND INFORMATION PROCESSING

a full word or a first letter, and guesses should be input as character strings to guard against an error in case the player enters a nonnumeric guess. The values of the sequence should be such that the nth member is generated by multiplying n times itself and adding to it the value $n-1$. A sample game is shown below:

```
RUNNH
CURRENT SEQUENCE
  1    5    11
DO YOU WANT TO SEE THE NEXT NUMBER  ? Y
CURRENT SEQUENCE
  1    5    11    19
DO YOU WANT TO SEE THE NEXT NUMBER  ? N
ENTER YOUR GUESS:   ? 29
THAT'S CORRECT
```

● **FIGURE VIII–12**
User-Defined String Function

```
00010 REM *** REVERSE A NAME ***
00020 REM
00030 DEF FNREV$(A$,B$) = B$ + "," + LEFT$(A$,1) + "."
00040 INPUT "ENTER FIRST NAME ";FIRST$
00050 INPUT "ENTER LAST NAME ";LAST$
00060 RNAM$ = FNREV$(FIRST$,LAST$)
00070 PRINT
00080 PRINT RNAM$
00099 END
```

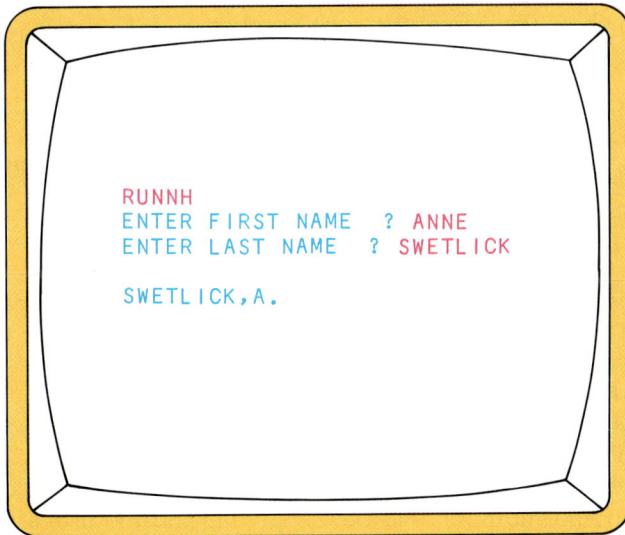

```
RUNNH
ENTER FIRST NAME   ? ANNE
ENTER LAST NAME    ? SWETLICK

SWETLICK,A.
```

MICROCOMPUTERS	DIFFERENCE
Apple	Only 1 argument allowed for user defined functions.
IBM/Microsoft	None
Macintosh/Microsoft	None
TRS-80	None

SOLUTION DESIGN

Because this is an interactive program, it is helpful to consider what steps must be taken to enable the player to enter a correct guess—the action that ends the program. In order to begin, the player must be able to see a part of the sequence. Each element is calculated according to the same formula, so a user-defined function could be used in generating the sequence.

The second major step, and therefore a second subroutine of the program, must give the player the option of seeing another number. In order to do this, the program must prompt the player with a yes or no question. The player's response at this point could be converted to a Y or N and checked by another subroutine. If the answer is yes, then the first step of the program (printing the current number sequence) must be performed again. This process of prompting the player and displaying the sequence can continue until the player answers no; the repetition should suggest a loop.

The third major step of the program is to allow a guess to be entered. This step involves prompting the user, checking to see if the guess is correct (and therefore generating the next number of the sequence), and then printing an appropriate message. The needed steps thus far are as follows:

1. Print first three numbers of sequence
2. Offer to show the player the next number
3. Offer the player the chance to guess

A correct guess ends the game; otherwise, the program must continue to offer the player more numbers and accept guesses until a correct guess is entered. These two processes could therefore be initiated within a loop.

2.a. Convert player response
2.b. Print next number in sequence

The structure chart for this solution is shown in Figure VIII–13. Each of the steps on the second level of the diagram represents a subroutine. Notice that the subroutine which offers the player another number calls two other subroutines, and that one of these is a subroutine that has already been called by the main program.

The variables needed by the program are relatively few. The input variables consist of the user's input, a Y/N response to the question of whether another number is to be displayed, and the user's guess. Program variables needed are a counter to keep track of the numbers in the currently displayed sequence, and a flag to indicate a correct guess. The only output is a message to the user, so no variable is required. The needed variables are summarized below:

Input variables

player response	(AN$)
player guess	(GUES$)

Program variables

count of numbers generated	(CNT)
flag for correct guess	(OK$)

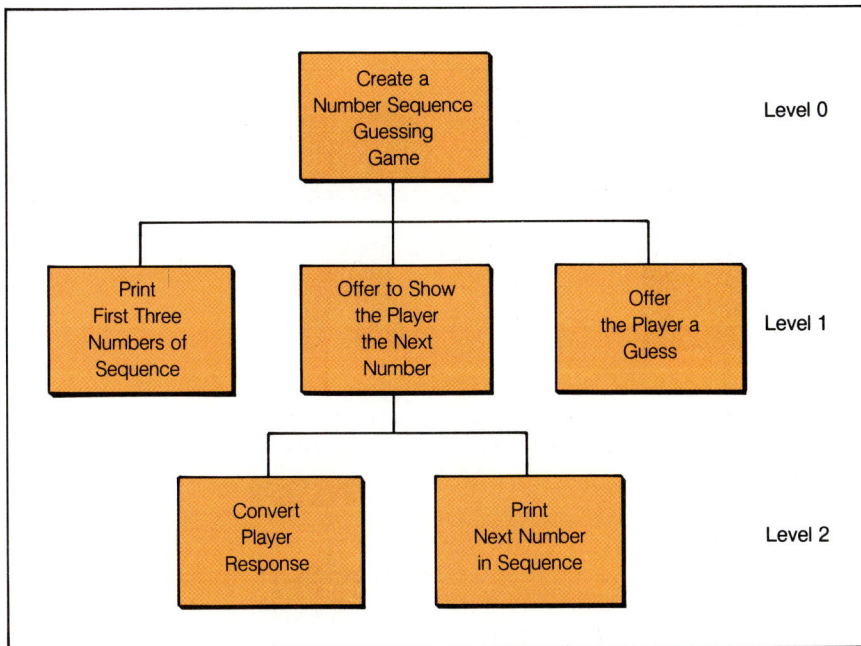

Level 0

Create a
Number Sequence
Guessing
Game

Print
First Three
Numbers of
Sequence

Offer to Show
the Player
the Next
Number

Offer
the Player a
Guess

Level 1

Convert
Player
Response

Print
Next Number
in Sequence

Level 2

THE PROGRAM

The program in Figure VIII–14 uses four subroutines and one user-defined function (defined in line 90) to solve the problem. The variable CNT is used to keep track of the quantity of numbers which have been displayed; this is initially set to 3 in line 120 to begin the game. The variable OK$, initialized to "N," is used as a flag that indicates whether a correct guess has been given and the game is to end.

The WHILE loop of lines 190 through 220 allows the player to see numbers and make guesses until the answer flag equals "Y." The subroutine of lines 1000 through 1100 displays the current sequence by calling the user-defined function FNNXT. The second subroutine asks the player if another number is needed; the answer is converted to a Y or N by calling the fourth subroutine in lines 4000 through 4090. Each time the player responds to a yes/no question, his or her answer is checked in this way.

When the player does not want to see more numbers, the subroutine beginning at line 3000 is called to accept a guess, which is entered as a string in line 3060. The next number of the sequence is computed in line 3100 and converted to a string to be compared to the guess. In line 3110, the flag OK$ is set to reflect a correct or incorrect guess, and control is passed back to the main program at line 220. The WHILE statement then checks the flag and either repeats the entire process or terminates the game.

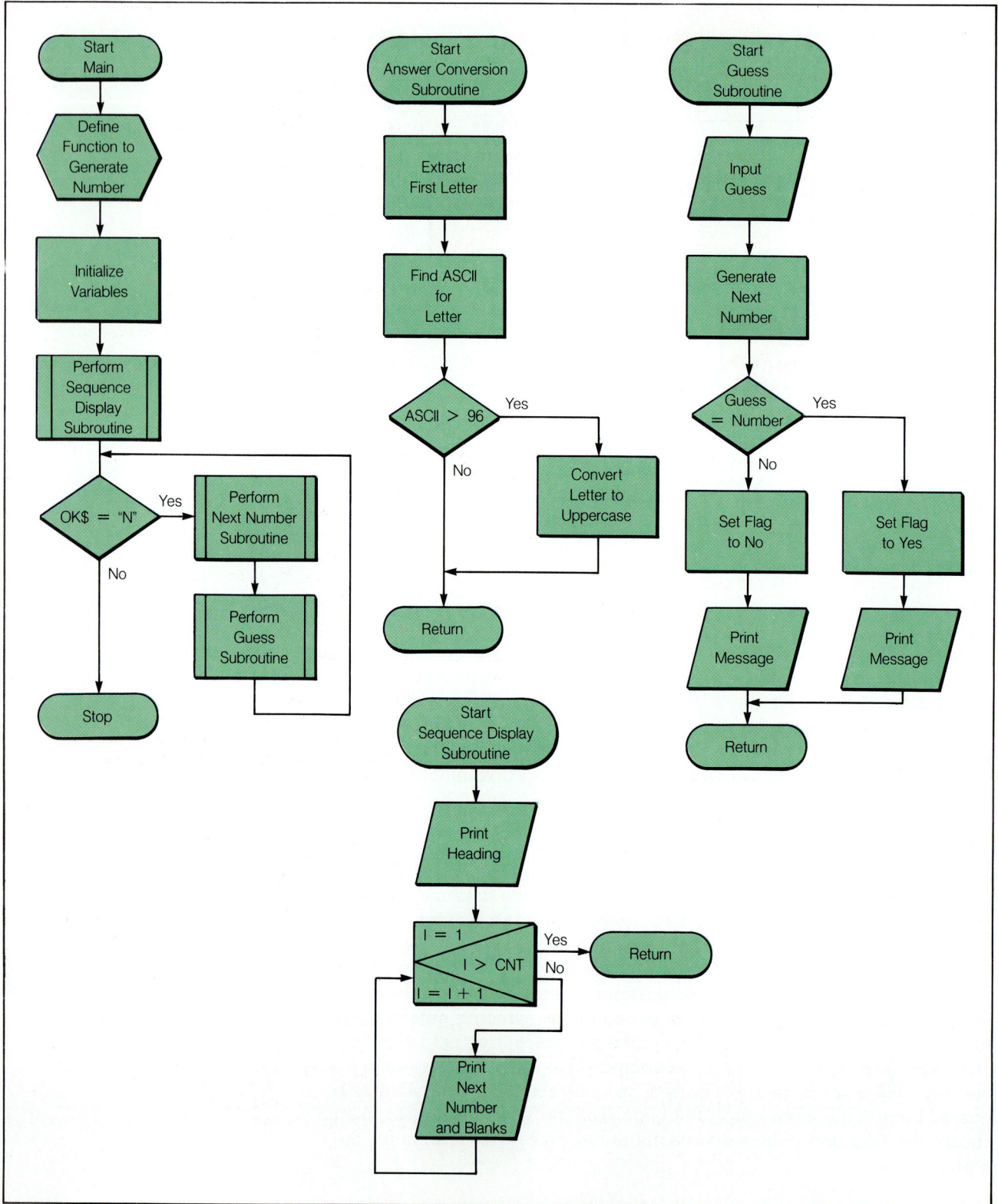

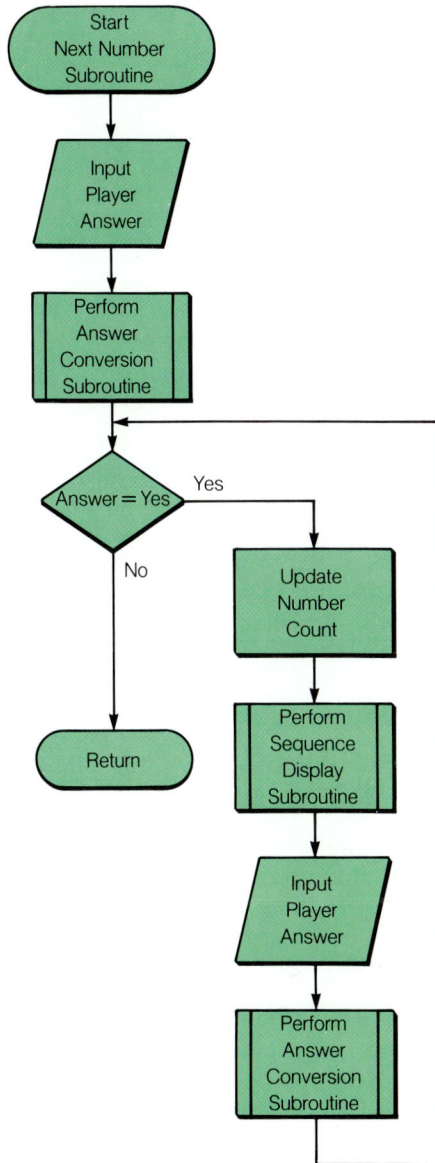

Pseudocode

Begin main program
Define function to generate sequence
Initialize number count and solution flag
Perform sequence display subroutine
Begin loop, do until solution flag = yes
    Perform next number subroutine
    Perform guess subroutine
End loop
End main program

Begin sequence display subroutine
Print heading
Begin loop, do for current value of number count times
    Print number and blanks
End loop
End sequence display subroutine

Begin next number subroutine
Ask player if a number is desired
Perform answer conversion subroutine
Begin loop, do until answer = no
    Update number count
    Perform sequence display subroutine
    Ask player if a number is desired
    Perform answer conversion subroutine
End loop
End next number subroutine

Begin guess subroutine
Ask player for guess
Generate next number
If guess = next number
    Then set solution flag to yes and print message
    Else set solution flag to no and print message
End if
End guess subroutine

Begin answer conversion subroutine
Extract first letter of answer
Get ASCII code of letter
If code > 96
    Then letter is lowercase so convert to uppercase
End if
End answer conversion subroutine

```
00010 REM *** NUMBER SEQUENCE GUESSING GAME    ***
00020 REM
00030 REM *** MAJOR VARIABLES:                 ***
00040 REM ***   CNT   COUNT OF NUMBERS GENERATED ***
00050 REM ***   AN$   PLAYER RESPONSE (Y/N)     ***
00060 REM ***   GUES  PLAYER GUESS              ***
00070 REM ***   OK    IS GUESS CORRECT? (Y/N)   ***
00080 REM
00090 DEF FNXT(X) = (X * X) + (X - 1)
00100 REM
```

```
00110 REM *** INITIALIZE VARIABLES ***
00120 CNT = 3
00130 OK$ = "N"
00140 REM
00150 REM *** DISPLAY INITIAL SEQUENCE ***
00160 GOSUB 1000
00170 REM
00180 REM *** LOOP TO DISPLAY NUMBERS AND ACCEPT GUESSES UNTIL CORRECT ***
00190 WHILE OK$ = "N"
00200  GOSUB 2000
00210  GOSUB 3000
00220 NEXT
00230 GOTO 9999
01000 REM
01010 REM *****************************************************************
01020 REM ***                    SUBROUTINE 1                        ***
01030 REM *****************************************************************
01040 REM ***               DISPLAY CURRENT SEQUENCE                 ***
01050 REM
01060 PRINT "CURRENT SEQUENCE "
01070 FOR I = 1 TO CNT
01080    PRINT FNXT(I);"  ";
01090 NEXT I
01100 RETURN
02000 REM
02010 REM *****************************************************************
02020 REM ***                    SUBROUTINE 2                        ***
02030 REM *****************************************************************
02040 REM ***              PROVIDE ADDITIONAL NUMBERS                ***
02050 REM
02060 PRINT
02070 INPUT "DO YOU WANT TO SEE THE NEXT NUMBER ";AN$
02080 GOSUB 4000
02090 WHILE AN$ = "Y"
02100    CNT = CNT + 1
02110    GOSUB 1000
02120    PRINT
02130    INPUT "DO YOU WANT TO SEE THE NEXT NUMBER ";AN$
02140    GOSUB 4000
02150 NEXT
02160 RETURN
03000 REM
03010 REM *****************************************************************
03020 REM ***                    SUBROUTINE 3                        ***
03030 REM *****************************************************************
03040 REM ***              ACCEPT AND TEST PLAYER'S GUESS            ***
03050 REM
03060 INPUT "ENTER YOUR GUESS: ";GUES$
03070 REM
03080 REM *** GENERATE NEXT NUMBER AND TEST GUESS ***
03090 TEMP = CNT + 1
03100 NXT$ = STR$(FNXT(TEMP)
03110 IF NXT$ = GUES$ THEN OK$ = "Y" \ PRINT "THAT'S CORRECT"
       ELSE OK$ = "N" \ PRINT "SORRY, INCORRECT "
03120 RETURN
04000 REM
04010 REM *****************************************************************
04020 REM ***                    SUBROUTINE 4                        ***
04030 REM *****************************************************************
04040 REM ***              CONVERT PLAYER RESPONSE TO Y/N            ***
04050 REM
04060 AN$ = LEFT$(AN$,1)
04070 B = ASCII(AN$)
04080 IF B > 96 THEN AN$ = CHR$(B - 32)
04090 RETURN
09999 END
```

```
RUNNH
CURRENT SEQUENCE
 1    5    11
DO YOU WANT TO SEE THE NEXT NUMBER  ? Y
CURRENT SEQUENCE
 1    5    11    19
DO YOU WANT TO SEE THE NEXT NUMBER  ? N
ENTER YOUR GUESS:   ? 29
THAT'S CORRECT
```

MICROCOMPUTERS	DIFFERENCE
Apple	No WHILE loop; 4070 B = ASC(AN$)
IBM/Microsoft	220 WEND; 2150 WEND; 4070 B = ASC(AN$)
Macintosh/Microsoft	220 WEND; 2150 WEND; 4070 B = ASC(AN$)
TRS-80	220 WEND; 2150 WEND; 4070 B = ASC(AN$)

● Summary Points

● The BASIC language includes several library functions that can make complicated mathematical operations easier to program.

● The trigonometric functions are SIN (X), COS (X), TAN (X), and ATN (X), where X is in radians.

● The exponential or EXP function calculates EXP (X) = e^x, and the natural logarithm or LOG (X) function is the reverse of that function.

● The SQR (X) function returns the square root of its argument.

● The INT (X) function computes the greatest integer less than or equal to the value specified as the argument.

● The SGN (X) function produces a 1, 0, or −1, depending on whether the argument is positive, zero, or negative respectively.

● The ABS (X) function returns the absolute value of its argument.

- The programmer can define functions by using the DEF statement. A user-defined function definition cannot exceed one line and must precede any reference to it in a program.
- BASIC string functions permit modification, concatenation, comparison, and analysis of the composition of strings.
- The concatenation operation (+) joins two strings together.
- The LEN function is used to find the number of characters in a string.
- The LEFT$ function returns a specified number of leftmost characters of a string.
- The RIGHT$ function returns the specified rightmost characters of a string.
- The MID$ function enables the programmer to gain access to characters in the middle of a string.
- The ASCII function returns the ASCII code for the first character in a string.
- The CHR$ function returns the string representation of the ASCII code of the expression.
- The VAL (X) function is used to find the numeric equivalent of a string expression.
- The STR$ function acts as a reverse of the VAL (X) function by converting a number to its string equivalent.

● Review Questions

1. What are the allowable arguments of a function?
2. How many values can be returned by a function?
3. What is the result of INT (−3.4)?
4. Write a BASIC statement using the INT (X) function to round a number to the nearest hundredth.
5. Where is the function definition placed in a program?
6. What is meant by string concatenation?
7. The _____ function returns the number of characters in a string.
8. Explain the use of the LEFT$, RIGHT$, and MID$ functions.
9. What will the output from this instruction be?

00030 PRINT STR$(342) + STR$(58)

10. Give the output from the following statement:

00020 PRINT MID$("MICHAEL JACKSON",9,4)

● Debugging Exercises

Identify the following program segments that contain errors and debug them.

```
1. 00010 READ X
   00020 PRINT FNA(X)
   00030 DEF FNA(Y) = EXP(Y) + 5
   00040 DATA 22
```

2.
```
00010 FOR I = 1 TO 5
00020    READ N$
00030    N = STR$(N$)
00040    N = N * .5
00050    PRINT N
00060 NEXT I
```

● Programming Problems

1. Write an interactive program that accepts a Fahrenheit temperature and prints the centigrade equivalent. Define one function to use the following formula:

$C = 5 / 9 (F - 32)$

A second function should round the results to the nearest tenth of a degree. Let the user enter temperatures as long as desired. Test the program with the following data: 32, 77, 120.

2. Write a program to print the trigonometric functions sine, cosine, and tangent for 1° to 15°. Define a function to convert degrees to radians and another function to round the results to four decimal places. The output should be printed in a format similar to this:

DEGREES	SIN X	COS X	TAN X
XX	X.XXXX	X.XXXX	X.XXXX
.	.	.	.
.	.	.	.

3. Write a program to simulate the throwing of a dice twenty times. After the twenty throws, print the total occurrence of each number (1 to 6). Generate random numbers to represent the tosses. Define a function to generate the needed random numbers.

4. Write a program that reads a list of words and prints only those words that begin with whatever prefix is entered by the user. Use the following data: EXCESS, EXCOMMUNICATE, EXCELLENT, REWARD, RENUMER-ATE, REWORD, RECEIVE, PREPARE, PREFIX, PREVIEW, SUBTOTAL, SUBMARINE, SUBTRACT.

5. An auto parts store has a system to help detect errors in recording inventory. The last two digits of every stock number must be the sum of the preceding three digits. For example, the stock number QB412.07 is valid because 07 is the sum of 4 + 1 + 2. Write a program that inputs stock numbers and prints a message for any invalid numbers. Use the following data:

QB371.11
UT491.14
UT307.11

Section IX
Arrays

Introduction

All of our programs thus far have used simple variables such as LBS, TITLE$, or HRS to represent single values. If a program was required to handle many single values of the same type (such as 100 student scores), a loop was used to allow one variable to represent these values one at a time. Now consider the problem of a TV network poll. A program is needed to read and retain the daily viewing times of ten random viewers, calculate the average viewing time, and print the difference between each person's viewing time and the average in the following format:

NAME	HRS	DIFFERENCE FROM AVG
P. BUSCH	1	−3
C. CARSTENS	5	1
J. DRAKE	0	−4
H. POIROT	2	−2
M. BULAS	7	3
D. ZONGAS	3	−1
C. HASTINGS	4	0
T. ZEKLEY	11	7
S. MCKINNIS	3	−1
G. BALDUCCI	4	0

AVERAGE VIEWING TIME = 4

Our past procedure for calculating averages has been to set up a loop to read and accumulate each value in a single variable. Each time a new value is read by this method, however, the previous value stored in the variable is destroyed. Thus, in the problem involving the TV poll, we would not be able to compare each person's viewing time with the calculated average viewing time. To make the comparison, we must store each person's viewing time in a separate memory location. It is possible to use ten different variables to hold these values, but this clearly is a cumbersome solution that would be even more impractical when dealing with a larger number of values.

There is an easier way: BASIC permits us to deal with many related data items as a group by means of a structure known as an **array.** This chapter shows how arrays can be used in a situation such as the television poll program, in which groups of data items must be stored and manipulated efficiently. Both one-dimensional and two-dimensional arrays are presented in Section 9. Various methods of sorting and searching arrays are also discussed.

● Subscripts

The individual data items within an array are called **elements.** An array consists of a group of consecutive storage locations in memory, each location containing a single value. The entire array is given one name; the programmer indicates an individual element in the array by referring to its position in the array. To illustrate, suppose that there are five test scores to be stored: 97, 85, 89, 95, 100. The scores could be put in an array called TESTS, which we might visualize like this:

Array TESTS

97	85	89	95	100

The array name TESTS now refers to all five storage locations containing the test scores. To gain access to a single test score within the array, an array **subscript** or **index** is used. A subscript is a value enclosed in parentheses that identifies the position of a given element in the array. For example, the first element of array TESTS (containing the value 97) is referred to as TESTS(1). The second test score is in TESTS(2), the third test score is in TESTS(3), and so on. Therefore, the following statements are true:

TESTS(1) = 97
TESTS(2) = 85
TESTS(3) = 89
TESTS(4) = 95
TESTS(5) = 100

The subscript enclosed in parentheses does not have to be an integer constant; it can consist of any legal numeric expression. When an array element subscript is indicated by an expression, the computer carries out the following steps:

● It evaluates the expression within the parentheses.
● It converts the result to an integer value. (This is done either by truncation, as on the DECsystem and the Apple, or by rounding, as on the IBM, Macintosh, and TRS-80).
● It accesses the indicated element in the array. Keep in mind that the subscript value of an array element is entirely different from the contents of that element. In the previous example, the value of TESTS(4) is 95; the subscript 4 tells where the value 95 is located in the array.

Variables that refer to specific elements of arrays (such as TESTS(4)) are called **subscripted variables.** In contrast, simple variables such as we have used in previous chapters are called **unsubscripted variables.** Both kinds of variables store a single value, numeric or string, and both can be used in BASIC statements in the same manner. The important difference between the two is that a subscripted variable refers to one value in a group; it is possible to access a different value in the group simply by changing the subscript. An unsubscripted variable, on the other hand, does not necessarily have any special relationship to the values stored before or after it in memory.

The same rules that apply to naming simple variables also apply to naming arrays. Remember that only numeric values can be stored in arrays with numeric variable names, and that character string arrays can contain only string values. It is possible to use the same name for both a simple variable and an array in a program, but this is not a good programming practice because it makes the logic of the program difficult to follow.

Assume that the array X and the variables A and B have the following values:

$X(1) = 2$ $A = 3$
$X(2) = 15$ $B = 5$
$X(3) = 16$
$X(4) = 17$
$X(5) = 32$

The following examples show how the various forms of subscripts are used.

Example	Reference
$X(3)$	Third element of X, or 16.
$X(B)$	$B = 5$; thus the fifth element of X, or 32.
$X(X(1))$	$X(1) = 2$; thus the second element of X, or 15.
$X(B - SQR(X(3)))$	$X(3) = 16$, $SQR(16) = 4$, $B - 4 = 1$; thus the first element of X, or 2.

● Dimensioning an Array

When a subscripted variable is found in a program, the BASIC system recognizes it as part of an array and automatically reserves a standard number of storage locations for the array. On most systems (including all those discussed here), space is set aside for eleven array elements, the subscripts of which run from 0 through 10. (Some systems reserve space for ten elements, 1 through 10.) The programmer does not have to fill all of the reserved array storage spaces with values; it is illegal, however, to refer to an array element for which space has not been reserved.

The DIM, or dimension, statement enables the programmer to override this standard array space reservation and reserve space for an array of any desired size. A DIM statement is not required for arrays of eleven or fewer elements, but it is good programming practice to specify DIM statements for all arrays to help document the array usage.

The general format of the DIM statement follows:

line# DIM variable1(limit1)[, variable 2(limit2),...]

The variables are the names of arrays. Each limit is an integer constant that specifies the maximum subscript value possible for that particular array. For example, if space is needed to store 25 elements in an array ITEM$, the following statement reserves the necessary storage locations:

```
00010 DIM ITEM$(24)
```

Although it may seem that this statement sets aside only 24 positions, remember that array positions 0 through 24 are actually equal to 25 locations. For the sake of clarity and program logic, programmers often ignore the zero element. If we choose not to use the zero position, we would dimension the array ITEM$ as shown below in order to have 25 positions:

```
00010 DIM ITEM$(25)
```

There is no problem if fewer than 25 values are read into array ITEM$. Array subscripts can vary in the program from 0 to the limit declared in the DIM statement, but no subscript can exceed that limit.

As indicated in the statement format, more than one array can be declared in a DIM statement. For example, the following statement declares ACCNT, NAM$, and OVERDRWN as arrays:

```
00010 DIM ACCNT(100),NAM$(150),OVERDRWN(50)
```

Array ACCNT may contain up to 101 elements, NAM$ up to 151 elements, and OVERDRWN up to 51 elements. (If the index begins at 1, then 100, 150, and 50 elements can be stored respectively.)

DIM statements must appear in a program before the first references to the arrays they describe; a good practice is to place them at the beginning of the program. The following standard preparation symbol is often used to flowchart the DIM statement:

● One-Dimensional Arrays

READING DATA TO AN ARRAY

A major advantage of using arrays is the ability to use a variable rather than a constant as a subscript. Because a single name such as TESTS(I) can refer to any element in the array TESTS, depending on the value of I, this subscripted variable name can be used in a loop that varies the value of the subscript I. A FOR/NEXT loop can be an efficient method of reading data to an array if the exact number of items to be read is known in advance. The following program segment reads a list of five numbers into the array TESTS:

```
00010 FOR I = 1 TO 5
00020    READ TESTS(I)
00030 NEXT I
00040 DATA 85,71,63,51,99
```

The first time this loop is executed, the loop variable I equals 1. Therefore, when line 20 is executed, the computer reads the first number from the data list (which is 85) and stores it in TESTS(I), which evaluates as TESTS(1) during this loop execution. The second time through the loop, I equals 2. The second number is read to TESTS(I), which now refers to TESTS(2)—the second location in the array. The loop processing continues until all five numbers have been read and stored. This process is outlined as follows:

FOR I =	Action	Array TESTS:				
1	READ TESTS(1)	85				
2	READ TESTS(2)	85	71			
3	READ TESTS(3)	85	71	63		
4	READ TESTS(4)	85	71	63	51	
5	READ TESTS(5)	85	71	63	51	99

An array can also be filled with values using an INPUT statement or an assignment statement within a loop. To initialize an array of ten elements to zero, the following statements could be used:

```
00050 FOR I = 1 TO 10
00060     SCORES(I) = 0
00070 NEXT I
```

It is often possible to read data to several arrays within a single loop. In the following segment, each data line contains data for one element of each of three arrays:

```
00010 DIM NAM$(5),AGE(5),SSN$(5)
00020 FOR I = 1 TO 5
00030     READ NAM$(I),AGE(I),SSN$(I)
00040 NEXT I
00050 DATA "TOM BAKER",41,"268-66-1071"
00060 DATA "LALLA WARD",28,"353-65-2861"
00070 DATA "MASADA WILMOT",33,"269-59-9064"
00080 DATA "PATRICK JONES",52,"255-65-9375"
00090 DATA "BERYL JONES",56,"249-50-8736"
```

When the exact number of items to be read to an array is unknown, a WHILE/NEXT loop and a trailer value can be used. This method is demonstrated in the following segment, where the data contains a trailer value of −1. Care must be taken, however, that the number of items read does not exceed the size of the array.

```
00010 DIM X(50)
00020 I = 1
00030 INPUT X(I)
00040 WHILE (I < 50) AND (X(I) <> -1)
00050     I = I + 1
00060     INPUT X(I)
00070 NEXT
```

PRINTING THE CONTENTS OF AN ARRAY

The FOR/NEXT loop can be used to print the contents of the array TESTS, as shown in the following segment.

● **COMPUTERS AND INFORMATION PROCESSING**

```
00070 FOR T = 1 TO 5
00080    PRINT TESTS(T)
00090 NEXT T
```

RUNNH
85
71
63
51
99

Because there is no punctuation at the end of the PRINT statement in line 80, each value will be printed on a separate line. The values could be printed on the same line instead by placing a semicolon at the end of the line:

```
00070 FOR T = 1 TO 5
00080    PRINT TESTS(T);
00090 NEXT T
```

RUNNH
85   71   63   51   99

As the loop control variable T varies from 1 to 5, so does the value of the array subscript, and the computer prints elements 1 through 5 of array TESTS.

PERFORMING CALCULATIONS ON ARRAY ELEMENTS

Now consider again the problem of the TV network viewing poll presented earlier in this chapter. The output format required that each line contain the viewer's name, his or her number of viewing hours, and the difference between those hours and the average hours of all the viewers. This problem is solved in the program in Figure IX–1. The solution can be broken into the following steps:

1. Read the data to two arrays: a character string array for the names and a numeric array for the hours.
2. Calculate the average viewing hours.
3. Calculate for each viewer the difference between his or her hours and the average; these differences can be stored in a third array.
4. Print the required information from the three arrays.

The viewers' names and hours are read to their appropriate arrays in line 200 as part of a FOR/NEXT loop. Line 210 performs an accumulation of all the elements of the array HRS. AS I varies from 1 to 10, the elements 1 through 10 of HRS are added to the total hours (THRS). Therefore, when this loop is exited, the arrays NME$ and HRS are filled with values, and the unsubscripted variable THRS contains the sum of all the values contained in HRS. The average number of viewing hours is then calculated in line 230.

The FOR/NEXT loop starting in line 260 calculates the difference from the average viewing time for each viewer and stores the results in the array DAVG. Thus the first element of each array contains some information about the first viewer, the second element of each array concerns the second viewer, and so on. All of the information can then be printed in the required format by the FOR/NEXT loop of lines 320 through 340.

```
00010 REM ***              NETWORK VIEWING TIME SURVEY         ***
00020 REM
00030 REM *** THIS PROGRAM DETERMINES THE AVERAGE VIEWING ***
00040 REM *** TIME BY A GROUP OF VIEWERS. IT THEN DETER-  ***
00050 REM *** MINES THE DIFFERENCE FOR EACH VIEWER FROM   ***
00060 REM *** THE AVERAGE AND THEIR ACTUAL VIEWING TIME.  ***
00070 REM *** MAJOR VARIABLES:                            ***
00080 REM ***    NME$     ARRAY OF VIEWERS                ***
00090 REM ***    HRS      ARRAY OF HOURS                  ***
00100 REM ***    DAVG     ARRAY OF DIFFERENCES FROM AVG   ***
00110 REM ***    AVG      AVERAGE VIEWING HRS             ***
00120 REM ***    THRS     TOTAL VIEWING HRS               ***
00130 REM
00140 REM *** DIMENSIONING THE ARRAY SIZES ***
00150 DIM NME$(10), HRS(10), DAVG(10)
00160 THRS = 0
00170 REM
00180 REM *** READ DATA AND CALCULATE TOTAL HOURS ***
00190 FOR I = 1 TO 10
00200    READ NME$(I),HRS(I)
00210    THRS = THRS + HRS(I)
00220 NEXT I
00230 AVG = THRS / 10
00240 REM
00250 REM *** CALCULATE DIFFERENCES ***
00260 FOR I = 1 TO 10
00270    DAVG(I) = HRS(I) - AVG
00280 NEXT I
00290 REM
00300 REM *** PRINT RESULTS ***
00310 PRINT "NAME","HRS";TAB(22);"DIFFERENCE FROM AVG"
00320 FOR I = 1 TO 10
00330     PRINT NME$(I),HRS(I),DAVG(I)
00340 NEXT I
00350 PRINT
00360 PRINT "AVERAGE VIEWING TIME = ";AVG
00370 REM
00380 REM *** DATA STATEMENTS ***
00390 DATA P. BUSCH, 1, C. CARSTENS, 5, J. DRAKE, 0, H. POIROT, 2
00400 DATA M. BULAS, 7, D. CSONGAS, 3, C. HASTINGS, 4, T. ZEKLY, 11
00410 DATA S. MCKINNIS, 3, G. BALDUCCI, 4
00999 END
```

```
RUNNH
NAME              HRS      DIFFERENCE FROM AVG
P. BUSCH          1              -3
C. CARSTENS       5               1
J. DRAKE          0              -4
H. POIROT         2              -2
M. BULAS          7               3
D. CSONGAS        3              -1
C. HASTINGS       4               0
T. ZEKLY          11              7
S. MCKINNIS       3              -1
G. BALDUCCI       4               0

AVERAGE VIEWING TIME =   4
```

Sometimes not every element of an array needs to be manipulated in the same way. If we wanted to find the product of only the odd-numbered entries in an array K containing 25 numbers, we could use the following statements:

```
00090 PROD = 1
00100 FOR I = 1 TO 25 STEP 2
00110    PROD = PROD * K(I)
00120 NEXT I
```

● Two-Dimensional Arrays

The arrays shown so far in this chapter have all been one-dimensional arrays; that is, arrays that store values in the form of a single list. Two-dimensional arrays enable a programmer to represent more complex groupings of data. For example, suppose that a fast-food restaurant chain is running a four-day promotional T-shirt sale at its three store locations. It might keep the following table of data concerning the number of shirts sold by each of the three restaurants.

| | | Store | | |
		1	2	3
	1	12	14	15
	2	10	16	12
Day	3	11	18	13
	4	9	9	10

Each row of the data refers to a specific day of the sale, and each column contains the sales data for one store. Thus, the number of shirts sold by the second store on the third day of the sale (18) can be found in the third row, second column.

Data items that can be grouped into rows and columns such as this can be stored easily in a two-dimensional array. A two-dimensional array named SHIRTS containing the preceding data can be pictured like this:

Array SHIRTS

12	14	15
10	16	12
11	18	13
9	9	10

The array SHIRTS consists of twelve elements arranged as four rows and three columns. In order to reference a single element of a two-dimensional array such as this, two subscripts are needed: one to indicate the row and a second to indicate the column. For instance, the subscripted variable SHIRTS(4,1) contains the number of shirts sold on the fourth day by the first store (9). In BASIC, the first subscript gives the row number and the second subscript gives the column number.

The rules regarding one-dimensional arrays also apply to two-dimensional arrays. Two-dimensional arrays are named in the same way as other variables, and cannot use the same name as another array (of one or two dimensions) in the same program. A two-dimensional array can contain only one type of data; numeric and character string values cannot be mixed.

As with one-dimensional arrays, subscripts of two-dimensional arrays can be indicated by any legal numeric expression:

```
SHIRTS(3,3)
SHIRTS(1,2)
SHIRTS(I,J)
SHIRTS(1,I + J)
```

Assume that I = 4 and J = 2, and that the array X contains the following 16 elements:

Array X:

10	15	20	25
50	55	60	65
90	95	100	105
130	135	140	145

The following examples show how the various forms of subscripts are used:

Example	Refers to
X(4,I)	X(4,4)—The element in the fourth row, fourth column of X, which is 145.
X(J,I)	X(2,4)—The element in the second row, fourth column of X, which is 65.
X(3,J + 1)	X(3,3)—The element in the third row, third column, which is 100.
X(I − 1,J − 1)	X(3,1)—The element in the third row, first column, which is 90.

As with one-dimensional arrays, most computers automatically reserve space for a two-dimensional array. Usually this default reservation allows for 11 elements (0 through 10) for each dimension, making 11 rows and 11 columns. (Some computers reserve 10 elements (1 through 10) per dimension.) Thus the default space for a two-dimensional array is usually $11 \times 11 = 121$ elements. As mentioned earlier, often the 0 elements (those in the 0 row and 0 column) are ignored.

The DIM statement can also be used to set the dimensions of a two-dimensional array. The general format of such a DIM statement is as follows:

line# DIM variable (limit1,limit2)

where the variable is the array name, and the limits are the highest possible values of the subscripts for each dimension. For example, the following statement reserves space for the two-dimensional character array STDNT$, with up to 16 rows and 6 columns, for a total of $16 \times 6 = 96$ elements (or $15 \times 5 = 75$ elements if the subscripts begin at 1):

```
00030 DIM STDNT$(15,5)
```

READING AND PRINTING WITH TWO-DIMENSIONAL ARRAYS

Recall from the previous sections of this chapter that a FOR/NEXT loop is a convenient means of accessing all the elements of a one-dimensional array. The loop control variable of the FOR statement is used as the array subscript, and as the loop control variable changes value, so does the array subscript:

```
00030 DIM X(5)
00040 FOR I = 1 TO 5
00050    READ X(I)
00060 NEXT I
```

FOR/NEXT loops can also be used to read data to and print information from a two-dimensional array. It may be helpful to think of a two-dimensional array as a group of one-dimensional arrays, with each row making up a single one-dimensional array. A single FOR/NEXT loop can read values to one row. This process is repeated for as many rows as the array contains; therefore, the FOR/NEXT loop that reads a single row is nested within a second FOR/NEXT loop controlling the number of rows being accessed.

The array SHIRTS of the previous example can be filled from the sales data table one row at a time, moving from left to right across the columns. The following segment shows the nested FOR/NEXT loops that do this:

```
00030 FOR I = 1 TO 4
00040    FOR J = 1 TO 3
00050       READ SHIRTS(I,J)
00060    NEXT J
00070 NEXT I
00080 DATA 12,14,15
00090 DATA 10,16,12
00100 DATA 11,18,13
00110 DATA 9,9,10
```

Notice that each time line 50 is executed, one value is read to a single element of the array; the element is determined by the current values of I and J. This statement is executed $4 \times 3 = 12$ times, which is the number of elements in the array.

The outer loop (loop I) controls the rows, and loop J controls the columns. Each time the outer loop is executed once, the inner loop is executed three times. While I = 1, J becomes 1, 2, and finally 3 as the inner loop is executed. Therefore, line 50 reads values to SHIRTS(1,1), SHIRTS(1,2), and SHIRTS(1,3), and the first row is filled:

	J = 1	2	3
	12	14	15
I = 1			

While I equals 2, J again varies from 1 to 3, and line 50 reads values to SHIRTS(2,1), SHIRTS(2,2) and SHIRTS(2,3) to fill the second row:

	J =		
	1	2	3
I = 2	12	14	15
	10	16	12

I is incremented to 3 and then to 4, and the third and fourth rows are filled in the same manner.

To print the contents of the entire array, the programmer can substitute a PRINT statement for the READ statement in the nested FOR/NEXT loops. The following segment prints the contents of the array SHIRTS, one row at a time:

```
00040 BLANK = 10
00050 FOR I = 1 TO 4
00060    FOR J = 1 TO 3
00070       PRINT TAB(BLANK * J);SHIRTS(I,J);
00080    NEXT J
00090    PRINT
00100 NEXT I
```

The semicolon at the end of line 70 tells the computer to print the three values on the same line. After the inner loop is executed, the blank PRINT statement in line 90 sets the carriage return so that the next row is printed on the next line. The program in Figure IX–2 shows how the data table for the T-shirt sales results can be read to a two-dimensional array and printed in table form with appropriate headings.

ADDING ROWS

Once data has been stored in an array, it is often necessary to manipulate certain array elements. For instance, the sales manager in charge of the T-shirt promotional sale might want to know how many shirts were sold on the last day of the sale.

Because the data for each day is contained in a row of the array, it is necessary to total the elements in one row of the array (the fourth row) to find the number of shirts sold on the fourth day. The fourth row can be thought of by itself as a one-dimensional array. One loop is therefore required to access all the elements of this row:

```
00030 D4SALES = 0
00040 FOR J = 1 TO 3
00050    D4SALES = D4SALES + SHIRTS(4,J)
00060 NEXT J
```

Notice that the first subscript of SHIRTS(4,J) restricts the computations to the elements in row 4, while the column,J, varies from 1 to 3. The process performed in line 50 is pictured in the following diagram:

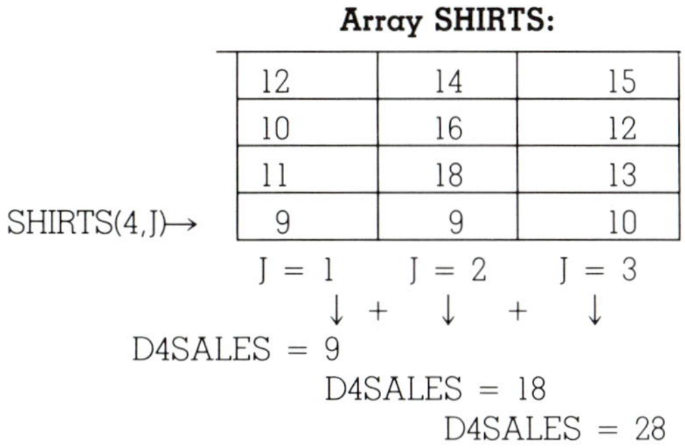

Array SHIRTS:

12	14	15
10	16	12
11	18	13
9	9	10

SHIRTS(4,J)→

$J = 1$ $J = 2$ $J = 3$

↓ + ↓ + ↓

D4SALES = 9

D4SALES = 18

D4SALES = 28

● **FIGURE IX–2**
Two Dimensional Array

```
00010 REM ***              T-SHIRT SALES REPORT           ***
00020 REM
00030 REM *** THIS PROGRAM PRINTS A REPORT ON THE NUMBER OF   ***
00040 REM *** T-SHIRTS SOLD PER STORE FOR 4 DIFFERENT DAYS.   ***
00050 REM *** MAJOR VARIABLES:                                ***
00060 REM ***     TSHIRT        ARRAY OF T-SHIRTS SOLD        ***
00070 REM ***     I,J           LOOP CONTROLS                 ***
00080 REM
00090 REM *** DIMENSION ARRAY ***
00100 DIM TSHIRT(4,3)
00110 REM
00120 REM *** READ THE DATA ***
00130 FOR I = 1 TO 4
00140     FOR J = 1 TO 3
00150         READ TSHIRT(I,J)
00160     NEXT J
00170 NEXT I
00180 REM
00190 REM *** PRINT TABLE OF QUANTITIES SOLD ***
00200 PRINT "DAY #";TAB(10);"STORE 1";TAB(20);"STORE 2";TAB(30);"STORE 3"
00210 FOR I = 1 TO 4
00220     PRINT I;
00230     FOR J = 1 TO 3
00240         PRINT TAB(J*10);TSHIRT(I,J);
00250     NEXT J
00260     PRINT
00270 NEXT I
00280 REM
00290 REM *** DATA STATEMENTS ***
00300 DATA 12,4,15,10,6,12,11,8,13,9,9,10
00999 END
```

```
RUNNH
DAY #      STORE 1    STORE 2    STORE 3
  1          12          4         15
  2          10          6         12
  3          11          8         13
  4           9          9         10
```

ADDING COLUMNS

To find the total number of T-shirts sold by the third store, it is necessary to total the elements in the third column of the array. This time we can think of the column by itself as a one-dimensional array of four elements. This operation calls for a FOR/NEXT loop, as shown here:

```
00040 S3SHOP = 0
00050 FOR I = 1 TO 4
00060    S3SHOP = S3SHOP + SHIRTS(I,3)
00070 NEXT I
```

In line 60, the second subscript (3) restricts the computations to the elements in the third column, while the row, I, varies from 1 to 4. This process is pictured in the following diagram:

Array SHIRTS

SHIRT(I,3)
↓

12	14	15
10	16	12
11	18	13
9	9	10

$I = 1 \rightarrow$ S3SHOP = 15
$I = 2 \rightarrow$ S3SHOP = 27
$I = 3 \rightarrow$ S3SHOP = 40
$I = 4 \rightarrow$ S3SHOP = 50

TOTALING A TWO-DIMENSIONAL ARRAY

Consider now the problem of finding the grand total of all T-shirts sold during the entire four-day special offer. The program must access all the elements of the array one at a time and add them to the grand total. Remember that nested FOR/NEXT loops were used to print or read values to a two-dimensional array. This same method can be used to total the elements of an array by substituting an addition operation for the READ or PRINT statement:

```
00050 TSHIRT = 0
00060 FOR I = 1 TO 4
00070    FOR J = 1 TO 3
00080       TSHIRT = TSHIRT + SHIRTS(I,J)
00090    NEXT J
00100 NEXT I
```

This segment adds the elements in a row-by-row sequence. While I equals 1, the inner loop causes J to vary from 1 to 3, thus adding the contents of the first row elements to the total accumulated in TSHIRT. When the outer loop terminates, the contents of all four rows will have been added to the total.

This totaling of all the elements of the array can also be performed in a column-by-column sequence:

```
00050 TSHIRT = 0
00060 FOR J = 1 TO 3
00070    FOR I = 1 TO 4
00080       TSHIRT = TSHIRT + SHIRTS(I,J)
00090    NEXT I
00100 NEXT J
```

Note that the two loops have been interchanged from the first example. Now the outer loop, loop J, controls the columns, and the inner loop, loop I, controls the rows. While J equals 1, I varies from 1 to 4 and the elements of the first column are added to the total: SHIRTS(1,1), SHIRTS(2,1), SHIRTS(3,1) and SHIRTS(4,1). J is then incremented to 2, the second column is added, and so on.

● The Bubble Sort

Many applications require that data items be sorted, or ordered, in some way. For example, names must be alphabetized, Social Security numbers arranged from lowest to highest, basketball players ranked from high scorer to low scorer, and the like.

Suppose that an array, X, contains five numbers that we would like ordered from lowest to highest:

It is a simple matter for us to mentally reorder this list as follows:

Array X (Unsorted)	Array X (Sorted)
10	2
30	10
15	15
100	30
2	100

What if there were seven hundred numbers instead of five? Then it would not be easy for us to order the number list. However, the computer is perfectly suited for such tasks. One method of sorting with the computer is illustrated in Figure IX–3. The **bubble sort** works by comparing two adjacent values in an array and then interchanging them according to the desired order—either ascending or descending order.

The program in Figure IX–3 sorts ten U.S. cities into alphabetical order. To the computer, the letter A is less than the letter B, B is less than C, and so on. Lines 110 through 140 simply read the city names into an array called C$ and print them. Lines 200 through 280 perform the bubble sort. Let us examine them carefully to see what happens.

Line 200 refers to the variable F, short for flag. It is initialized to 0. Its value is checked later by the computer to determine if the entire array has been sorted.

Notice the terminal value of the FOR/NEXT loop that sorts the array. The terminal value is one less than the number of items to be sorted. This is because two items at a time are compared. I varies from 1 to 9, which means that the computer eventually will compare item 9 and item 9 + 1. If the terminal value were 10 (the number of cities), the computer would try to compare item 10 with item 11, which does not exist in our array.

The IF/THEN statement in line 220 tells the computer whether to interchange two compared values. For example, when I = 1, the computer compares LOS ANGELES with CHICAGO. Since C comes before L in the alphabet, the positions of these two items must be switched:

LOS ANGELES	I = 1	CHICAGO	
	Switch		
CHICAGO	I = 2	LOS ANGELES	DETROIT
	Switch		
DETROIT	I = 3	LOS ANGELES	
	No Switch		
NEW YORK CITY	I = 4		

.
.
.

DENVER

Then I is incremented to 2, and LOS ANGELES is compared with DE-TROIT. These two names must be interchanged. This is performed by lines 230 through 250. Note that we have created a holding area, H$, so that the switch can be made. We move LOS ANGELES to the holding area, H$, and then move DETROIT to LOS ANGELES'S previous position.

● FIGURE IX–3
Bubble Sort Program

```
00010 REM ************************************************************
00020 REM ***   THIS PROGRAM SORTS THE CITIES INTO ALPHABETIC ORDER ***
00030 REM ************************************************************
00040 REM
00050 DIM C$(10)
00060 PRINT "UNSORTED LIST OF CITIES"
00070 PRINT
00080 REM **************************************************
00090 REM ***      READ THE NAMES INTO AN ARRAY       ***
00100 REM **************************************************
00110 FOR I = 1 TO 10
00120     READ C$(I)
00130     PRINT C$(I)
00140 NEXT I
00150 PRINT
00160 PRINT
00170 REM **************************************************
00180 REM ***                  THE BUBBLE SORT        ***
00190 REM **************************************************
00200 F = 0
00210 FOR I = 1 TO 9
00220     IF C$(I) <= C$(I + 1) THEN 270
00230     H$ = C$(I)
00240     C$(I) = C$(I + 1)
00250     C$(I + 1) = H$
00260     F = 1
00270 NEXT I
00280 IF F = 1 THEN 200
00290 PRINT "SORTED LIST OF CITIES"
00300 PRINT
00310 FOR I = 1 TO 10
00320     PRINT C$(I)
00330 NEXT I
00340 DATA LOS ANGELES,CHICAGO,DETROIT,NEW YORK CITY,DALLAS
00350 DATA CLEVELAND,BOSTON,WASHINGTON,MIAMI,DENVER
00999 END
```

● COMPUTERS AND INFORMATION PROCESSING

Now LOS ANGELES is placed in the position previously occupied by DETROIT. Whenever the computer interchanges two values, F is set to 1 in line 260. This loop continues until every item in the array has been examined. After once through this entire loop, the array C$ looks like this:

CHICAGO
DETROIT
LOS ANGELES
DALLAS
CLEVELAND
BOSTON
NEW YORK CITY
MIAMI
DENVER
WASHINGTON

● **FIGURE IX–3**
Continued

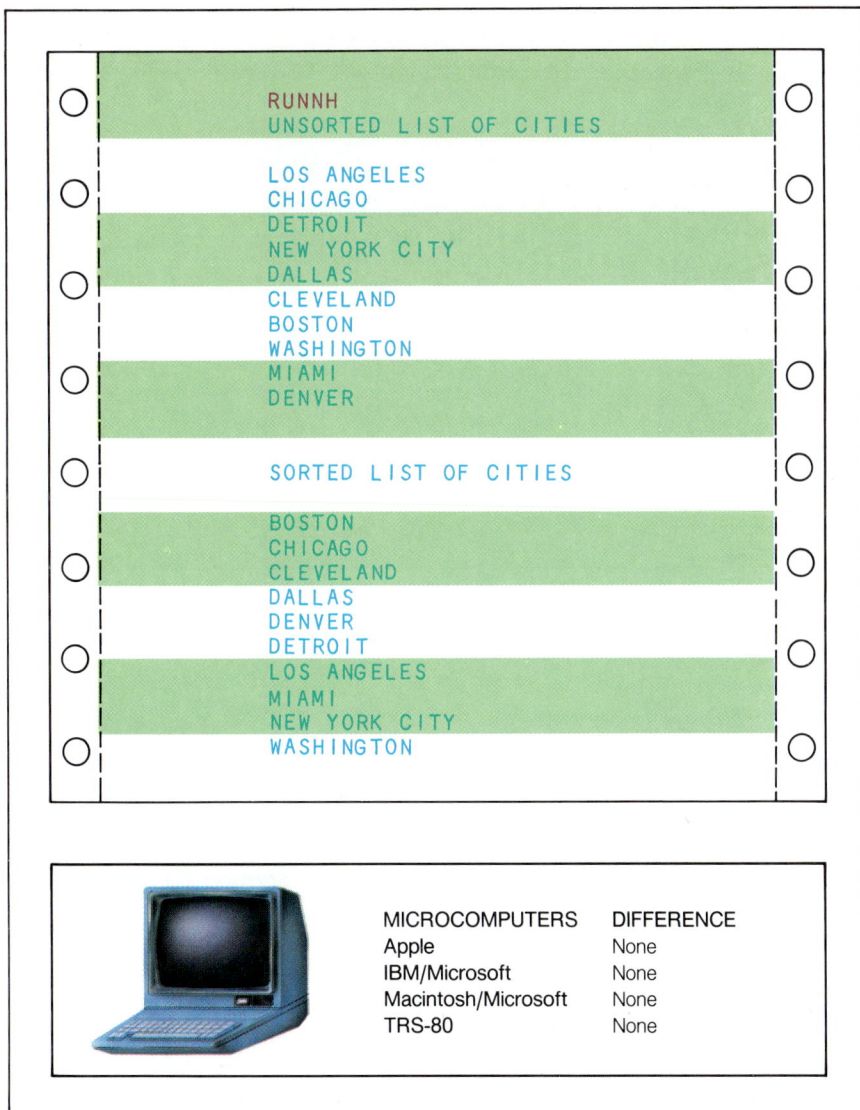

```
RUNNH
UNSORTED LIST OF CITIES

LOS ANGELES
CHICAGO
DETROIT
NEW YORK CITY
DALLAS
CLEVELAND
BOSTON
WASHINGTON
MIAMI
DENVER


SORTED LIST OF CITIES

BOSTON
CHICAGO
CLEVELAND
DALLAS
DENVER
DETROIT
LOS ANGELES
MIAMI
NEW YORK CITY
WASHINGTON
```

MICROCOMPUTERS	DIFFERENCE
Apple	None
IBM/Microsoft	None
Macintosh/Microsoft	None
TRS-80	None

Although several switches have been made, the list is not sorted completely. That is why we need line 280. As long as F equals 1, the computer knows that switches have been made, and the sorting process must continue. When the computer loops through the entire array without setting F equal to 1—that is, when no switches are made—the computer finds F equal to 0 and knows that the list is ordered.

Numbers, of course, can be sorted by this same method. Two-dimensional arrays can be sorted with nested loops.

● SWAP

The Macintosh and the IBM/Microsoft have additional capabilities which allow the use of the SWAP statement. The SWAP statement exchanges the values of two variables and is useful when sorting. The general format of the SWAP statement is shown below.

line# SWAP variable 1, variable 2

Following is a sorting subroutine using the SWAP statement.

```
01000 REM ******************************************
01010 REM ***         SUBROUTINE BUBBLE SORT      ***
01020 REM ******************************************
01030 REM *** SORT ARRAY D$ IN ASCENDING          ***
01040 REM *** USING THE SWAP STATEMENT.           ***
01050 REM
01060 FLAG = 0
01070 FOR K = 1 TO 9
01080     IF D$(K) <= D$(K + 1) THEN 1110
01090     SWAP D$(K),D$(K + 1)
01100     FLAG = 1
01110 NEXT K
01120 IF FLAG = 1 THEN 1060
01130 RETURN
```

● A Programming Problem

PROBLEM DEFINITION

The scorekeepers of the Centrovian Open Ice Skating Championships need a program to determine the winner of the final round. Each competitor is given six scores, of which the highest and lowest are discarded. The remaining four scores are then averaged to obtain the final score. The maximum score for each event is 6.0. Write a program that will read the names and scores of the ten finalists and produce a listing of the skaters' names and final scores in order of finish. Sample input and needed output are shown in the following table.

Input:

BALDUCCI, G.	5.7	5.3	5.1	5.0	4.7	4.8
CREED, A.	3.1	4.9	4.1	3.7	4.6	3.9
WILLIAMS, E.	4.1	5.3	4.9	4.4	3.9	5.4
HAMILTON, S.	5.1	5.7	5.6	5.5	4.4	5.3
LORD, P.	5.9	4.8	5.5	5.0	5.7	5.7
STRAVINSKY, I.	5.1	4.7	4.1	3.1	4.6	5.0
MONTALBAN, R.	5.1	5.1	4.9	3.4	5.5	5.3
SCHELL, M.	4.9	4.3	5.2	4.5	4.6	4.9
CRANSTON, T.	6.0	6.0	5.7	5.8	5.9	5.9
CROWLEY, S.	4.3	5.2	6.9	5.3	4.3	6.0

Needed Output:

PLACE	NAME	SCORE
1	BALDUCCI, G.	5.7
.	.	.
.	.	.
.	.	.

SOLUTION DESIGN

The problem provides us with seven items of data for each skater—a name and six scores—and asks for a list of names and averages, sorted by average. Once the data items have been read (the first step), two basic operations must be performed in order to produce the listing: the averages must be calculated, and these averages with their associated names must be sorted. Thus, the problem can be broken into four major tasks: (1) read the data, (2) calculate the averages, (3) sort the names and averages, and (4) print the sorted information. The stepwise refinement is shown below.

1. Read names and scores
2. Calculate averages
3. Sort by averages
4. Print results

The structure chart for this problem is shown in Figure IX–4.

The input for this problem consists of two types of data, alphabetic and numeric, so two arrays must be used to store them. The output calls for

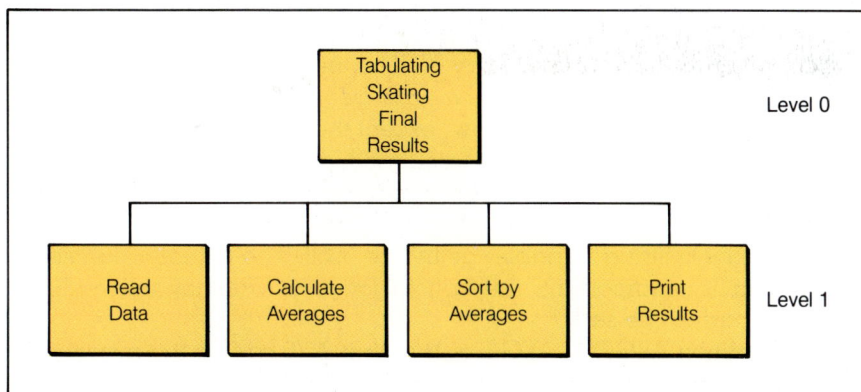

● **FIGURE IX–4**
Structure Chart for Skating Scores Program

the names already stored plus a new set of values, the averages, so another array can be used to store these averages. In calculating the averages, variables will also be needed to keep track of the high and low scores. The main variables needed can be summarized as follows.

Input variables

array of names	(SKNM$)
array of scores	(PTS)

Program variables

high score for a competitor	(HI)
low score for a competitor	(LO)
total of four scores	(TPTS)

Output variables

array of averages	(AVG)

In order to calculate the averages, each of the six scores of each skater must be examined to find the high and low scores. For any given skater, each score must be compared with the highest and lowest score found so far for that skater.

A sort is required in the third step of our algorithm. A descending-order bubble sort could be effective here, because the number of items to be sorted is relatively small. A crucial point is that, as the averages are rearranged, the corresponding skater's name must be carried with each average. This means, for example, that the average for the fourth skater (SKNM$(4)) must be stored in AVG(4).

THE PROGRAM

The program of Figure IX–5 shows the solution to the problem. Line 140 of the main program reserves space for a two-dimensional array for the scores. Each row of array PTS contains the scores for one skater, so ten rows with six columns each are needed.

The first subroutine called by the main program reads the names and scores to their respective arrays. The second subroutine finds the average score of each skater. It does this by performing a sequential search on each row of the scores array (array PTS) in lines 2050 through 2110. When the low and high scores for the row have been found, lines 2150 through 2170 add all the scores for that row, except the low and high, to the total; then the average for that row is calculated.

The sorting of the final averages is performed in the bubble sort of the third subroutine. Notice that the flag indicating that a switch has been made can be a string variable, as in line 3050. The actual value stored in the flag is unimportant; the critical factor is whether that value is changed during the sort.

The condition AVG(I) > AVG(I + 1) in line 3070 causes the averages to be sorted from highest to lowest. Every time an average is moved, its corresponding name from the array SKNM$ is also moved. The sorted results are printed by the fourth subroutine in lines 4000 through 4090.

● COMPUTERS AND INFORMATION PROCESSING

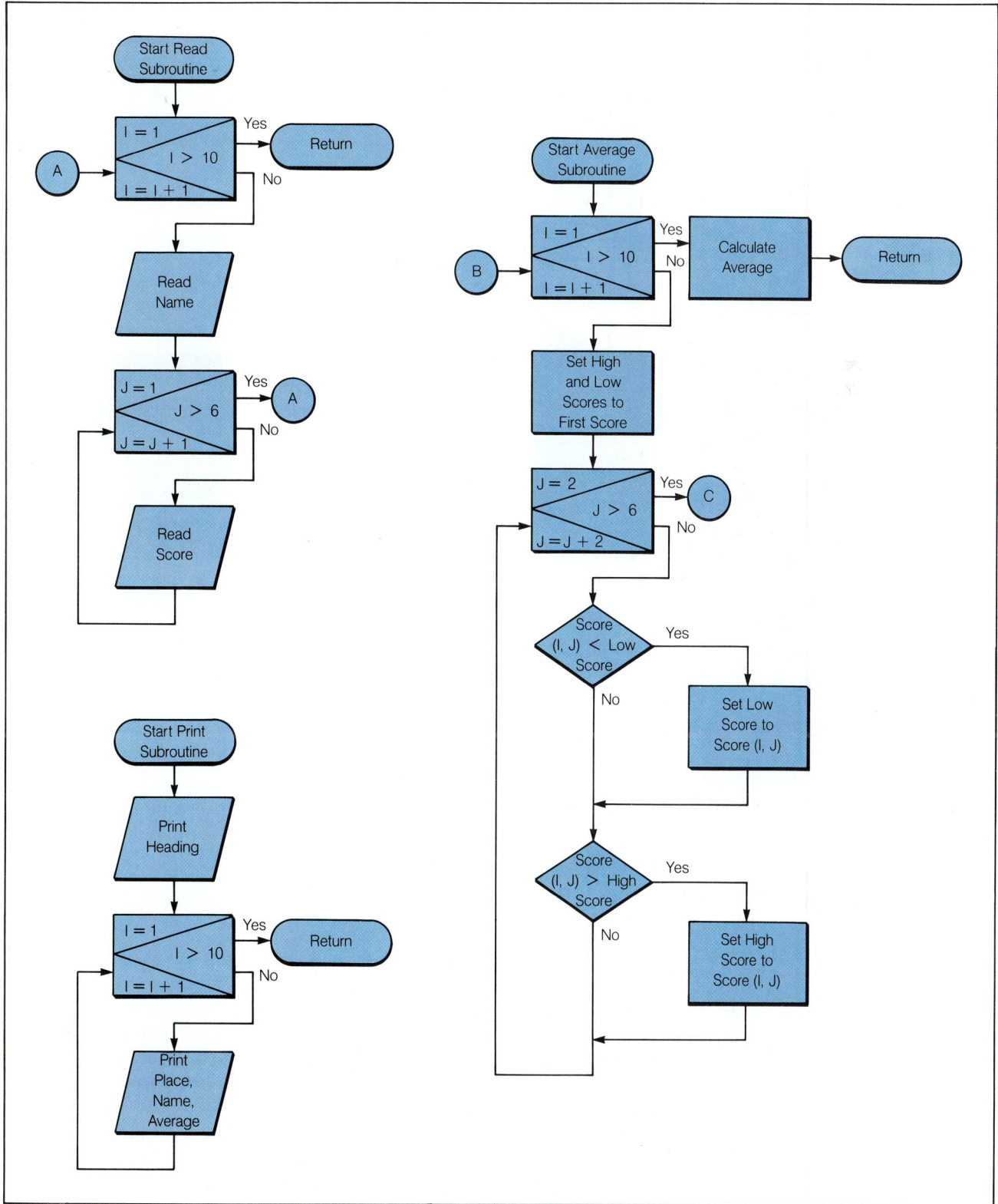

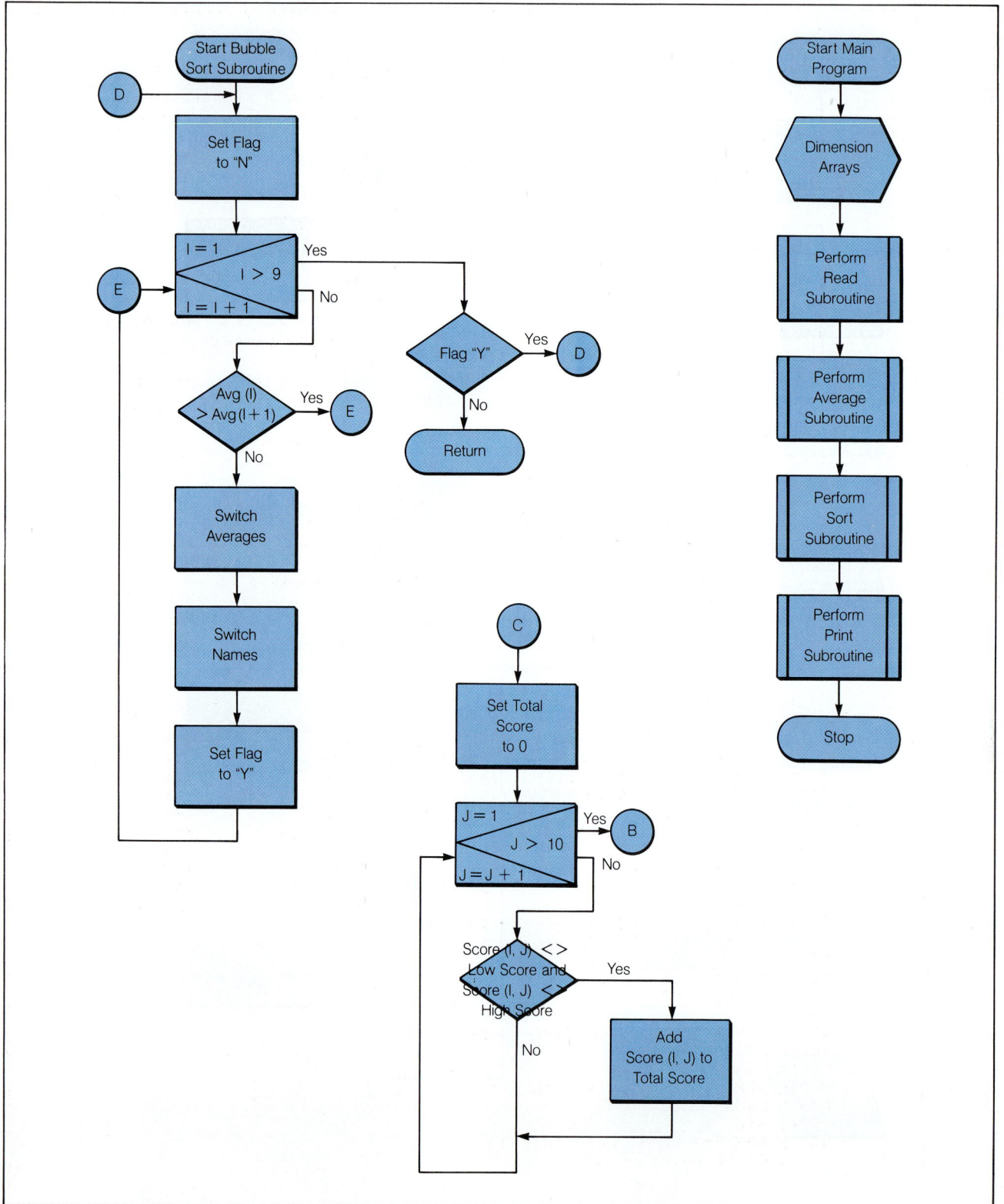

● COMPUTERS AND INFORMATION PROCESSING

Pseudocode

Begin main program
Dimension arrays
Perform subroutine to read data
Perform subroutine to calculate averages
Perform subroutine to sort information
Perform subroutine to print information
End main program

Begin read subroutine
Begin loop, do 10 times
    Read name
    Begin loop, do 6 times
       Read score
    End loop
End loop
End read subroutine

Begin average subroutine
Begin loop, do 10 times
    Set low and high scores to first score
    Begin loop, do 5 times
       If current score < low score
          Then set low score to current score
       End if
       If current score > high score
          Then set high score to current score
       End if
    End loop

Set total of scores to 0
Begin loop, do 6 times
       If current score is not low or high score,
          Then add current score to total score
       End if
    End loop
    Calculate average
End loop
End average subroutine

Begin sort subroutine
Initialize flag
Begin loop, do 9 times
    If adjacent scores are already in ascending order
       Then proceed to next pair
    End if
    Switch scores and corresponding names
    Set flag to indicate switch
End loop
If flag indicates switch
    Then repeat entire process
End if
End sort subroutine

Begin print subroutine
Print headings
Begin loop, do 10 times
    Print place, name, average
End loop
End print subroutine

```
00010 REM ***                    SKATING  FINAL  RESULTS                 ***
00020 REM
00030 REM *** THIS PROGRAM COMPUTES THE AVERAGES OF SKATING ***
00040 REM *** SCORES, USING SIX SCORES AND DROPPING THE LOW ***
00050 REM *** AND HIGH SCORES. IT THEN SORTS ALL THE AVERAGE***
00060 REM *** SCORES IN ASCENDING ORDER.                    ***
00070 REM *** MAJOR VARIABLES:                              ***
00080 REM ***     SKNM$           ARRAY OF SKATERS NAMES    ***
00090 REM ***     PTS             ARRAY OF SCORES           ***
00100 REM ***     AVG             ARRAY OF AVERAGES         ***
00110 REM ***     HI,LO           HIGHEST/LOWEST SCORES     ***
00120 REM
00130 REM *** DIMENSION THE ARRAYS ***
00140 DIM SKNM$(10),PTS(10,6),AVG(10)
00150 REM
00160 REM *** READ NAMES AND SCORES ***
00170 GOSUB 1000
00180 REM
00190 REM *** CALCULATE FINAL AVERAGE ***
00200 GOSUB 2000
00210 REM
00220 REM *** SORT BY AVERAGE ***
00230 GOSUB 3000
00240 REM
00250 REM *** PRINT RESULTS ***
00260 GOSUB 4000
```

```
00270 GOTO 9999
01000 REM ********************************************************
01010 REM ***              SUBROUTINE READ              ***
01020 REM ********************************************************
01030 REM ***      READS THE NAMES AND SIX SCORES       ***
01040 REM
01050 FOR I = 1 TO 10
01060    READ SKNM$(I)
01070    FOR J = 1 TO 6
01080       READ PTS(I,J)
01090    NEXT J
01100 NEXT I
01110 RETURN
02000 REM ********************************************************
02010 REM ***            SUBROUTINE AVERAGE             ***
02020 REM ********************************************************
02030 REM ***  DROP HIGH/LOW SCORES, THEN AVERAGE SCORE  ***
02040 REM
02050 FOR I = 1 TO 10
02060     HI = PTS(I,1)
02070     LO = PTS(I,1)
02080     FOR J = 2 TO 6
02090        IF PTS(I,J) < LO THEN LO = PTS(I,J)
02100        IF PTS(I,J) > HI THEN HI = PTS(I,J)
02110     NEXT J
02120     REM
02130     REM *** AVERAGE REMAINING SCORES ***
02140     TPTS = 0
02150     FOR J = 1 TO 6
02160        IF PTS(I,J) <> LO OR PTS(I,J) <> HI THEN
              TPTS = TPTS + PTS(I,J)
02170     NEXT J
02180     AVG(I) = TPTS / 4
02190 NEXT I
02200 RETURN
03000 REM ********************************************************
03010 REM ***           SUBROUTINE BUBBLE SORT          ***
03020 REM ********************************************************
03030 REM ***        SORT AVERAGES IN ASCENDING ORDER    ***
03040 REM
03050 SWITCH$ = "N"
03060 FOR I = 1 TO 9
03070     IF AVG(I) > AVG(I + 1) THEN 3150
03080     TEMP = AVG(I)
03090     STEMP$ = SKNM$(I)
03100     AVG(I) = AVG(I + 1)
03110     SKNM$(I) = SKNM$(I + 1)
03120     AVG(I + 1) = TEMP
03130     SKNM$(I + 1) = STEMP$
03140     SWITCH$ = "Y"
03150 NEXT I
03160 IF SWITCH$ = "Y" THEN 3050
03170 RETURN
04000 REM ********************************************************
04010 REM ***              SUBROUTINE PRINT             ***
04020 REM ********************************************************
04030 REM ***    PRINT THE HEADINGS AND THE RESULTS     ***
04040 REM
04050 PRINT "PLACE";TAB(10);"NAME";TAB(30);"SCORE"
04060 PRINT
```

```
04070 FOR I = 1 TO 10
04080     PRINT I;TAB(10);SKNM$(I);TAB(30);AVG(I)
04090 NEXT I
04100 RETURN
04200 REM
04210 REM ***  DATA STATEMENTS  ***
04220 DATA "BALDUCCI,G",5.7,5.3,5.1,5.0,4.7,4.8
04230 DATA "CREED,A",3.1,4.9,4.1,3.7,4.6,3.9,
04240 DATA "WILLIAMS,E.",4.1,5.3,4.9,4.4,3.9,5.4,
04250 DATA "HAMILTON,S",5.1,5.7,5.6,5.5,4.4,5.3
04260 DATA "LORD,P",5.9,4.8,5.5,5.0,5.7,5.7
04270 DATA "STRAVINSKY,I",5.1,4.7,4.1,3.1,4.6,5.0
04280 DATA "MONTALBAN,R",5.1,5.1,4.9,3.4,5.5,5.3
04290 DATA "SCHELL,M",4.9,4.3,5.2,4.5,4.6,4.9
04300 DATA "CRANSTON,T",6.0,6.0,5.7,5.8,5.9,5.9
04310 DATA "CROWLEY,S",4.3,5.2,6.9,5.3,4.3,6.0
09999 END
```

```
RUNNH
PLACE       NAME                    SCORE

  1         CRANSTON,T              8.825
  2         LORD,P                  8.15
  3         CROWLEY,S               8
  4         HAMILTON,S              7.9
  5         BALDUCCI,G              7.65
  6         MONTALBAN,R             7.325
  7         SCHELL,M                7.1
  8         WILLIAMS,E.             7
  9         STRAVINSKY,I            6.65
 10         CREED,A                 6.075
```

MICROCOMPUTERS	DIFFERENCE
Apple	None
IBM/Microsoft	None
Macintosh/Microsoft	None
TRS-80	None

● Summary Points

● Arrays are lists or tables of related values stored under a single variable name.

● Access to individual elements in an array can be gained through the use of subscripts.

● A subscript of an array element can be any legal numeric expression.

● The DIM statement sets up storage for arrays and must appear before the first reference to the array it describes.

- Array manipulation is carried out through the use of loops.
- A two-dimensional array stores values as a table or matrix, grouped into rows and columns.
- The first subscript of a two-dimensional array refers to the element's row, and the second subscript refers to the column.
- The bubble sort places elements of an array in ascending or descending order by comparing adjacent elements.

● Review Questions

1. What is an array?

2. We can make reference to individual elements in an array by referring to their position. This is done through the use of _____.

3. What is the purpose of the DIM statement?

4. DIM statements must appear where in a program?

5. Only one array can be dimensioned in a DIM statement. True or false?

6. Assume $X = 1$, $Y = 2$, and $Z = 3$. What are the values of the variables $A(X)$, $A(Y-X)$, and $A(X*Z)$ if array A contains the following values?

Array A

11
42
37
90
17

7. Write a set of instructions that will find the sum of the four elements in array A.

8. Reading data into and printing data from two-dimensional arrays can be accomplished using _____statements.

9. Give two advantages of arrays.

10. Describe how a bubble sort works.

● Debugging Exercises

Identify the following programs or program segments that contain errors, and debug them.

```
1. 00010 DIM L(15)
   00020 FOR I = 1 TO 16
   00030    PRINT L(I)
   00040 NEXT I
2. 00100 DIM X(3,2)
   00110 FOR I = 1 TO 2
   00120    FOR J = 1 TO 3
   00130       READ X(I,J)
   00140    NEXT J
   00150 NEXT I
```

● Programming Problems

1. A stereo equipment store is holding a sale. The manager needs a program that will place the prices of all sale items in one array and the corresponding rate of discount in a second array. A third array should be used to hold the sale price of each item (sale price = price − (rate * price)). Use the following data:

Price	Rate of Discount
$178.89	0.25
59.95	0.20
402.25	0.30
295.00	0.25
589.98	0.30
42.99	0.20

Print the original prices and their corresponding sale prices.

2. Read 12 numbers to array A and 12 numbers to array B. Compute the product of the corresponding elements of the two arrays, and place the results in array C. Print a table similar to the following:

A	B	C
2	3	6
7	2	14

3. Your teacher has a table of data concerning the semester test scores for your class:

Name	Test 1	Test 2	Test 3
Mathey, S.	88	83	80
Sandoval, V.	98	89	100
Haggerty, B.	75	65	79
Drake, J.	60	85	99
Jenkins, J.	75	89	89

Your teacher would like to know the test average for each student, and the class average for each test. The output should include the preceding table.

4. The following list of employee names and identification numbers is in alphabetical order. Use a bubble sort to print the list in ascending order by I.D. number. (Remember that when you change the position of a number in the array, the position of the name also must be changed so that they correspond.)

Name	I.D. #
Altt, D.	467217
Calas, M.	624719
Corelli, F.	784609
Kanawa, K.	290013
Lamas, F.	502977
Lehman, B.	207827
Shicoff, N.	389662
Talvela, M.	443279
Tousteau, J.	302621
Wymer, E.	196325

5. The manager of the Epitome Books store would like a program that will generate a report regarding the sales of the various types of books the store carries. The program should use the following data:

Year	Pop. Fiction	Classics	Biography	Instruction
1982	4,561	549	973	3,702
1983	5,140	632	1,375	4,300
1984	5,487	581	1,798	4,345
1985	5,952	605	2,204	5,156

The report should indicate what percentage of each year's total sales consisted of each book type. The format for the report is as follows:

SALES PERCENTAGES FOR EACH YEAR:

YEAR	POP. FICTION	CLASSICS	BIOGRAPHY	INSTRUCT.
1982	XX.XX%	XX.XX%	XX.XX%	XX.XX%
1983				
1984				
1985				

● Section X
File Processing

● Introduction

Up to this point, we have been storing data in variables using either DATA statements or INPUT statements. The storage locations where these variables are kept are in the primary storage unit of the computer. This method of storing data is adequate for some applications, but not for others.

Suppose that a large amount of data needs to be stored. Two problems arise: the data is difficult to organize, and the computer's primary storage unit may be too small to hold all of it. These problems occur often in business and scientific applications. For instance, a large insurance corporation needs many pieces of data for each of its policy holders. This data might include the policyholder's name, address, age, social security number, the type of policy, the amount of the policy, what the policy covers, and so on. The amount of memory in the corporation's computer would almost certainly be too small to store all of this data, and the data would not be organized in a useful fashion.

Another problem also arises. What if the same data needs to be accessed by more than one program? For example, the data used by the accounting department in one program might need to be used by the sales department in a different program. It would not be efficient to have duplicate DATA statements in both programs, and updating all the DATA statements would likely result in some errors.

Using files can help us solve these problems. A **file** is a collection of related data items organized in a meaningful way and kept in secondary storage. In this section, you will learn to use files in BASIC programs. Unfortunately, however, there is no standardized method for performing operations on files. Many BASIC implementations include unique file manipulation commands, although the principles on which these commands are based are similar. We will discuss the general concepts of file handling before explaining how the necessary commands are implemented on each of the BASIC systems discussed here.

● What Is a File?

Files provide an alternative means of organizing and storing related data. A major advantage of using files is that they make use of secondary storage, which is virtually unlimited; thus the problem of inadequate space in the primary storage unit is solved. Another advantage is that the data contained in a file can be organized and stored using a variety of methods, depending on the needs of the user. Also, many users can access the same file. Thus, data can be used more efficiently, and updating data is simpler and less error-prone.

Although files help to solve these problems, they have one major disadvantage. It takes longer to retrieve data stored in a file than data stored in the computer's primary storage unit. When using files, the computer must locate the data in secondary storage, move it into the primary storage unit, and then retrieve it. Even though program execution is slower using files, the advantages of greater storage space and data organization outweigh this disadvantage.

There are two major divisions within a file. The smallest of these divisions, the *field*, contains a single unit of information. A student's name is an example of a **field** value. Fields are grouped together to form the second major division, the **record.** A record consists of one or more fields that describe a single entity. Therefore, an example of a record might contain a name field, a course field, and a grade field; together, these fields would constitute a student's record for a single course. The finished product, a file, consists of a group of records. An example of a file is a group of student records, each containing a name field, a course field, and a grade field.

A computer file can be compared to a drawer in a filing cabinet. A particular file drawer usually contains related information about one general topic. For example, it might contain information about a company's employees. A computer file also contains information about a single subject. Within each file cabinet drawer there are probably folders, each containing information regarding a single employee. Records for computer files also contain information about individual entities. Each record in file drawer folder consists of a collection of individual pieces of information, such as an employee's name, address, and so on. Each field in a computer file also contains a single piece of information. Figure X–1 illustrates this concept.

Now that the divisions of a computer file have been explained, the organization within a file can be described. In many companies or or-

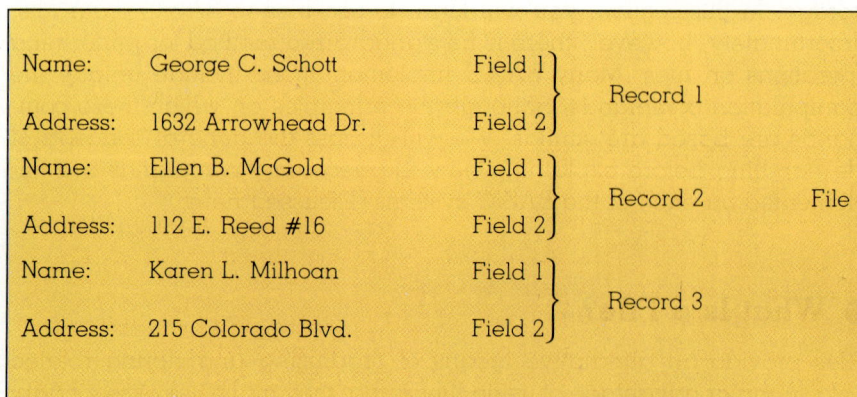

● **FIGURE X–1**
Parts of a File

● **COMPUTERS AND INFORMATION PROCESSING**

ganizations, special filing systems are used. For example, the records within a file cabinet might be arranged alphabetically or from the oldest to the newest. Computer records can also be organized in several different ways. This organization of records within a file is referred to as **file organization.**

● File Organization

The method used to organize records within a file determines how these records will be stored and retrieved by the BASIC system. The method of organization is specified when a file is created. Three possible methods of file organization are implemented on BASIC systems, although some systems allow only two of them to be used.

The first method of organization, **sequential organization,** stores records in a sequence. The order in which records are written to a file determines the order in which the records are stored. In order to access a record with sequential organization, all preceding records must be accessed before the record needed can be accessed. Therefore, if the fifth record of a file needs to be accessed, the first four records must be sequentially accessed first.

To help in understanding this concept, imagine four rooms, each with one door that connects it to the room next to it:

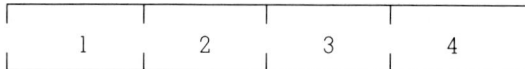

```
 _____
|     |      |      |       |
|  1  |  2   |  3   |   4   |
|_____|_____|_____|_____|
```

In order for a person to enter the third room, he or she must open the door at the left and walk through the first room, open the next door and walk through the second room, and then open the third door and walk through the third room. This concept is analogous to sequential organization of files.

A second method of organization, **relative organization,** stores each record in a numbered location in secondary storage. A record can be accessed either in order from the first record to the needed record, or randomly by using the record's numbered location. Now imagine that there is a hallway adjacent to the four connected rooms. Each room still has a door that connects it to the next room, but now each room also has another door that enters in the hallway:

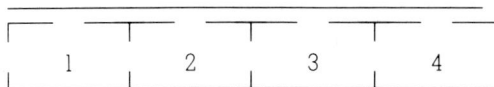

```
 _____
|                                       |
 _____
|    |      |      |      |
| 1  |  2   |  3   |  4   |
|____|_____|_____|_____|
```

In order for a person to enter the third room, he or she can walk through the first two rooms and enter the third room, or enter the hallway and open the door to the third room. This concept is similar to that of relative organization of computer files.

The third method of file organization, **indexed organization,** stores records according to a primary key. A **primary key** is a field that uniquely identifies a particular record and by which that record is accessed. Records cannot be accessed by their physical order when using indexed organization. The primary key field of each record must be different from that of every other record in the file. An example of a primary key is a person's social security number. Because no two people have the same social security number, an individual's record can be uniquely identified by this value.

Records in a file using indexed organization may contain more than one key. The additional keys, called **secondary keys,** are unique or nonunique fields that can also be used to access and retrieve records. However, a record must be accessed through its primary key before the secondary key can be used.

Let's now compare indexed organization with our analogy of the four rooms. The rooms now have no doors between them; there is only the hallway with a door entering into each room. In order for a person to find a specific room, he or she must know the room number (that is, the primary key value). By knowing the room number, a person can find the needed room and enter it. This concept is illustrated as follows:

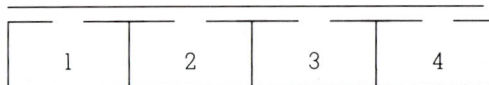

1	2	3	4

Because records are organized within files using different methods, it might seem that the retrieval of records for each type of file organization would be different. This is not the case, however; only two access methods exist. One access method can be used with all three types of file organization, and the other can be used with two types of file organization. We will discuss these methods next.

● Methods of Accessing Files

An **access method** is a way in which the computer transmits data between secondary storage and the primary storage unit when reading data to or writing data from a file. Two types of access methods are used in BASIC: random access and sequential access.

Random access allows the BASIC program, not the manner in which the file is organized, to control which record is to be accessed. The record is accessed directly because the program specifies which record is to be retrieved. A record location number is used if the record is in a relative file, and a key value is used if the record is in an indexed file. Random access cannot be used with a record in a sequential file, because there is no primary key field or record location number by which to access it.

The other access method, **sequential access,** retrieves a record based on its sequential position within the file. Sequential access uses the physical ordering of the sequential file or the position number of the relative file to access a record sequentially. Note that a sequential file is not the same as sequential access. The term "sequential file" refers to the organization of a file, whereas "sequential access" refers to the manner in which individual records within the file are retrieved.

The next section discusses the type of secondary storage medium that is used by the computer to store the file. The type of medium is an important factor in file organization and access.

● Secondary Storage

Secondary storage refers to storage media outside the primary storage unit on which files are permanently kept. Some forms of secondary storage media are magnetic tapes, magnetic disks, and floppy diskettes. Home computers such as the Macintosh, Apple, IBM PC, and TRS-80 most frequently use floppy diskettes. Larger computers, such as the DEC-system, use magnetic tapes or disks.

A reel of magnetic tape looks similar to a reel of movie film. Magnetic tape is usually 2400 feet long and is spun by a tape drive, as shown in Figure X–2. Because of the design of a tape drive, records must be read sequentially. The read/write head, which performs the actual reading and writing of the data, cannot skip to a particular record on the tape; the tape must spin until the read/write head locates the needed record. Figure X–3 shows how records are stored on magnetic tape.

A magnetic disk looks like a record album. Data is stored on the disk in tracks, which are series of concentric circles on the surface of the magnetic disk (see Figure X–4). A collection of concentric disk tracks with

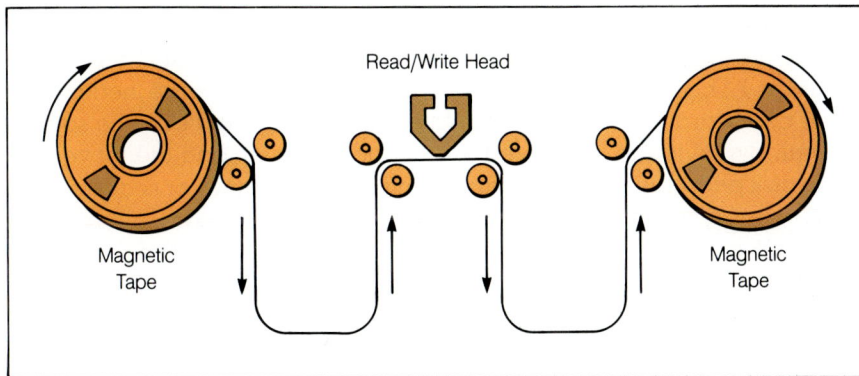

● FIGURE X–2
Read/Write Head

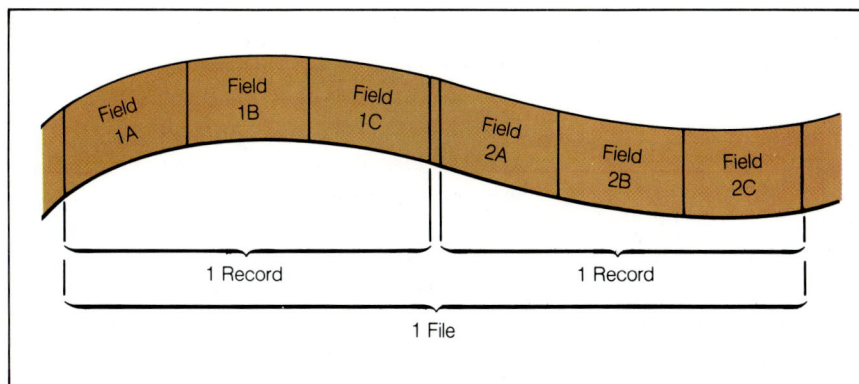

● FIGURE X–3
Data Storage on Magnetic Tape

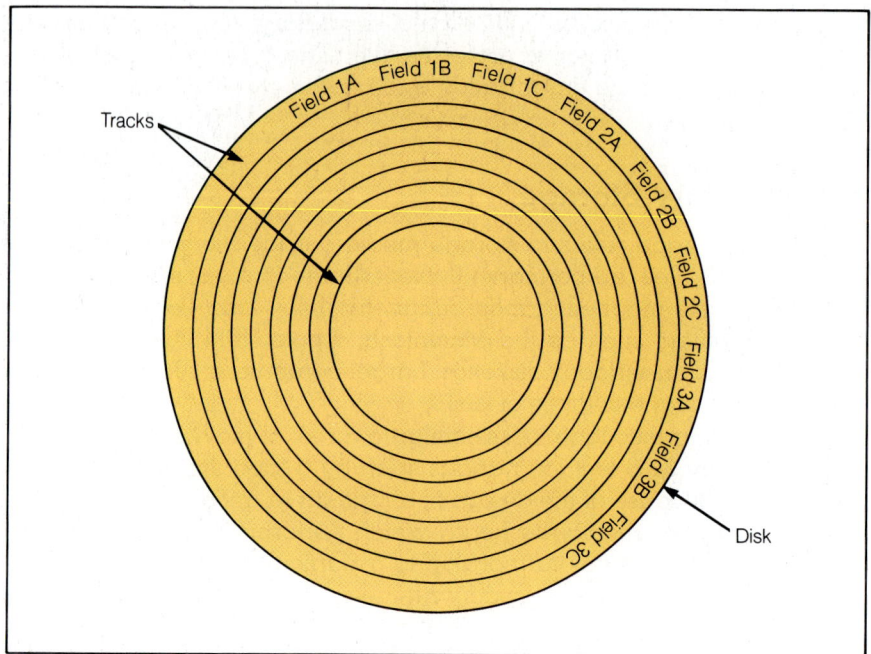

Tracks

Field 1A Field 1B Field 1C Field 2A Field 2B Field 2C Field 3A Field 3B Field 3C

Disk

the same radius is called a cylinder. Both cylinders and tracks are numbered. A group of disks is a disk pack, which looks like a stack of record albums with a spindle passing through the middle, as shown in Figure X-5. Notice that there are two read/write heads for each disk: one for the upper surface and one for the lower surface. (The top and bottom disk in the disk pack each have only one read/write head for control purposes.) The read/write arm, which holds the read/write heads, can move backward and forward, and the disk pack can rotate on the spindle as well. By using the numbered tracks and cylinders and the movement of the disk pack, the computer can find a record randomly or sequentially.

A floppy diskette (Figure X-6) looks like a small record album in its cover. To locate a record, the computer uses tracks that are located on the diskette. Each track is divided into sectors. The diskette contains an index hole, which the computer uses to calculate the location of a particular sector by timing the diskette's rotation. Figure X-7 shows the parts of a floppy diskette.

Data file programs never have to specify the physical address when accessing a record. However, the file organization and the access method

● FIGURE X-5
A Disk Pack

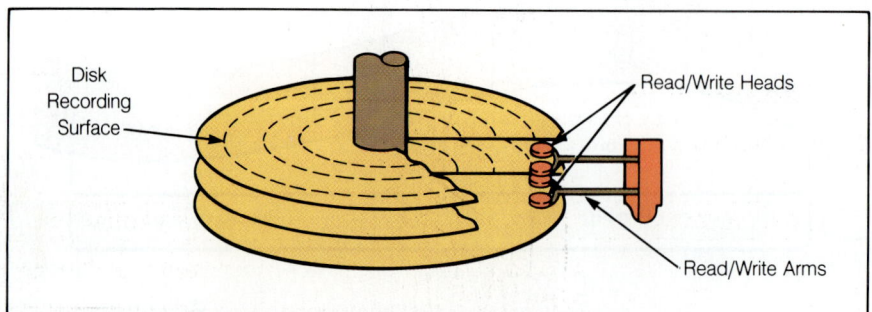

Disk
Recording
Surface

Read/Write Heads

Read/Write Arms

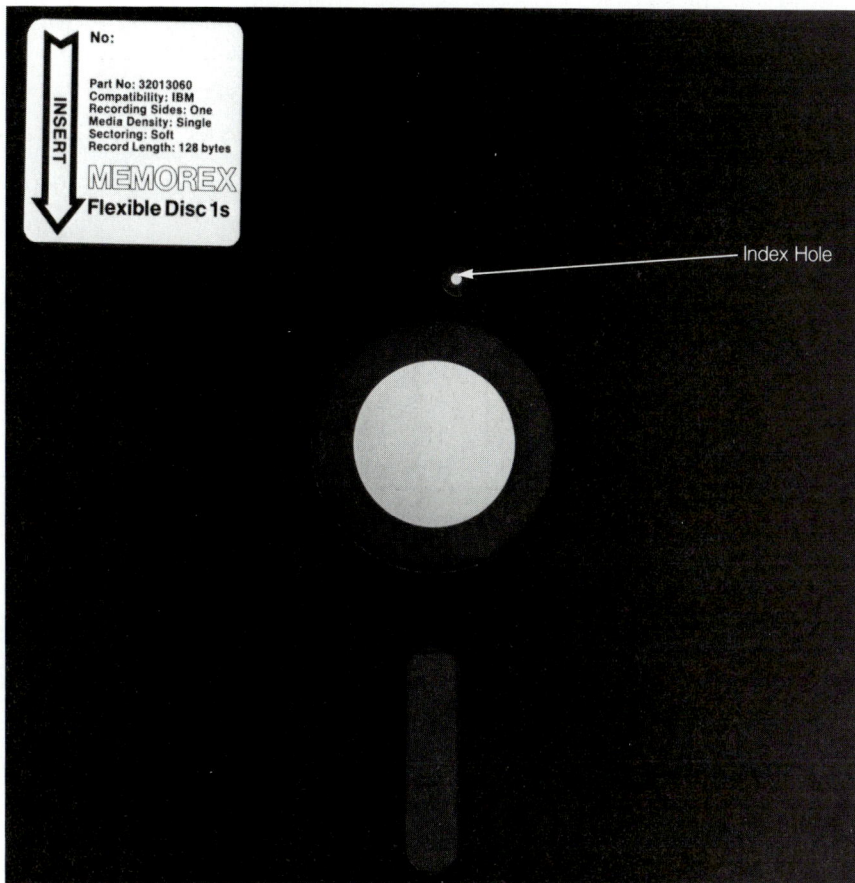

Index Hole

must be determined before the program is written. Not all file organizations can be used with all access methods on all types of secondary storage, as shown in Figure X–8.

● Using Sequential Files With Sequential Access and Relative Files With Random Access

Now that we have explained the general concepts of what a file is, how it is organized, and how it is stored, we can describe specific applications. This section will not explain how to use all the possible file organizations with all the types of BASIC systems presented in this textbook. An entire book could be written on this subject. We will explain only the most

● FIGURE X–7
Parts of a Floppy Diskette

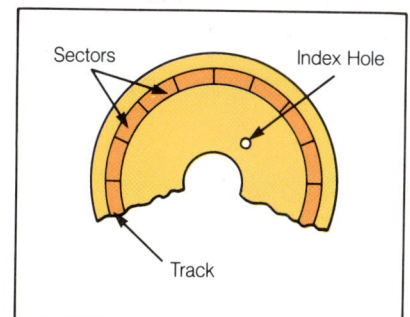

Sectors   Index Hole

Track

● FIGURE X–8
Possible Combinations of Storage Media, File Organizations, and Access Methods

FILE ORGANIZATION	ACCESS METHOD	STORAGE MEDIA
Sequential	Sequential	Tape, Disk, Diskette
Relative	Random or Sequential	Disk, Diskette

frequently used combinations: sequential files with sequential access and relative files with random access.

In sequential files, records are stored in the order in which they were written to the file. Therefore, when a programmer needs to write to or read from a sequential file, all records that precede the needed one must be accessed first. This is referred to as a predecessor-successor record relationship. For each successfully accessed record (except the last) there is a succeeding record somewhere in the file.

Sequentially organized files allow only sequential access. In these files, the predecessor-successor relationship is physical (that is, each record except the last is physically adjacent to the next record). Sequential access to a sequential file means that records are accessed in the order in which they were inserted into the file. A record can be processed only after each preceding record has been successfully accessed. Similarly, once a record is processed, you must start at the beginning of the file before preceding records can be accessed. For example, imagine four houses on a one-way street where house number one is the first house as you enter the street. For a driver to get to the third house he or she would have to turn on to the one-way street and drive past the first and the second house. If the driver should then wish to go to the first house it would be necessary for him or her to go around the block and return to the beginning of the one-way street.

Programs that use random access to relative files must specify a particular record number, which represents the record location. Remember that a relative file consists of records in numbered locations: location 1 contains the first record relative to the start of the file, location 2 contains the second record, and so forth. Because the record locations are numbered, records do not have to be read or written in sequential order. The records are still in sequential order from the beginning of the file, however, so they can be sequentially accessed. Relative files that use random access are referred to as random files by all of the BASIC systems. Specific instructions for sequential files will be explained for the DECsystem 20/ 60, Apple, IBM, Macintosh, and TRS-80.

● File Position Pointers

Associated with each file is a file position pointer that indicates the current position in the file; i.e., the next record to be processed. The computer itself manipulates this pointer when a file command is executed in a program. For instance, when a file is accessed the pointer is moved to the beginning of the specified file so that the first record in the file is available for processing. If a program then retrieves a record, the file pointer is automatically advanced, after the operation is performed, to the next record. For example, in the diagram below of file NAMES the file pointer points to the name MIKE after the file is accessed.

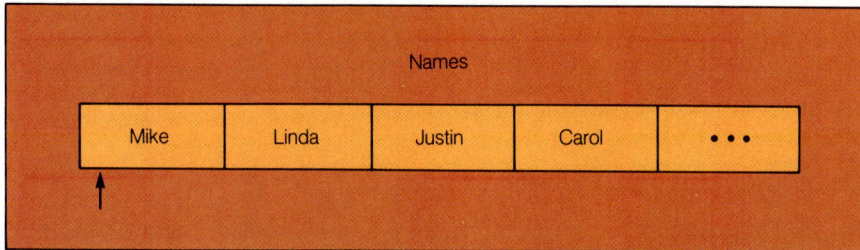

If a record retrieval is then executed, the name MIKE would be read and the file pointer would advance to the next record; the pointer would then be at LINDA.

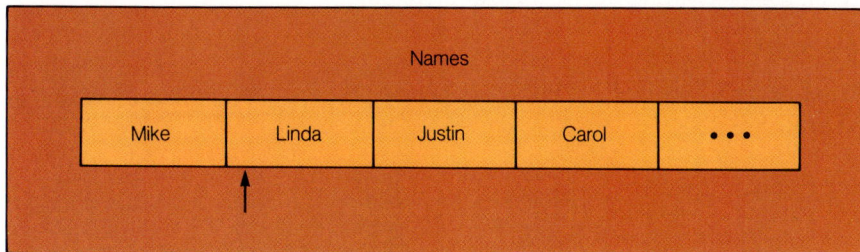

The file position pointer has no effect on the data contained in the file; it simply indicates the current position in the file. This information will be useful when processing sequential and relative files.

● DECsystem 20/60

MAPPING

Before a file is opened, a buffer must be created in memory. A buffer is a space set aside in main memory that contains a record that has been read from secondary storage or a record that will be written to secondary storage. The MAP statement establishes and names this buffer, and also describes the fields contained in each of the records in the file. It lists the variables into which each of these fields will be placed. The general format of the MAP statement is as follows:

line# MAP (buffer-name) fieldname,fieldname

Buffer-name is the name given to the buffer (the parentheses around it are optional). **Fieldname** assigns a name to each field of the record. The length of each string field must be specified by the syntax:

string variable fieldname = n

where string variable **fieldname** is any string variable, and *n* is the maximum number of characters that will ever need to be placed in that field. An example of the MAP statement is as follows:

```
00010 MAP BUFF1 P$ = 16,H$ = 2
```

This MAP statement indicates that each record in this file has two fields. The maximum length of the first field is 16 characters, and the maximum length of the second field is 2 characters.

CREATING AND ACCESSING A FILE

The OPEN statement enables you to create a new file or access an existing file. The following syntax is used when opening an existing file or creating a new sequential file:

line# OPEN filename FOR $\begin{Bmatrix} \text{INPUT} \\ \text{OUTPUT} \end{Bmatrix}$

AS FILE #integer,SEQUENTIAL,MAP mapname

MAP mapname

(The braces ({}) indicate a choice. Choose one from the enclosed options.) where:

filename	is a string expression representing the name of the file.
FOR INPUT	requires that the specified file exists. If the file does not exist, an error results.
FOR OUTPUT	creates a new file with the specified name.

(If you leave the FOR INPUT/OUTPUT clause out entirely, BASIC searches for an existing file of the specified name. If the search fails, BASIC creates a new file. It is good programming practice always to specify this clause in the OPEN statement.)

AS FILE #integer	Associates the file with a file number; zero is invalid.
SEQUENTIAL	Arranges the records in the file by order of input.
MAP mapname	References a MAP statement that defines the record layout buffer used to store the file's data temporarily.

The following example opens a sequential file:

```
00020 OPEN "COMMITTEE" FOR OUTPUT AS FILE #2,
         SEQUENTIAL MAP BUFF1
```

Because the file is opened FOR OUTPUT, a new file named COMMITTEE is created. BUFF 1 is the mapname for the buffer that contains the record layout.

CLOSING A FILE

Files should be closed when no longer needed. The CLOSE statement closes all types of files. It has the following format:

● **COMPUTERS AND INFORMATION PROCESSING**

line# CLOSE #filenumber 1[,filenumber 2...]

For example:

```
00070 CLOSE #1
00080 CLOSE #2,#4
```

These statements close the three files represented by the filenumbers 1, 2, and 4. If you do not specify a file number, BASIC closes all files, as shown below:

```
00070 CLOSE
```

FILE OPERATIONS

There are several operations that you can perform on individual records in a file. These operations allow you to add, modify and examine the records within a file. The following section describes the available options for sequential file organization.

Writing to a File

When a file is opened for output, a new file is created; however, no records are in the file. To place records in a newly created file, the PUT statement is used. The PUT statement writes a new record from the buffer to the file. The general format of the PUT statement for sequential files is as follows:

line# PUT #filenumber

Figure X–9 is an example of a program creating a new file and adding records to it. Notice that the input variables are the same as the MAP (buffer) variables. This causes the buffer to be filled with the record's data, so that when line 110 is encountered the buffer data is written to the file represented by the file number 2.

When sequential files are used, the order in which the records occur in the file is determined by the order in which they were written to the file. This is because each time a PUT statement is executed, the record in the buffer is written to the file and the file position pointer points to the end of the newly inserted record (also referred to as the next available record position). In Figure X–9 the record SARA 21 is the first record in the file COMMITTEE because it was entered first, TONY 43 is second, and so forth.

If it is necessary to append (add to the end) records to an existing file, a few alterations to the OPEN statement are necessary. Because the file is already created, the file must be opened for INPUT. The reason for this is that if an existing file is opened for OUTPUT the file is deleted and a new file is created. When a file is opened for INPUT, the file position pointer points to the first record in the file; however, records can only be added to the end of a sequential file. Thus it becomes necessary to have the file position pointer point to the end of the file. This can be done by adding an ACCESS APPEND clause to the statement:

line# OPEN filename FOR INPUT ,AS FILE #integer,SEQUENTIAL, MAP mapname, ACCESS APPEND

```
00060 MAP BUFF1 NME$ = 15, HRWK
00070 OPEN "COMMITTEE" FOR OUTPUT AS FILE #2, SEQUENTIAL, MAP BUFF1
00080 INPUT "ENTER THE NAME (FINISH TO QUIT) ";NME$
00090 WHILE NME$ <> "FINISH"
00100    INPUT "ENTER THE HOURS WORKED ";HRWK
00110    PUT #2
00120    INPUT "ENTER THE NAME (FINISH TO QUIT) ";NME$
00130 NEXT
00140 CLOSE #2
00999 END
```

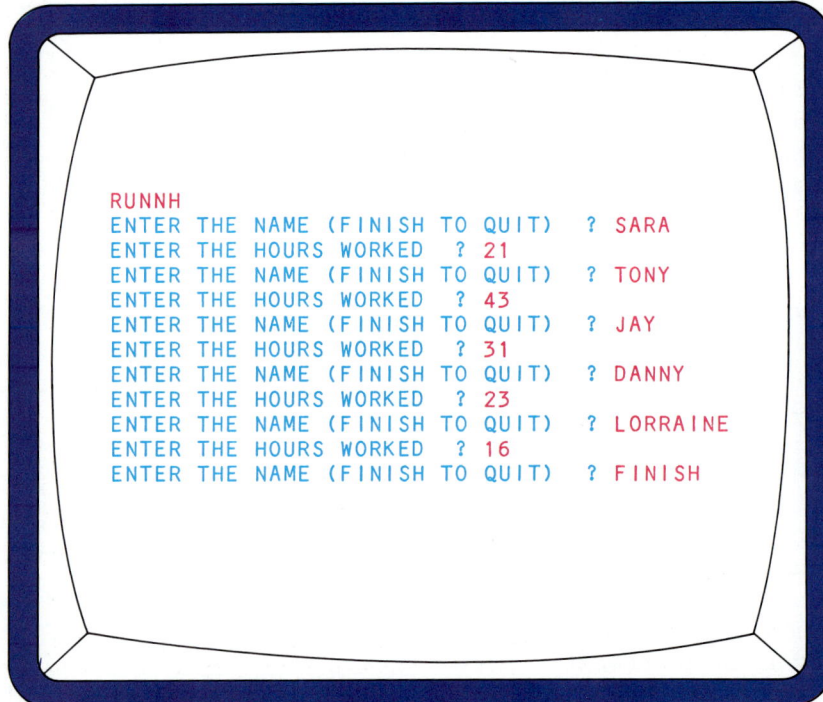

```
RUNNH
ENTER THE NAME (FINISH TO QUIT)  ? SARA
ENTER THE HOURS WORKED  ? 21
ENTER THE NAME (FINISH TO QUIT)  ? TONY
ENTER THE HOURS WORKED  ? 43
ENTER THE NAME (FINISH TO QUIT)  ? JAY
ENTER THE HOURS WORKED  ? 31
ENTER THE NAME (FINISH TO QUIT)  ? DANNY
ENTER THE HOURS WORKED  ? 23
ENTER THE NAME (FINISH TO QUIT)  ? LORRAINE
ENTER THE HOURS WORKED  ? 16
ENTER THE NAME (FINISH TO QUIT)  ? FINISH
```

● **FIGURE X–9**
Writing to a Sequential File

This clause sets the file pointer initially to the end of the file. Now records can be appended in the same manner as they are added to a new file.

Figure X–10 shows a program adding records to the file COMMITTEE, which was created in Figure X–9. The only change made was in the OPEN statement; the file is opened for INPUT and the ACCESS APPEND clause has been added.

Reading from a File

To read a record from a file you need to open the file for input and then use the GET statement. The general format of the GET statement for sequential files is as follows:

● **COMPUTERS AND INFORMATION PROCESSING**

```
00060 MAP BUFF1 NME$ = 15, HRWK
00070 OPEN "COMMITTEE" FOR INPUT AS FILE #2, SEQUENTIAL, MAP BUFF1,
        ACCESS APPEND
00080 INPUT "ENTER THE NAME (FINISH TO QUIT) ";NME$
00090 WHILE NME$ <> "FINISH"
00100   INPUT "ENTER THE HOURS WORKED ";HRWK
00110   PUT #2
00120   INPUT "ENTER THE NAME (FINISH TO QUIT) ";NME$
00130 NEXT
00140 CLOSE #2
00999 END
```

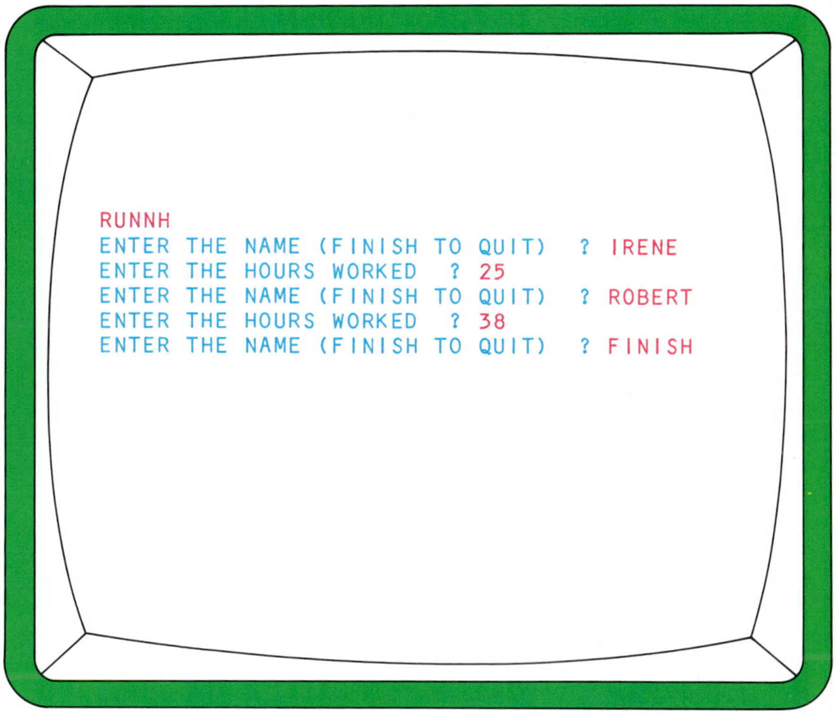

```
RUNNH
ENTER THE NAME (FINISH TO QUIT)  ? IRENE
ENTER THE HOURS WORKED  ? 25
ENTER THE NAME (FINISH TO QUIT)  ? ROBERT
ENTER THE HOURS WORKED  ? 38
ENTER THE NAME (FINISH TO QUIT)  ? FINISH
```

● FIGURE X–10
Appending Records to a Sequential File

line# GET #filenumber

This statement reads the record pointed to by the file position pointer, from the file specified, and places it in the buffer. After the GET statement is executed, the file position pointer is automatically advanced to the next record.

In a sequential file a GET operation is performed on succeeding records starting at the beginning of the file (because the OPEN statement sets the pointer at the first record). Each successive GET statement retrieves the next record in the file and places it in the buffer. Unless the user knows the exact number of records in a file, it is impossible to know how many GET statements should be executed in order to read the entire file. If the program attempts to read more than the number of records in a file an error will occur and the program will stop executing prematurely.

This situation can be avoided by an ONERROR statement. This statement allows the user to read the file until the end of the file is found, and then continue with the rest of the program. This syntax is as follows:

line# ONERROR GOTO line number

Figure X–11 reads the data records stored in the file COMMITTEE, which was created and added to Figures X–9 and X–10.

Line 130 causes the program flow to branch around the printing of the records when the end of the file is found. Line 140 retrieves a record from the file and places it in the buffer; notice that the variables printed are the same as those in the buffer.

Within a subroutine, a RESUME statement must be used in conjunction with the ONERROR statement. The RESUME statement has the following format:

line # RESUME transfer line number

The transfer line number, which is optional, specifies the line to which control is transferred. If the transfer line is omitted, control passes to the line where the error occurred. If the program code appearing in Figure X-11 were used in a subroutine, a RESUME statement would be included to cause execution to continue beyond the end of the loop:

```
00130 ONERROR GOTO 170
00140    GET #2
00150     PRINT NME$;TAB(15);HRWK
00160 GOTO 130
00170 RESUME 180
00180 CLOSE #2
00190 RETURN
```

● **FIGURE X11**
Reading a Sequential File

```
00060 MAP BUFF1 NME$ = 15, HRWK
00070 OPEN "COMMITTEE" FOR INPUT AS FILE #2, SEQUENTIAL, MAP BUFF1
00090 REM
00100 REM *** PRINT THE HEADINGS ***
00110 PRINT "NAME";TAB(15);"HOURS WORKED"
00120 PRINT
00130 ONERROR GOTO 170
00140      GET #2
00150       PRINT NME$;TAB(15);HRWK
00160 GOTO 130
00170 CLOSE #2
00999 END
```

```
RUNNH
NAME            HOURS WORKED

SARA            21
TONY            43
JAY             31
DANNY           23
LORRAINE        16
IRENE           25
ROBERT          38
```

● COMPUTERS AND INFORMATION PROCESSING

● IBM/Microsoft and Macintosh/Microsoft

For our purposes here the IBM/Microsoft and Macintosh/Microsoft implementations of files are very similar. Therefore, we will discuss these two implementations together, noting any differences. (Remember that line numbers are optional on the Macintosh.)

CREATING AND ACCESSING A FILE

The OPEN statement enables the programmer to create a new file or access an existing file. The following syntex is used when creating a new, or accessing an existing, sequential file:

line# OPEN "filename" FOR $\begin{Bmatrix} \text{INPUT} \\ \text{OUTPUT} \\ \text{APPEND} \end{Bmatrix}$ AS #filenumber

where:

filename	is a string expression representing the name of the file.
FOR INPUT	requires that the specified file exist; if not, an error results. Used for sequential files.
FOR OUTPUT	creates a new file with the specified name. Used for sequential files.
FOR APPEND	used for sequential files. Sets the file pointer to the end of the file.

If the FOR INPUT/OUTPUT/APPEND is omitted, the computer defaults to random files and searches for an existing random file of the specified name. If found, the file is opened for input; if the search fails, BASIC creates a new random file.

AS #filenumber   associates a file with a number; zero is invalid.

For example, the following statement opens a sequential file named COMMITTEE and gives it filenumber 3:

```
470 OPEN "COMMITTEE" FOR INPUT AS #3
```

CLOSING A FILE

Files need to be closed when no longer needed. The CLOSE statement closes all types of files. It has the following format:

920 CLOSE #filenumber[,#filenumber...]
where:
#filenumber   represents the file to be closed.
For example:
```
70 CLOSE #1
80 CLOSE #2,#3,#5
```

These statements close the four files represented by the filenumbers 1,2,3, and 5. If no filenumber is supplied, as shown below, BASIC closes all files.

```
70 CLOSE
```

FILE OPERATIONS

Several operations can be performed on individual records in a file, depending on the file's organization. These operations allow you to add, modify, and examine the records within a file. The following section describes the available options in relation to sequential file organization.

Writing to a File

When a file is opened for output, a new file is created; however no records are in the file. To place records in a newly created file the WRITE# statement is used. The WRITE# statement writes a new record to the file. The general format is as follows:

WRITE #filenumber,expression-list

The filenumber is the number under which the file was opened with the OPEN statement. The expressions in the list can be either string or numeric expressions. They must be separated by commas.

Figure X–12 is an example of a program creating a new file and adding records to it. With sequential files the order in which the records occur in the file is the order in which they are written to the file. This is because each time a WRITE# statement is executed, the record is written to the file and the file position pointer is advanced to the next record position. Therefore, in Figure X–12 the record SARA 21 is the first record in the file COMMITTEE because it was entered first, TONY 43 is second, and so on.

If it is necessary to add records to an existing file the OPEN statement must contain the FOR APPEND clause. When a file is opened for input or output the file position pointer is placed at the first record in the file; however, you can only write records at the end of a sequential file. The FOR APPEND clause sets the file position pointer to the end of the specified file and permits the user to insert new records.

Figure X–13 shows a program adding records to the file COMMITTEE, which was created in the program in Figure X–12. The only change made was in the OPEN statement; the file is opened for APPEND.

Reading from a File

To read a record from a file, the file must be opened for input; then the INPUT# statement is used. The general format of this statement is as follows:

line# INPUT #filenumber,variable-list

The filenumber is the number used when the file was opened for input. The variable-list contains the names used that will be assigned to the items in the file (the data types must match).

This statement reads the record pointed to by the file position pointer from the file specified and places its contents in the variables in the variable list. After the INPUT# statement is executed, the file position pointer is automatically advanced to the next record.

```
70 OPEN "COMMITTEE" FOR OUTPUT AS #3
80 INPUT "ENTER THE NAME (FINISH TO QUIT) ";NME$
90 WHILE NME$ <> "FINISH"
100     INPUT "ENTER THE HOURS WORKED ";HRWK
110     WRITE #3,NME$,HRWK
120     INPUT "ENTER THE NAME (FINISH TO QUIT) ";NME$
130 WEND
140 CLOSE #3
999 END
```

```
RUN
ENTER THE NAME (FINISH TO QUIT) ? SARA
ENTER THE HOURS WORKED ? 21
ENTER THE NAME (FINISH TO QUIT) ? TONY
ENTER THE HOURS WORKED ? 43
ENTER THE NAME (FINISH TO QUIT) ? JAY
ENTER THE HOURS WORKED ? 31
ENTER THE NAME (FINISH TO QUIT) ? DANNY
ENTER THE HOURS WORKED ? 23
ENTER THE NAME (FINISH TO QUIT) ? LORRAINE
ENTER THE HOURS WORKED ? 16
ENTER THE NAME (FINISH TO QUIT) ? FINISH
```

In a sequential file, an INPUT# operation is performed on succeeding records starting at the beginning of the file (because the OPEN statement sets the pointer to the first record). Each successive INPUT# statement retrieves the next record in the file and places it in the variable list. Unless the user knows the exact number of records in a file it is impossible to know how many INPUT# statements should be executed in order to read the entire file. If the program attempts to read more records than are in the file, an error will occur and program execution will stop prematurely. This can be avoided by the EOF function. This function tests for the end-of-the-file, thus allowing the user to read the file until the end is found. The syntax is as follows:

EOF (filenumber)

```
 70 OPEN "COMMITTEE" FOR APPEND AS #3
 80 INPUT "ENTER THE NAME (FINISH TO QUIT) ";NME$
 90 WHILE NME$ <> "FINISH"
100      INPUT "ENTER THE HOURS WORKED ";HRWK
110      WRITE #3,NME$,HRWK
120      INPUT "ENTER THE NAME (FINISH TO QUIT) ";NME$
130 WEND
140 CLOSE #3
999 END
```

```
RUN
ENTER THE NAME (FINISH TO QUIT) ? IRENE
ENTER THE HOURS WORKED ? 25
ENTER THE NAME (FINISH TO QUIT) ? ROBERT
ENTER THE HOURS WORKED ? 38
ENTER THE NAME (FINISH TO QUIT) ? FINISH
```

Figure X–14 reads the data records stored in the file COMMITTEE, which was created and added to in Figures X–12 and X–13.

The WHILE statement in line 120 uses the EOF function to find the end of the file. Once the WHILE condition is false (that is, the end of the file has been reached), the file is closed and execution stops. Line 130 retrieves a record from the file and places its contents in the variables listed.

● TRS-80 Model 4

CREATING AND ACCESSING A FILE

The OPEN statement enables the programmer to create a new file or access an existing file. The following is used when creating a new or accessing an existing sequential file:

● COMPUTERS AND INFORMATION PROCESSING

```
70 OPEN "COMMITTEE" FOR INPUT AS #3
80 REM
90 REM *** PRINT THE HEADINGS ***
100 PRINT "NAME";TAB(15);"HOURS WORKED"
110 PRINT
120 WHILE NOT EOF(3)
130    INPUT #3,NME$,HRWK
140    PRINT NME$;TAB(15);HRWK
150 WEND
160 CLOSE #3
999 END
```

```
RUN
NAME           HOURS WORKED

SARA           21
TONY           43
JAY            31
DANNY          23
LORRAINE       16
IRENE          25
ROBERT         38
```

$$\text{line\# OPEN} \left\{ \begin{array}{c} \text{"I"} \\ \text{"O"} \\ \text{"E"} \end{array} \right\}, \text{filenumber}, \text{filename}$$

where:

I	instructs the computer to open for input an existing sequential file. If the file specified does not exist, an error results.
O	instructs the computer to create a new sequential file with the filename specified.
E	is used with sequential files; it opens an existing file and sets the file pointer to the end of the file.
filenumber	associates a file with a number; zero is invalid.
filename	is a string expression representing the name of the file.

For example, the following statement opens a sequential file named COMMITTEE and gives it filenumber 3:

```
130 OPEN "I",3,"COMMITTEE"
```

CLOSING A FILE

Files need to be closed when no longer needed. The CLOSE statement closes all types of files. It has the following format:

line# CLOSE filenumber[,filenumber...]

where filenumber represents the file to close. For example:

```
70 CLOSE 1
80 CLOSE 2,3,5
```

These statements close the four files represented by the filenumbers 1, 2, 3, and 5. If you do not specify any filenumber, all files are closed:

```
70 CLOSE
```

FILE OPERATIONS

Several operations can be performed on individual records in a file. These operations allow you to add, modify, and examine the records within a file.

The following section describes the options in relation to sequential file organization.

Writing to a File

When a file is opened for output, a new file is created; however, no records are in the file. To place records in a newly created file you use the WRITE# statement. The WRITE# statement writes a new record to the file. The general format of this statement for sequential files is as follows:

WRITE# filenumber, expression-list

The filenumber is the number under which the file was opened with the OPEN statement. The expressions in the list are string or numeric expressions. They must be separated by commas.

Figure X–15 is an example of a program creating a new file and adding records to it. With sequential files the order in which they are written to the file is the order in which they occur in the file. This is because each time a WRITE# statement is executed the record is written to the file and the file pointer is advanced to the next record position. Therefore, in Figure X–15 the record SARA 21 is the first record in the file COMMITTEE because it was entered first; TONY 43 is second, and so on.

If it is necessary to add records to an existing file, the OPEN statement must be formatted as follows:

line# OPEN "E",filenumber,filename

When a file is opened for input/output, the file position pointer is placed at the first record in the file; however, records can only be appended to the end of a sequential file. Thus it becomes necessary to have the file position pointer point to the end of the file. Opening the file with "E" sets the file position pointer to the end of the specified file and permits the user to append new records.

Figure X–16 shows a program adding records to the file COMMITTEE, which was created in the program in Figure X–15. The only change made was in the OPEN statement.

Reading from a File

To read a record from a file, the file must be opened for input:

line# OPEN "I",filenumber,filename

```
70   OPEN "O",2,"COMMITTEE"
80   INPUT "ENTER THE NAME (FINISH TO QUIT) ";NME$
90   WHILE NME$ <> "FINISH"
100    INPUT "ENTER THE HOURS WORKED ";HRWK
110    WRITE #2,NME$,HRWK
120    INPUT "ENTER THE NAME (FINISH TO QUIT) ";NME$
130  WEND
140  CLOSE 2
999  END
```

```
RUN
ENTER THE NAME (FINISH TO QUIT) ? SARA
ENTER THE HOURS WORKED ? 21
ENTER THE NAME (FINISH TO QUIT) ? TONY
ENTER THE HOURS WORKED ? 43
ENTER THE NAME (FINISH TO QUIT) ? JAY
ENTER THE HOURS WORKED ? 31
ENTER THE NAME (FINISH TO QUIT) ? DANNY
ENTER THE HOURS WORKED ? 23
ENTER THE NAME (FINISH TO QUIT) ? LORRAINE
ENTER THE HOURS WORKED ? 16
ENTER THE NAME (FINISH TO QUIT) ? FINISH
```

Then the INPUT# statement is used to read the needed data:

line# INPUT #filenumber,variable-list

The filenumber is the number used when the file was opened for input. The variable list contains the names used that will be assigned to the items in the file (the data types must match).

This statement reads the record pointed to by the file position pointer, from the file specified, and places its contents in the variables of the variable list. After the INPUT# statement is executed, the file position pointer is automatically advanced to the next record.

In a sequential file, an INPUT# operation is performed on succeeding records starting at the beginning of the file (because the OPEN statement sets the pointer at the first record). Each successive INPUT# statement retrieves the next record in the file and places it in the variable list.

```
70   OPEN "E",2,"COMMITTEE"
80   INPUT "ENTER THE NAME (FINISH TO QUIT) ";NME$
90   WHILE NME$ <> "FINISH"
100    INPUT "ENTER THE HOURS WORKED ";HRWK
110    WRITE #2,NME$,HRWK
120    INPUT "ENTER THE NAME (FINISH TO QUIT) ";NME$
130 WEND
140 CLOSE 2
999 END
```

```
RUN
ENTER THE NAME (FINISH TO QUIT) ? IRENE
ENTER THE HOURS WORKED ? 25
ENTER THE NAME (FINISH TO QUIT) ? ROBERT
ENTER THE HOURS WORKED ? 38
ENTER THE NAME (FINISH TO QUIT) ? FINISH
```

Unless the user knows the exact number of records in a file it is impossible to know how many INPUT# statements should be executed in order to read the entire file. If the program attempts to read more records than are in the file, an error will occur and the program will stop executing prematurely. This can be avoided by using the EOF (*End Of File*) function. This function tests for the end of a data file, thus allowing the program to read the file until the end is encountered. The syntax is as follows:

EOF (filenumber)

Figure X–17 reads the data records stored in the file COMMITTEE, which was created and added to in Figures X–15 and X–16.

The WHILE statement in line 120 uses the EOF function to find the end of the file. Once the WHILE condition is false (that is, the end of the file is reached), the file is closed and execution stops. Line 130 retrieves a record from the file and places its contents in the variables listed.

```
70   OPEN "I",2,"COMMITTEE"
80   REM
90   REM *** PRINT THE HEADING ***
100  PRINT "NAME";TAB(15);"HOURS WORKED"
110  PRINT
120  WHILE NOT EOF(2)
130     INPUT #2,NME$,HRWK
140     PRINT NME$;TAB(15);HRWK
150  WEND
160  CLOSE 2
999  END
```

● FIGURE X–17
Reading a Sequential File

```
RUN
NAME              HOURS WORKED

SARA              21
TONY              43
JAY               31
DANNY             23
LORRAINE          16
IRENE             25
ROBERT            38
```

● Apple

CREATING AND ACCESSING A FILE

Data files, referred to as text files by Apple, are stored on floppy diskettes. In order to access a disk for text files from within a BASIC program, the user must press the CTRL key and the D key simultaneously. An alternative method of accessing files is to have the program reference a string variable that has been set equal to CHR$(4), the ASCII code character for <CTRL><D>. It is common practice to call this variable D$. The following statement should come at the beginning of a text file program:

```
10 D$ = CHR$(4)
```

(We will use D$ from here on, and assume it has been initialized to CHR$(4).) Next, the file must be opened. The general format for the OPEN statement on the Apple when creating a new, or accessing an existing, sequential file is as follows:

line# PRINT $\left\{ \begin{array}{c} \text{D\$} \\ \text{<CTRL><D>} \end{array} \right\}$; "OPEN filename"

where:

PRINT $\left\{ \begin{array}{c} \text{D\$} \\ \text{<CTRL><D>} \end{array} \right\}$ tells the computer that a file on disk is going to be accessed. D$ must have been initialized to CHR$(4).

OPEN   opens the specified file.
filename   identifies the file.

For example, the following statement opens a sequential file named COMMITTEE.

```
290 PRINT D$;"OPEN COMMITTEE"
```

CLOSING A FILE

Files need to be closed when no longer needed. The CLOSE statement closes all types of files. It has the following format:

line# PRINT D$;"CLOSE filename"

where filename represents the file to be closed. For example:

```
80 PRINT D$;"CLOSE COMMITTEE"
```

This statement closes the file COMMITTEE. If no filename is specified, then all opened files will be closed.

FILE OPERATIONS

Several operations can be performed on individual records in a file. These operations allow the programmer to add, modify, and examine the records within a file. The following section describes the available options in relation to sequential file organizations.

Writing to a File

Before data can be written to a file, the operating system must be instructed that all subsequent PRINT statements are to write to the file instead of the display screen. The syntax for the statement to do this is as follows:

line# PRINT D$;"WRITE filename"

This statement does not write anything to the file; it just indicates to the operating system that any data is now to be written to the stated file. Now PRINT statements can be used to write data to the file. However, there is one difference between the standard PRINT statement and the PRINT statement used for files. An example is shown below:

```
70 PRINT "MONDAY",31,"MARCH"
```

The above PRINT statement appears to write three values. However, when the program tries to read the first data item back (MONDAY), all the values will come back combined into one value:

```
MONDAY31MARCH
```

In Applesoft, fields must be separated in the file by a comma or a carriage return. To solve the above problem, the programmer must assign a comma to a string variable and write that variable between every value in the PRINT statement, separated by a semicolon as follows:

```
60 C$ = ","
70 PRINT "MONDAY";C$;31;C$;"MARCH"
```

● COMPUTERS AND INFORMATION PROCESSING

A PRINT statement always generates a carriage return, thus indicating the end of a record.

Remember that the WRITE command causes all output to be written to the file, including any output that would normally appear on the display screen. Therefore, if you use an INPUT statement such as a prompt after the WRITE command has been executed, the prompt which would normally be output to the display screen would be written to the file instead. If an INPUT statement needs to be used with a prompt after the WRITE command has been executed, the WRITE command must first be cancelled by issuing the PRINT D$ statement:

```
50 PRINT D$
```

In order to continue writing data to the file you must reissue the WRITE command. Figure X–18 is an example of a program creating a new file and adding records to it.

● FIGURE X–18
Writing to a Sequential File

```
5 C$ = ","
10 D$ = CHR$ (4)
20 PRINT D$;"OPEN COMMITTEE"
40 INPUT "ENTER THE NAME (FINISH TO QUIT) ";NME$
50 IF NME$ = "FINISH" GOTO 100
60 INPUT "ENTER THE HOURS WORKED ";HRWK
65 PRINT D$;"WRITE COMMITTEE"
70 PRINT NME$;C$;HRWK
75 PRINT D$
80 INPUT "ENTER THE NAME (FINISH TO QUIT) ";NME$
90 GOTO 50
100 PRINT D$;"CLOSE COMMITTEE"
999 END
```

```
]RUN
ENTER THE NAME (FINISH TO QUIT) SARA
ENTER THE HOURS WORKED 21
ENTER THE NAME (FINISH TO QUIT) TONY
ENTER THE HOURS WORKED 43
ENTER THE NAME (FINISH TO QUIT) JAY
ENTER THE HOURS WORKED 32
ENTER THE NAME (FINISH TO QUIT) DANNY
ENTER THE HOURS WORKED 25
ENTER THE NAME (FINISH TO QUIT) LORRAINE
ENTER THE HOURS WORKED 16
ENTER THE NAME (FINISH TO QUIT) FINISH
```

Line 5 assigns a comma to the variable string C$ and the PRINT statement in line 70 uses the variable string to separate the fields in the record written to the file. The WRITE command is issued in line 65 directly prior to the PRINT statement in line 70, which indicates the data to be written to the file. Line 75, however, cancels the WRITE command. This is so that the INPUT prompts will not be written to the file, but rather to the display screen.

Each time this program is executed, whatever is in the PRINT statement will overwrite the old file, thus deleting the data already stored in the file. If fewer characters are written than are already in the file, the tail end of the previous data will remain following the new data. To avoid this problem, the old file should be erased before new data is stored in it. To delete the file, type DELETE filename at the system prompt (]). This process is only necessary when a given file is created more than once.

With sequential files the order in which the records occur in the file is the order in which they are written to the file. If you wish to add records to an existing file you must add the records to the end of the file. Because the OPEN statement sets the file pointer to the first record in the file, it cannot be used when adding records. The APPEND statement is used instead. The format of the APPEND statement is:

line# PRINT D$;"APPEND filename"

The APPEND statement places the pointer at the end of the file; therefore records can be added to an existing file. The APPEND statement requires that the specified file already exists; if it does not, the error message FILE NOT FOUND is printed. Figure X–19 shows a program adding records to the file COMMITTEE, which was created in the program in Figure X–18. The only change made was that the OPEN statement was replaced by the APPEND statement.

Reading from a File

Just as output can be directed to a file, so input can be accepted from a file. Again, it is necessary to tell the operating system that all subsequent INPUT statements are to receive data from the specified file until the READ command is cancelled. The format is as follows:

line# PRINT D$;"READ filename"

This command does not read anything from the file; it just indicates to the operating system that data is now to be read from the file. After the READ command is executed, all subsequent input will be read from the file. Once the computer has been directed to read input from the specified file, the INPUT statement is used to read the data from the file.

All data values in a record must be read by a single INPUT statement. Each INPUT statement always reads all the data up to the next carriage return (which marks the next record's starting point), no matter how many values that may involve. The values are assigned one by one to the variables listed in the INPUT statement. If the INPUT statement does not list enough variables for all the values, the extra values are lost and the message EXTRA IGNORED appears.

● COMPUTERS AND INFORMATION PROCESSING

```
 5 C$ = ","
10 D$ = CHR$ (4)
20 PRINT D$;"APPEND COMMITTEE"
40 INPUT "ENTER THE NAME (FINISH TO QUIT) ";NME$
50 IF NME$ = "FINISH" GOTO 100
60 INPUT "ENTER THE HOURS WORKED ";HRWK
65 PRINT D$;"WRITE COMMITTEE"
70 PRINT NME$,C$,HRWK
75 PRINT D$
80 INPUT "ENTER THE NAME (FINISH TO QUIT) ";NME$
90 GOTO 50
100 PRINT D$;"CLOSE COMMITTEE"
999 END
```

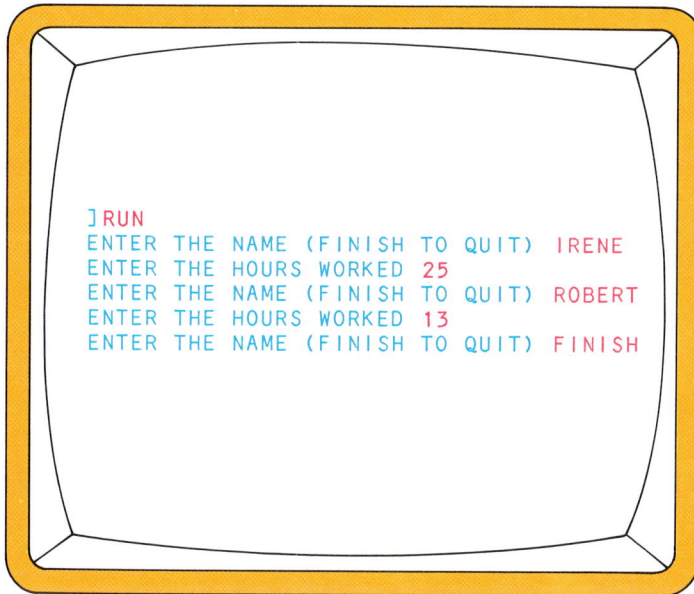

```
]RUN
ENTER THE NAME (FINISH TO QUIT) IRENE
ENTER THE HOURS WORKED 25
ENTER THE NAME (FINISH TO QUIT) ROBERT
ENTER THE HOURS WORKED 13
ENTER THE NAME (FINISH TO QUIT) FINISH
```

For example, assuming the WRITE command is in effect, the following PRINT statement would write one record to the file, but three data values (record fields).

```
390 C$ = ","
400 PRINT "MONDAY";C$;31;C$;"MARCH"
```

The INPUT statement necessary to read this record from the file is as follows:

```
420 INPUT DY$,DTE,MNTH$
```

In Applesoft, the INPUT statement interprets every comma it encounters in a file's record as the end of a value; therefore, the commas separate data in the records. This is the reason why commas must be used in the PRINT statement when writing to the file.

In a sequential file, an INPUT operation is performed on succeeding records starting at the beginning of the file (because the OPEN command sets the pointer to the first record). Each successive INPUT statement retrieves the next record in the file and places it in the variable list. Unless the user knows the exact number of records in a file it is impossible to know how many INPUT statements should be executed in order to read the entire file. If the program attempts to read more than the number of records in the file an error will occur and your program will stop executing prematurely. This situation can be avoided by an ONERR statement. This statement allows the user to read the file until the end of the file is found and then continue with the rest of the program. The syntax is:

line# ONERR GOTO line#

Figure X–20 reads the data records stored in the file COMMITTEE, using the ONERR statement to find the end of the file. Without this statement, when the end of the file is encountered, the program would stop executing and an error message would be printed. With the statement, the file will be closed and then program execution stopped because the error causes the program to branch to line 85.
Line 40 activates the READ command so the INPUT statement in line 50 will read from the file.

● A Programming Problem

PROBLEM DEFINITION

Safeway National Bank keeps a file of all its customers and their savings account balances. They have asked you to write a program that will update their master file by using a transaction file they have processed for you. Up to twenty customers and their account balances are described on a file called MASTER. Twenty or fewer customers and the amounts

● **FIGURE X–20**
Reading a Sequential File

```
5  ONERR GOTO 85
10 D$ = CHR$ (4)
20 PRINT D$;"OPEN COMMITTEE"
40 PRINT D$;"READ COMMITTEE"
50 INPUT NME$,HRWK
60 PRINT NME$,HRWK
70 GOTO 50
85 PRINT D$;"CLOSE COMMITTEE"
99 END
```

```
]RUN
SARA        21
TONY        43
JAY         32
DANNY       25
LORRAINE    16
IRENE       25
ROBERT      13
```

● COMPUTERS AND INFORMATION PROCESSING

of their transactions are on a file called TRANSACTN. A negative amount on the TRANSACTN indicates a withdrawal, while a positive amount shows a deposit. Your program will be run on the DECsystem 20/60.

SOLUTION DESIGN

In order to produce an updated account file, the data in the master file and transaction file must be compared. This can be done by copying data from these files into arrays. Next, the transaction amounts must be added to the appropriate accounts. To find the needed account in the master arrays, each name in the transaction array can be compared to a master name array until a match is found. Then the transaction amount can be added to the old balance and placed in another array. Finally, the old customer names and the new balances can be written to the new updated file and printed. Thus, the steps needed are as follows:

1. Place the contents of the master file into arrays and print them.
2. Place the contents of the transaction file into arrays and print them.
3. Add the transaction amounts for the appropriate accounts.
4. Write the customer names and new balances from the arrays to a file and print them.

These steps are shown in the diagram in Figure X–21.

THE PROGRAM

Figure X–22 gives the program listing. Line 300 sets the dimensions for the arrays that will hold the data from the files. Lines 350 and 360 open the master and transaction files, respectively, to be read. Line 370 opens for output the new master file that will be an updated version of the master file. The appropriate buffers for each of these files are set in lines 320 through 340.

The first subroutine puts data from the master file into the arrays CUSTARAY$ and BALARAY, prints the contents of those arrays, and counts the customers in that file. Line 1170 closes the master file. The second subroutine does the same for the transaction file, putting the data in the arrays TRANSARAY$ and AMTARAY.

● **FIGURE X–21**
Structure Chart for Savings Account Update Problem

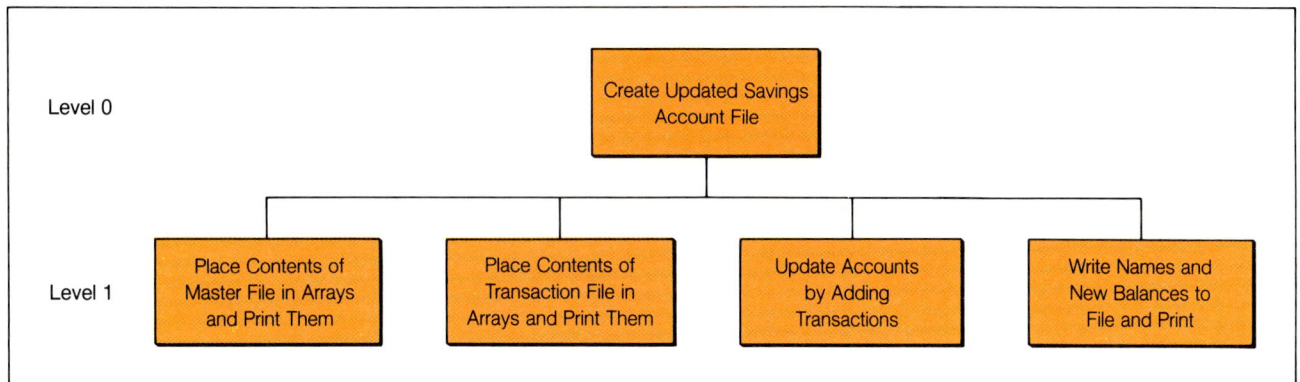

Level 0 — Create Updated Savings Account File

Level 1:
- Place Contents of Master File in Arrays and Print Them
- Place Contents of Transaction File in Arrays and Print Them
- Update Accounts by Adding Transactions
- Write Names and New Balances to File and Print

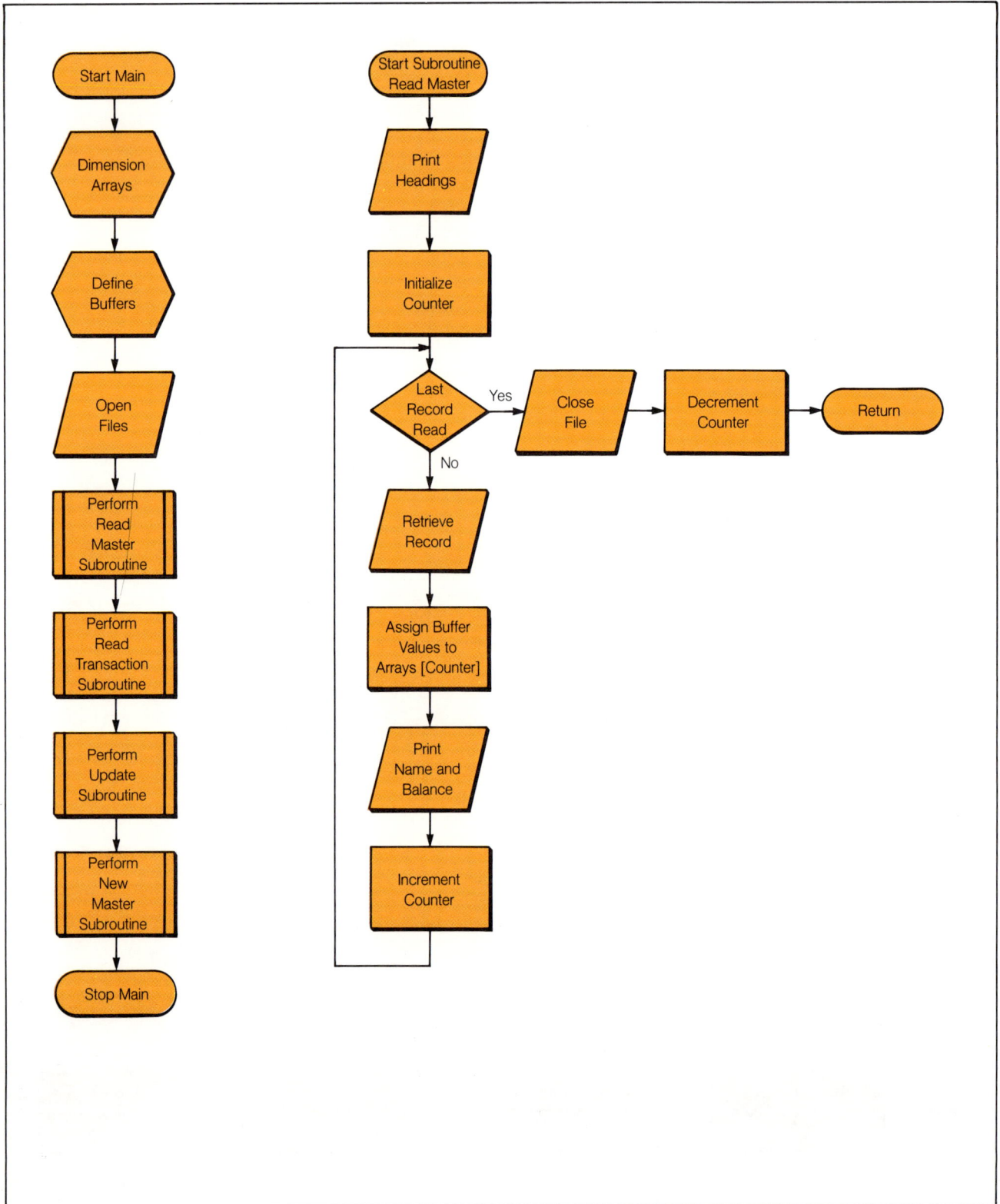

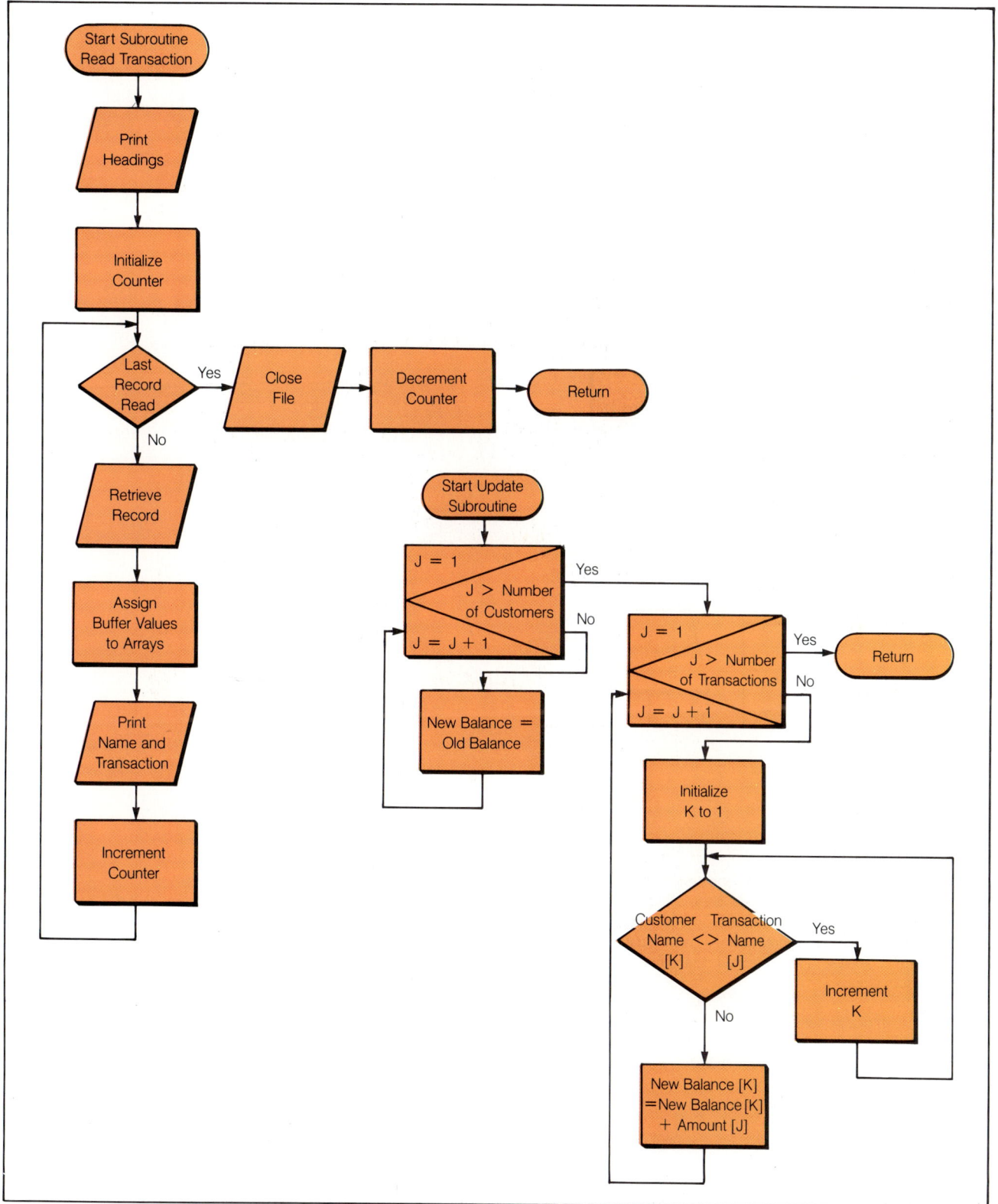

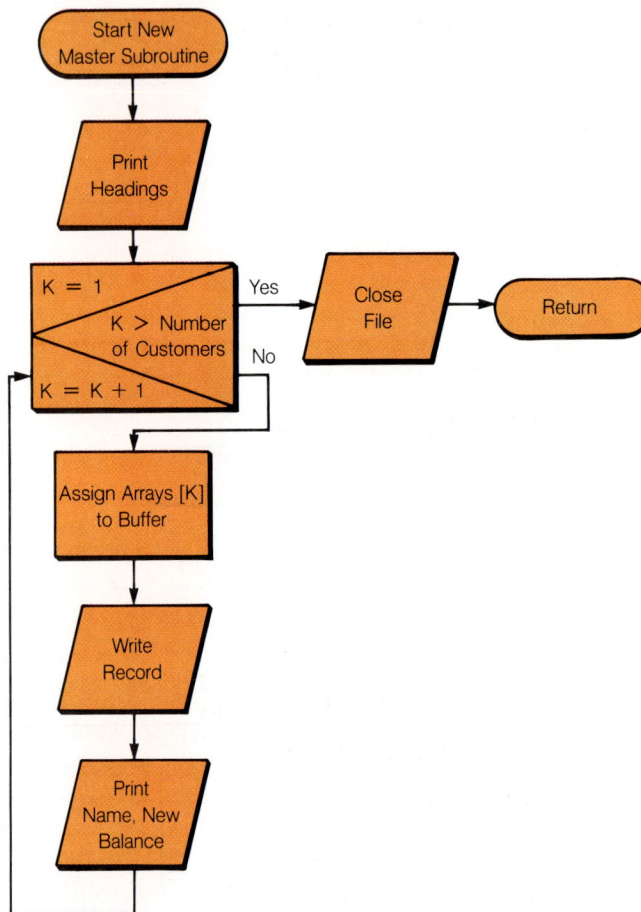

Pseudocode

Begin main program
Dimension arrays
Define buffers
Open master file, transaction file, and new master file
Perform subroutine to read master file to arrays and print them
Perform subroutine to read transaction file to arrays and print them
Perform subroutine to update account balance data
Perform subroutine to write updated data to new master file and print
End main program

Begin read master subroutine
Print headings
Begin loop, repeat until no more records
    Retrieve record
    Assign buffer values to arrays
    Print name and balance
    Update count of records
End loop

Close master file
End read master subroutine

Begin read transaction subroutine
Print headings
Begin loop, repeat until no more records
    Retrieve record
    Assign buffer values to arrays
    Print name and transaction amount
    Update count of records
End loop
Close transaction file
End read transaction subroutine

Begin update subroutine
Begin loop, repeat for number of master records
    Copy old balance to new balance
End loop

Begin loop, repeat for number of transaction records
    Initialize master array index
    Begin loop, repeat until master array name equals transaction array name
        Increment master array index
    End loop
    New balance equals old balance plus transaction amount
End loop
End update subroutine

Begin new master subroutine
Print headings
Begin loop, repeat for number of master records
    Assign name from master array to new master buffer
    Assign new balance from array to new master buffer
    Write record
    Print name and new balance
End loop
Close new master file
End new master subroutine

```
00010 REM ***                    SAVINGS ACCOUNT UPDATE                    ***
00020 REM
00030 REM ***  THIS PROGRAM ACCESSES A SEQUENTIAL FILE CALLED MASTER   ***
00040 REM ***  AND UPDATES ITS DATA USING THE SEQUENTIAL FILE TRANS-   ***
00050 REM ***  ACTN.   THE CONTENTS OF THE FILES ARE READ INTO ARRAYS, ***
00060 REM ***  THE TRANSACTION AMOUNTS ARE ADDED TO THE APPROPRIATE     ***
00070 REM ***  CUSTOMER ACCOUNTS, AND THE RESULTS ARE PLACED IN A       ***
00080 REM ***  THIRD SEQUENTIAL FILE CALLED NMASTER.                    ***
00090 REM
00100 REM
00110 REM *** FIELDS OF THE FILE MASTER:                                ***
00120 REM ***     CUST$ - CUSTOMER NAME                                 ***
00130 REM ***     BAL   - CURRENT ACCOUNT BALANCE                       ***
00140 REM *** FIELDS OF THE FILE TRANSACTN:                             ***
00150 REM ***     NME$ - CUSTOMER NAME                                  ***
00160 REM ***     AMOUNT - AMOUNT OF TRANSACTION                        ***
00170 REM *** FIELDS OF THE FILE NMASTER:                               ***
00180 REM ***     NCUST$ - CUSTOMER NAME                                ***
00190 REM ***     NBAL - NEW BALANCE OF ACCOUNT                         ***
00200 REM
00210 REM *** MAJOR VARIABLES:                                          ***
00220 REM ***     MCOUNT - COUNT OF CUSTOMERS IN MASTER                 ***
00230 REM ***     TCOUNT - COUNT OF CUSTOMERS IN TRANSACTN              ***
00240 REM ***     CUSTARAY$ - ARRAY OF CUSTOMER NAMES                   ***
00250 REM ***     BALARAY$ - ARRAY OF CURRENT BALANCES                  ***
00260 REM ***     TRANSARAY$ - ARRAY OF TRANSACTION CUSTOMERS           ***
00270 REM ***     AMTARAY - ARRAY OF TRANSACTION AMOUNTS                ***
00280 REM ***     NBALARAY - ARRAY OF UPDATED BALANCES                  ***
00290 REM
00300 DIM CUSTARAY$(20),BALARAY(20),TRANSARAY$(20),AMTARAY(20),NBALARAY(20)
00310 REM
00320 MAP BUFF1 CUST$ = 10,BAL
00330 MAP BUFF2 NME$ = 10,AMOUNT
00340 MAP BUFF3 NCUST$ = 10,NBAL
00350 OPEN "MASTER" FOR INPUT AS FILE #1,SEQUENTIAL, MAP BUFF1
00360 OPEN "TRANSACTN" FOR INPUT AS FILE #2,SEQUENTIAL, MAP BUFF2
00370 OPEN "NMASTER" FOR OUTPUT AS FILE #3,SEQUENTIAL, MAP BUFF3
00380 REM
```

● **FIGURE X-22**
Continued

```
00390 REM *** READ FILES INTO ARRAYS ***
00400 GOSUB 1000
00410 GOSUB 2000
00420 REM
00430 REM *** DETERMINE UPDATED ACCOUNTS ***
00440 GOSUB 3000
00450 REM
00460 REM *** WRITE UPDATED ARRAY TO FILE AND PRINT ***
00470 GOSUB 4000
00480 GOTO 9999
00490 REM
01000 REM ********************************************************
01010 REM ***                    SUBROUTINE READ MASTER         ***
01020 REM ********************************************************
01030 REM *** READ FILE MASTER TO ARRAYS AND PRINT ARRAYS.      ***
01040 REM
01050 PRINT TAB(5);"MASTER FILE"
01060 PRINT "ACCOUNT","BALANCE"
01070 PRINT
01080 K = 1
01090 ONERROR GOTO 1160
01100    GET #1
01110    CUSTARAY$(K) = CUST$
01120    BALARAY(K) = BAL
01130    PRINT CUSTARAY$(K),BALARAY(K)
01140    K = K + 1
01150 GOTO 1090
01160 RESUME 1170
01170 CLOSE #1
01180 MCOUNT = K - 1
01190 RETURN
01200 REM
02000 REM ********************************************************
02010 REM ***                  SUBROUTINE READ TRANSACTION      ***
02020 REM ********************************************************
02030 REM *** READ FILE TRANSACTN TO ARRAYS AND PRINT THEM.     ***
02040 REM
02050 PRINT
02060 PRINT TAB(2);"TRANSACTION ACCOUNT"
02070 PRINT "ACCOUNT","AMOUNT"
02080 PRINT
02090 K = 1
02100 ONERROR GOTO 2170
02110    GET #2
02120    TRANSARAY$(K) = NME$
02130    AMTARAY(K) = AMOUNT
02140    PRINT TRANSARAY$(K),AMTARAY(K)
02150    K = K + 1
02160 GOTO 2100
02170 RESUME 2180
02180 TCOUNT = K - 1
02190 CLOSE #2
02200 RETURN
02210 REM
03000 REM ********************************************************
03010 REM ***                   SUBROUTINE UPDATE               ***
03020 REM ********************************************************
03030 REM *** COPY ALL BALANCES INTO ARRAY NBALARAY AND ADD TRANS- ***
03040 REM *** ACTION AMOUNTS TO UPDATED ACCOUNTS.               ***
03050 REM
```

```
03060 FOR J = 1 TO MCOUNT
03070    NBALARAY(J) = BALARAY(J)
03080 NEXT J
03090 REM
03100 REM *** SEARCH MASTER ARRAY FOR ACCOUNTS TO BE UPDATED ***
03110 FOR J = 1 TO TCOUNT
03120    K = 1
03130    WHILE CUSTARAY$(K) <> TRANSARAY$(J)
03140       K = K + 1
03150    NEXT
03160    NBALARAY(K) = NBALARAY(K) + AMTARAY(J)
03170 NEXT J
03180 RETURN
03190 REM
04000 REM *************************************************************
04010 REM ***                    SUBROUTINE NEW MASTER            ***
04020 REM *************************************************************
04030 REM *** WRITE THE NEW BALANCE ARRAY TO THE FILE NMASTER WITH ***
04040 REM *** THE OLD MASTER NAMES AND PRINT THEM.                 ***
04050 REM
04060 PRINT
04070 PRINT TAB(3);"NEW MASTER FILE"
04080 PRINT "ACCOUNT","BALANCE"
04090 PRINT
04100 FOR K = 1 TO MCOUNT
04110    NCUST$ = CUSTARAY$(K)
04120    NBAL = NBALARAY(K)
04130    PUT #3
04140    PRINT CUSTARAY$(K),NBALARAY(K)
04150 NEXT K
04160 CLOSE #3
04170 RETURN
09999 END
```

Now we must update the master file. Lines 3060 through 3080 set each new customer balance (NBALARAY) equal to each old account balance (BALARAY). If the name from the master file (CUSTARAY$) does not equal the name from the transaction file (TRANSARAY$) in line 3130, then the next master file name is checked until the two names are equal. When the names are equal, then line 3160 replaces the number in NBALARAY with the result of the transaction amount (AMTARAY) added to the old balance.

The fourth subroutine writes each customer's name and new balance to the file NMASTER and prints the contents of the new file. Line 4160 closes NMASTER.

● Summary Points

● Files are used to organize large amounts of data. Because they are kept in secondary storage, they solve the problem of limited space in the computer's primary storage unit.
● A given file can be accessed by many different programs.
● Files are divided into records, which in turn are divided into fields.
● Files can be organized in one of three ways: sequential organization, relative organization, or indexed organization.
● In sequential organization, records are stored in a sequence, one after another.
● In relative organization, each record is stored in a numbered location.
● When indexed organization is used, records are stored according to a primary key that uniquely identifies each record.
● Two access methods exist: random access and sequential access.
● Random access allows a program to access a particular record within a file directly, regardless of its position.
● Sequential access retrieves a record based on the record's sequential order within the file. If it is necessary to access the fifth record, for example, records 1 through 4 must be accessed first.
● Secondary storage media are a factor in determining the type of file organization and access method that will be used.
● Before a file can be accessed, it must be opened.
● When processing is completed on a file, it must be closed so that its contents are not lost.
● No standardized method exists among the various BASIC systems for performing operations on files. Therefore, it is necessary to become familiar with the specific statements used on your system.

● Review Questions

1. What is a data file?
2. What are the advantages and disadvantages of using a data file?
3. Name the divisions of a file, explain how they are related to each other, and give an example of each.
4. Explain sequential file organization.

5. Explain relative file organization.
6. Explain indexed file organization.
7. What is meant by an access method?
8. Differentiate between random access and sequential access.
9. Why can a magnetic tape only contain sequential files?
10. Why must a file be closed?

○ Debugging Exercises

Identify the following programs and program segments that contain errors and debug them. These exercises are written for the DECsystem 20/60 implementation of files.

```
1. 00010 MAPP BUFF J$ = 20,PS = 5
   00020 OPEN "PAYSCALE" FOR OUTPUT AS FILE #4,SEQUENTIAL,MAP BUFF
   00030 FOR I = 1 TO 4
   00040    PRINT "JOB TITLE?"
   00050    INPUT J$
   00060    PRINT "HOURLY WAGE?"
   00070    INPUT HW
   00080    PUT #2
   00090 NEXT I
   00100 CLOSE
   00999 END
```

```
2. 00010 MAP BUFF S$ = 20,A$ = 20
   00020 OPEN "SUBSCRIBERS" FOR OUTPUT AS FILE #4,SEQUENTIAL,
              MAP BUFFER
   00030 FOR X = 1 TO 20
   00040    GET #4
   00050    PRINT S$
   00060    PRINT A$
   00070    PRINT
   00080 NEXT X
   00099 END
```

○ Programming Problems

1. The Hoytville Hardware store has just taken inventory. Create a sequential file using the following data:

Stock #	Unit Price	Quantity
A1123	$4.82	50
B2132	9.73	70
C2134	5.00	20
D1955	4.35	60
D3356	0.55	90

Write the contents of the file to the screen, with appropriate headings.

2. Using the file created in Problem 1, determine the value of inventory on hand for each item and the total inventory value. Print these values using appropriate headings.

3. Create a sequential file with the following information:

SSN	Name	Sex	Height	Birthday
269670053	Cochran, K.	M	75	04/04/62
268441124	Veryser, A.	F	64	07/08/63
267768456	Simpson, L.	F	66	02/19/57
268770786	Bulas, M.	M	68	06/24/60
269556874	Rivera, P.	M	71	11/23/63

4. Print the average age and height of all females, and the average age and height of all males, from the file created in Problem 3.

5. Write a program to determine if a student is eligible for graduation from Washington High School. Read 10 students' names, ages, credits, and grade point averages. To qualify for graduation, a student must be at least 16 years old, have 20 credits, and a grade point average of at least 2.5. Print all eligible students' records to a sequential file. Create your own data for this program. Then access the file and print it to the display screen.

BASIC GLOSSARY

Access method   A way in which the computer transmits data between secondary storage and the primary storage unit.

Algorithm   The sequence of steps needed to solve a problem. Each step must be listed in the order in which it is to be performed.

Alphanumeric data   Any combination of letters, digits, and/or special characters.

Argument   A value used by a function to obtain its final result.

Array   A group of related data items, stored in consecutive storage locations, with a single variable name.

Assignment statement   A statement that causes a value to be stored in a variable.

Boolean operator   See **Logical operator.**

Branching   Altering the normal flow of execution.

Bubble sort   A sort that progressively arranges the elements of an array in ascending or descending order by making a series of comparisons of the adjacent array values and exchanging values that are out of order.

Character string   A group of alphanumeric characters enclosed in quotation marks.

Concatenation   The joining of data items, such as character strings, to form a single item.

Conditional transfer   Program control is transferred to another point only if a stated condition is satisfied.

Constant   A value that does not change during program execution.

Control statement   A statement that allows the programmer to alter the order in which program instructions are executed.

Conversational mode   See **inquiry-and-response mode.**

Counter   A method of loop control in which a numeric variable is assigned a specific value that is tested each time the loop is executed until the desired number of repetitions is reached.

Data   Facts that have not been organized in a meaningful way.

Data list   A single list containing the values in all of the data statements in a program. The values appear in the list in the order in which they occur in the program.

Debug   To locate and correct program errors.

Documentation   Comments that explain a program to people; documentation is ignored by the computer. In BASIC, the REM statement is used to denote a comment.

Driver program   A program whose main purpose is to call subroutines, which do the actual work of the program.

Element   A single data item within an array; elements are referred to by using a subscript along with the variable name.

Exponentiation   The process of raising a number to a stated power.

Field   The smallest division within a file, consisting of a single unit of data. Fields group together to form records.

File   A collection of related data items, organized in a meaningful way and kept in secondary storage.

File organization   The method used to arrange records within a file. There are three types of file organization: sequential organization, relative organization, and indexed organization.

Flowchart   A graphic representation of the solution to a programming problem.

Function   A subprogram that performs a specific task and results in a single value.

Hierarchy of operations   The order in which arithmetic operations are performed in BASIC; the order is (1) anything in parentheses; (2) exponentiation; (3) multiplication and division; (4) addition and subtraction.

Immediate-mode commands   A command executed as soon as the RETURN or ENTER key is pressed; it is used without line numbers.

Index   See **Loop control variable.**

Indexed organization   Records are stored according to a primary key.

Indirect mode   The mode in which statements are not executed until the RUN command is given. The statements must have line numbers (except in those implementations, such as Macintosh/Microsoft, in which line numbers are optional).

Infinite loop   A loop with no exit point; it therefore will never stop executing.

Information   Data that has been processed so that it is meaningful to the user.

Input   Data that is entered into the computer for processing.

Inquiry-and-response mode   A mode of operation in which the program asks a question and the user enters a response.

Library function   A function that is prewritten as part of the language.

Line number   A number preceding a BASIC statement which is used to reference that statement and which can determine its order of execution.

Literal   Any expression containing any combination of letters, numbers, and/or special characters.

Logical operator   An operator that acts on one or more conditions to produce a value of true or false.

Loop   A structure that allows a given section of a program to be repeated as many times as necessary.

Loop control variable   A variable the value of which is used to determine the number of loop repetitions.

Menu   A screen display of a program's functions. The user enters a code at the keyboard to make a selection.

Module   See **Subprogram.**

Numeric constant   A number (excluding line numbers) that is included in a statement.

Numeric variable   A variable used to store a number.

Predefined function   See **Library function.**

Primary key   A field that uniquely identifies a particular record; the record can then be accessed by this field.

Programming   The process of writing instructions for a computer to use to solve a problem.

Programming process   The steps used to develop a solution to a programming problem.

Prompt   A message telling the user what data should be entered at this point.

Pseudocode   An English-like description of a program's logic.

Random   A term describing a set (such as a set of numbers) in which every member has an equal chance of occurring.

Random access   Accessing a record directly by means of a record location number or a primary key.

Record   One or more fields that together describe a single entity. Records group together to form files.

Relational symbol   A symbol used to specify a relationship between two values.

Relative organization   Each record is stored in a numbered location.

Reserved word   A word that has a specific meaning to the BASIC system and therefore cannot be used as a variable name.

Secondary key   A field that can be used to access a record after it has been accessed through its primary key.

Secondary storage   Storage that is used to supplement the primary storage unit. Because it is external to the computer, it takes longer to access than primary storage, but it is less costly.

Sequential access   Accessing a record by accessing all records sequentially until the needed record is reached.

Sequential organization   A method of organizing records within a file, whereby the records are stored in the same order in which they are written to the file.

Software   A program or a series of programs.

Stepwise refinement   The process used in top-down design to divide a problem into smaller and smaller sub-problems.

String variable   A variable used to store a character string. In BASIC, the last character in a string variable name must always be a $.

Structure chart   A diagram that visually illustrates how a problem solution has been developed using stepwise refinement. The structure chart not only displays the modules of the problem solution but also the relationships between modules.

Structured programming   A method of programming in which programs have easy-to-follow logic and are divided into subprograms, each designed to perform a specific task.

Stub   A subroutine containing only a PRINT statement, which indicates that the subroutine has not yet been implemented, and a RETURN statement. Stubs are used when implementing a program in a top-down fashion.

Subprogram   A distinct part of a larger program, designed to perform a specific task. In structured programming, subprograms are used to make a program's logic easier to follow.

Subroutine   A module in a BASIC program containing a sequence of statements designed to perform a specific task; it follows the main program.

Subscript   A value enclosed in parentheses that identifies the position in an array of a particular element.

Subscripted variable   A variable that refers to a specific element of an array.

Syntax   The grammatical rules of a language.

Syntax error   A violation of the grammatical rules of a language.

System command   A command that instructs the computer's operating system to manipulate a program.

Top-down design A method of solving a problem that proceeds from the general to the specific.

Trailer value A method of controlling loop repetition in which a unique data value signals the termination of the loop.

Unary operator An operator used with one operand.

Unconditional transfer Program control is always passed elsewhere, regardless of any program conditions.

Unsubscripted variable A simple variable; one that does not refer to an array element.

User-defined function A function that is written by the programmer.

Variable A storage location containing a value that can change during program execution.

Variable name The name used to represent the memory location in which a variable is stored.

BASIC INDEX

● **BASIC INDEX**